Recreation Programming

A Benefits-Driven Approach

Richard Kraus

Department of Sport Management and Leisure Studies
Temple University

Allyn and Bacon

Boston • London • Toronto • Sydney • Tokyo • Singapore

Executive Editor: Suzy Spivey
Editorial Assitant: Amy Braddock
Marketing Manager: Quinn Perkson
Editorial-Production Administrator: Rob Lawson
Composition Buyer: Linda Cox
Manufacturing Buyer: Suzanne Lareau
Cover Administrator: Suzanne Harbison

Copyright © 1997 by Allyn & Bacon
A Viacom Company
Needham Heights, MA 02194
Internet: www.abacon.com
America Online: keyword: College Online

Library of Congress Cataloging-in-Publication Data

Kraus, Richard G.
    Recreation programming : a benefits-driven approach / Richard
Kraus.
      p.   cm.
    Includes bibliographical references and index.
    ISBN 0–205–16574–5
     1. Recreation—Planning.   2. Recreation leadership.
  3. Recreation—Management.   4. Leisure industry—Management.
I. Title.
GV181.5.K65   1997
790′.06′9—dc20
                                   96–34224
                                        CIP

Photo Credits
See p. 258

Printed in the United States of America
10 9 8 7 6 5 4 3 2 1 01 00 99 98 97 96

Contents

Preface

This book is designed to serve as a text in college and university courses in recreation, park, and leisure-service programming. Almost all undergraduate curricula in this field offer such courses as part of professional preparation. Since the field itself has undergone marked changes over the past two decades, it is essential that textbooks in recreation programming reflect these changes.

Until recently, the leisure-service movement focused primarily on the work of public, local recreation and park departments. Today, however, it has become far more diversified, with a broad range of career opportunities in public, nonprofit, commercial, private, therapeutic, armed forces and other types of agencies. *Recreation Programming: A Benefits-Driven Approach* provides a wealth of information about the full spectrum of leisure-service programs in the United States and Canada today, including examples of partnerships among agencies.

In the past, recreation programs tended to focus heavily on such traditional elements as playground and recreation center activities, intended to serve chiefly children and youth. Today, program elements are immensely varied and include a full range of sports, creative, social, educational, personality-enrichment, and human-service activities.

In addition to serving all age groups, including those with disabilities, today's recreation programs reflect increasing racial and ethnic diversity in the United States and Canada, and strive to promote multicultural understanding and positive relationships. The leisure needs and interests of girls and women are given fuller attention than in the past, and many agencies also seek to play a significant role with respect to at-risk youth in increasingly complex family constellations, addressing such difficult problems as drug and alcohol abuse, and gang violence.

Design of the Text

Each chapter of this book begins with a set of learning objectives for undergraduate programs in recreation, park resources, and leisure services. These objectives are based on those established by the Council on Accreditation of the National Recreation and Park Association, and the American Association for Leisure and Recreation.

Chapters 1 through 5 explore the social context of recreation and leisure in the United States and Canada, describe the program planning process, analyze the leisure-service system, and present the major approaches that have influenced this movement. While emphasis is given to the human-service and marketing models of recreation, parks, and leisure service, the newer benefits-driven approach, emphasizing significant program outcomes, is featured.

Chapters 6 through 8 analyze the key components of the recreation programming process: (1) the participants; (2) ten categories of activities and services; (3) leadership; and (4) facilities.

Chapters 9 through 11 present detailed analyses of three key stages of programming: development of the program plan, plan implementation, and evaluation of program quality and outcomes. Throughout, the text seeks to be as realistic as possible, with a minimum of excessively detailed, theoretical, or irrelevant background information, and with a wealth of examples drawn from leisure-services agencies in both the United States and Canada.

Each chapter ends with a set of discussion questions, or with individual and group projects and assignments. Typically, three or four class activities are suggested for each chapter, so instructors and students must decide how to use these activities to make the factual material come alive. In addition, chapters are heavily illustrated, with numerous photographs, material drawn from brochures, activity listings, promotional materials, and department forms showing how recreation, park, and leisure services are actually organized and presented to the public.

Sources Used

Appreciation is due to a great many organizations and other sources for the materials used in *Recreation Programming: A Benefits-Driven Approach.*

Public Agencies.   Many program illustrations were drawn from public recreation and park departments in the U.S. cities of Long Beach, Oakland, and Sunnyvale, California; Phoenix, Arizona; and Fort Worth, Texas; and in Canadian cities including Dartmouth, Nova Scotia; Edmonton, Alberta; Kamloops, British Columbia; Saskatoon, Saskatchewan; and Ottawa and York, Ontario. Other public sources included recreation and park departments in the following U.S. counties: Montgomery County and Prince George's County, Maryland; Oakland County, Michigan; Prince William County, Virginia; and Westchester County, New York.

Nonprofit Organizations.   Numerous other youth-serving and special-interest organizations also contributed materials, including the American Bowling Congress; Boys' and Girls' Clubs of America; Catholic Charities and Catholic Youth Organization in Cleveland, Ohio; Girl Scouts of the U.S.A.; the Jewish Community Center Association; Little League Baseball; the Mormon Church; the National Outdoor Leadership School; the Police Athletic League; and the Young Women's Christian Association in New York City.

Therapeutic or special-recreation agencies included RCH, Inc., in San Francisco; the South East Consortium for Special Services, Inc., in Mamaroneck, New York; and the Capistrano-by-the-Sea Hospital in California. A wealth of information about armed forces recreation was provided by John "Pat" Harden of the U.S. Naval Training Unit in Patuxent River, Maryland. Varied commercial recreation sources included Carnival Cruise Lines, Cypress Gardens, and Weeki Wachee Springs in Florida, Sugar Bush Ski Center in Vermont, and Ungava Bay Outfitters in Quebec, Canada. Material on company-sponsored recreation was generously provided by the National Employee Services and Recreation Association in Oak Brook, Illinois.

Much valuable information was drawn from the writings of such educators and researchers as John Crompton, B.L. "Bev" Driver, Christopher and Susan Edginton, Patricia Farrell and Herberta Lundegren, Christine Howe and Gaylene Carpenter, Carol Peterson and Scout Gunn, J. Robert Rossman and Ruth Russell. To them and to dozens of other authors whose work has appeared in professional publications, the author expresses his deep appreciation for the important contributions they have made to theory and practice in the recreation, park, and leisure-service field.

Acknowledgments

The author would also like to express his appreciation for the valuable feedback provided by the following reviewers:

Dr. M. Jean Keller, University of North Texas; Professor Chris A. Wilsman, University of North Carolina at Chapel Hill; Dr. Deb Jordan, The University of Northern Iowa; Dr. Mary G. Parr, Kent State University; Dr. Therese Sheehan, St. Cloud State University; Professor Ron Puhl, Bloomsburg University; Dr. David L. Holmes, University of Nevada at Las Vegas; Dr. Linda L. Powell, Western Michigan University; Professor Douglas M. Turco, Illinois State University; Professor Roger W. Riley, Illinois State University; Dr. Christine Howe, SUNY at Brockport.

Richard Kraus
Temple University

Chapter *1*

Recreation Programming: The Social Context

Let's try to look at ourselves [recreation and park managers] as our public might view *our* role in *their* community. They might be apt to tell us that we provide every individual in our community with an opportunity for life enrichment, physical development, creation of self-esteem, life-long learning, diversion from daily routine, self-discovery, catharsis, wellness, socialization, and cultural growth.

[We also provide] community pride; crime prevention and deterrence; opportunities to develop and maintain family unity; economic development and tourism enhancement; community unity and a sense of belonging; environmental protection/education/stewardship; [and] ethnic and cultural understanding.[1]

Recreation, park, and leisure-service programs play a vital role in the lives of millions of Americans and Canadians. Program planning and management are essential elements in assuring the success of leisure services for people of all ages and backgrounds.

This chapter describes the role of organized recreation programs in contemporary life. It defines a number of key terms that appear throughout the text, and identifies the important personal, social, economic, and environmental values of positive and constructive leisure experiences. A brief overview of the history of recreation and parks in the United States and Canada is followed by a discussion of major social trends affecting the field, with their implications for leisure-service program development.

This chapter addresses the following learning objectives, established for undergraduate programs in recreation, park resources, and leisure services by the Council on Accreditation of the National Recreation and Park Association (NRPA), and the American Association for Leisure and Recreation (AALR):

Understanding of the conceptual foundations of play, recreation, and leisure for all populations and settings. (8.01)

Understanding of the psychological, sociological, and physiological significance of play, recreation, and leisure from an historical perspective of all populations and settings. (8.02)

Understanding of the significance of play, recreation, and leisure throughout the life cycle relative to the individual's attitudes, values, behaviors, and use of resources. (8.04)

Understanding of the interrelationship between leisure behavior and the natural environment. (8.05)

Understanding of the economic impact of leisure-service programs upon the general economy. (9A.04)

Knowledge of the role and content of leisure programs and services. (8.15)

Recreation and Leisure in the Modern Community

One of the unique developments of the twentieth century has been the emergence of recreation and leisure as vital concerns of government officials, business leaders, and others concerned with personal health and social well-being in the United States and Canada.

From an earlier era in which people satisfied their limited leisure needs with simple forms of family play or village pastimes, we have witnessed the striking growth of organized recreation as a major form of civic responsibility, social service, and business enterprise. Several hundred billion dollars a year are spent by consumers on outdoor recreation, sports, entertainment, travel and tourism, hobbies, cultural activities, and other free-time pursuits, and recreation and park management has been transformed into a diversified field of professional career opportunity.

The Role of Programming

Programming is the process that uses the human, fiscal, and other physical resources of an agency to provide recreation and leisure activities and services to community residents or to members of an organization. All other agency functions should be directed to the end of delivering such services and ensuring that they are as appealing, healthful, morally and socially desirable, and creative as possible.

We live in an era in which community life is marked by a growing number of social pathologies, conflicts, and tensions, many of them involving unwise or self-destructive uses of leisure, such as substance abuse, compulsive gambling, and varied forms of exploitative sexual activity. It should be a responsibility of all recreation, park, and leisure-service agencies to provide enjoyable and personally enriching alternatives to these negative social forces. At the same time, organized recreation services must function as efficiently as possible from fiscal and benefits-based points of view, in order to justify themselves as viable community functions.

The important goals and responsibilities of recreation programming are therefore presented in detail throughout this text, along with guidelines for successful program planning, implementation, and evaluation, drawn from leading leisure-service agencies throughout the United States and Canada. First, however, it is essential to provide a brief conceptual and historical background of recreation and leisure.

Basic Concepts of Recreation, Play, and Leisure

Many readers of this text will have had earlier courses dealing with the meaning and history of recreation, play, and leisure. However, others may not have taken such courses. The key definitions and implications of these terms are therefore reviewed in the following pages.

Meaning of Recreation

Recreation traditionally has been viewed as a form of human activity carried on in one's free or non-work time, that is voluntarily chosen and pleasurable. During the industrial era, recreation was seen chiefly as a form of relaxation or a means of restoring one's energies after toil, in order to engage in renewed work. As free time and growing affluence resulted in a host of popular new forms of recreation in U.S. and Canadian life, the principle evolved that recreation, when provided by established community agencies, must be socially and morally acceptable in terms of prevailing values and standards.

Recreation must be recognized as a major aspect of modern community life, and as a significant social institution. Thousands of public, private, commercial, and therapeutic agencies sponsor recreation programs. Millions of men and women work in leadership roles in such agencies, and the money spent on admissions, rentals, the purchase of recreational supplies and equipment, membership fees, and related expenditures contributes significantly to the economies of numerous states, provinces, and regions in the United States and Canada.

Today, recreation is seen not so much as free-time activity itself as the experience that one undergoes while participating. Emotional, social, creative, and cognitive experiences are all part of recreation and satisfying involvement is seen as contributing to full self-actualization, reaching one's fullest potential as a human being.

It is generally understood that pleasure is not the only purpose of recreation. People may engage in free-time pursuits to meet needs for excitement and challenge, social acceptance and friendship, feelings of accomplishment and self-mastery, creative expression, and improvement of physical and emotional health.

Meaning of Play

The term *play* has often been used interchangeably with the term *recreation*. Obviously, the two have much in common. We play at many forms of recreational activities, chiefly games and sports and other pastimes involving a playlike spirit. Children take part in recreation in playgrounds, and what began in North America as the play movement was ultimately transformed into the recreation and park movement.

How is play to be defined, and how does it differ from recreation? While it is easy enough to give examples of play, it is not as easy to capture its essential character. Philosophers and historians such as Johan Huizinga have stressed that play is non-serious (that is, not compelled by physical necessity or practical purpose) and that it is separated from ordinary life in terms of its location, time of participation, and special rules or values. It may be defined as a form of activity or a behavioral style that involves competition, mimicry or play-acting, exploration, and creative inventiveness.

Meaning of Leisure

The term *leisure* is usually thought of as non-work time that may be used in ways of one's own choice. The adjective *leisurely* implies an unpressured, often unstructured, slow-paced, relaxed use of time. In the past, it was considered that leisure belonged primarily to the upper classes in European and American society.

Today, leisure's meaning has changed dramatically from these earlier views. When regarded as non-work time, it tends to be more freely available to the lower socioeconomic classes, and less so to busy business executives, managers, and other professionals. Instead of being relaxed and unstructured, leisure today is often challenging and highly organized; it often demands a high degree of personal effort or commitment.

Leisure should be regarded as broader than either recreation or play, in that it provides the framework within which these activities are carried on, but it may extend beyond them. Leisure may consist of simply doing nothing—relaxing in a hammock or "hanging out"—or may include such activities as adult education undertaken for nonvo-cational purposes, religious or spiritual pursuits, or community-service volunteerism. Leisure thus may be seen as the opportunity for a host of enjoyable and enriching experiences—discovering one's talents, exploring the world, strengthening family life, or contributing to community well-being.

Recreation Then and Now: An Overview

Having explored their meanings, we must ask, "Why do we study recreation, play, and leisure? Why is recreation programming an important concern?" The answers to these questions may be found both in an historical review of recreation and leisure in past societies, and in an examination of their functions in the modern community.

As indicated earlier, leisure was the special possession of the rich and influential classes in pre-industrial European societies. Although common folk certainly engaged in games, music, dance, and sport that were part of their folk heritage, they were often constrained by a lack of time and money, by laws prohibiting, for instance, their hunting game, or by the efforts of religious authorities to limit or control their play.

With the onset of the Industrial Revolution in Europe and the United States, and with the shift from a rural, agricultural economy to an urban, factory-based lifestyle, most holidays were eliminated and free time become even less available to the struggling poor. By the mid-nineteenth century, however, work hours began to be decreased, and leisure became increasingly available again to the lower and middle classes. At this point, church, government, and business leaders in both England and the United States began to identify the need to provide socially constructive leisure opportunities, in order to prevent or minimize worker involvement in such pursuits as drinking and gambling.

Public Parks and Playgrounds

In the latter half of the nineteenth century, beginning with the establishment of Central Park in New York City, communities throughout North America began to develop park systems that provided open space, fresh air, and greenery to urban environments that had become constricted by bricks and concrete, huge factories, and crowded slums.

Initially, these parks were valued for their scenic beauty, or as places where carriage rides, boating, or band concerts might take place. Gradually, however, parks grew to include zoos, botanical gardens, sports fields, and other facilities suited for varied forms of recreation.

During the same period, governmental agencies in the United States and Canada on federal, state, and provincial levels began to develop major park systems. Intended to preserve scenic wonders, historic sites, or wilderness areas, before long most of them came to be used widely for hiking, camping, sightseeing, and other outdoor recreation activities.

Urban Playgrounds.

A simultaneous development in the late nineteenth and early twentieth centuries was the establishment of city playgrounds to provide places for safe and constructive play for children and youth. Initially sponsored to serve youngsters in crowded slums, and supported by volunteer efforts or neighborhood associations, gradually city governments and school systems assumed responsibility for building and staffing playgrounds.

With convincing testimony from police officials and judges that playgrounds helped reduce juvenile delinquency, the playground movement expanded rapidly in smaller cities and towns, as well as in larger communities. Supported chiefly by tax dollars, playgrounds evolved into a more diversified recreation movement, serving all age groups year-round. In Canada, the social welfare role of play was stressed by the National Council of Women, which encouraged communities to sponsor vacation schools and develop recreational facilities. By 1920, most Canadian urban centers had organized public recreation and park systems.[2]

In the 1950s and 1960s, with increasing government sponsorship of leisure-service programs and facilities, the formerly separate recreation and park movements merged, in terms of combined local agencies, professional organizations and training programs, and national identities.

Youth-Serving and Special-Interest Organizations

During the latter half of the nineteenth century and the first few decades of the twentieth, numerous nonprofit youth-serving organizations that provided recreation along with other character-building functions were established throughout the United States and Canada.

Some were sponsored by religious denominations, such as the Young Men's and Young Women's Christian Associations, the Catholic Youth Organization, and the Young Men's and Young Women's Hebrew Association. While they included religious training and celebration as part of their overall missions, many organizations sponsored sports, camping, social programs, family events, and other leisure pursuits that promoted spiritual or religious values.

Other youth-serving organizations, such as Boy Scouts, Girl Scouts, Boys' and Girls' Clubs, Four-H Clubs, Camp Fire Girls, and Police Athletic Leagues, were established to serve a broad range of children and youth in socially and environmentally purposeful group activities.

Growth of Popular Culture

Another important element in the expansion of recreation and leisure programming in the United States and Canada was the establishment of special organizations designed to promote popular culture.

Many of these groups focused generally on adult education and cultural enrichment in small towns and agricultural areas in both countries. For example, during the nineteenth century the Lyceum movement was responsible for hundreds of local organizations that sponsored lectures, traveling performing arts companies, current events, and literary-discussion clubs that enriched the cultural lives of community residents.

Many school systems initiated community-school centers or offered extracurricular activities (sports, clubs, publications, and special events) for their students and, in time, evening classes and recreational programs for adults. Linked to this development in the early decades of the twentieth century was a growing awareness of the need to "educate for leisure." Supported by educational authorities in the United States and Canada, this effort was seen both as a great opportunity for cultural enrichment and as a means of developing literate and involved citizens on a mass scale.

Growth of the "Leisure Industry"

During the early decades of the twentieth century, recreation began to emerge as a vast, diversified commercial enterprise. In the post-World War I era, varied forms of popular leisure and entertainment gained millions of enthusiasts. Radio, motion pictures, night clubs, dance halls, and musical theater all appealed to the mass tastes of the public for exciting entertainment.

College and professional sports became large-scale sponsors of spectator events, with the emergence of successful professional leagues and highly publicized million-dollar heavyweight boxing events. As sports heroes captured the public imagination, the manufacture of sports clothing and equipment, the featuring of sports in the press, and widespread competition on all levels had a major impact on U.S. and Canadian leisure patterns. Giant college and professional stadiums were built, and with the expansion of country clubs and public recreation facilities, participation in golf, tennis, softball, and other forms of recreation also grew dramatically.

Based on all these developments, it became apparent in the 1970s and 1980s that recreation had become an immense new industry, and a major component in the economic structure of nations throughout the world. In the United States, for example, consumer spending on recreation rose steadily from $91.3 billion per year in 1970, to $304.1 billion in the early 1990s.[3] Impressive as these statistics are, they did not include spending on related leisure pursuits, such as travel and tourism, vacation homes, public and voluntary agency facilities and programs, and such difficult-to-measure activities as gambling and varied illicit pastimes. Other estimates of annual recreation spending in the United States put the early 1990s figure as high as a trillion dollars per year.[4]

Public, local recreation agencies offer a wide range of leisure pursuits. Here, the Westchester County, New York, Department of Parks, Recreation and Conservation sponsors coed beach volleyball, "Bicycle Sundays" on a scenic county parkway, and varied special events, such as this Ukrainian Heritage Day.

Professional Development and Identity

Paralleling the growth of public involvement in varied forms of organized recreation programs has been continuing progress toward achieving professional status for leisure-service practitioners. Key elements in this movement have included the establishment of higher education programs for the professional preparation of recreation and park personnel, and the formation of professional societies that developed certification and other credentialing procedures needed to identify qualified leisure-service practitioners.

In the United States, the Playground Association of America, founded in 1908, was later transformed into the National Recreation Association and ultimately into the National Recreation and Park Association, which embraces varied specialized aspects of the leisure-service field. In Canada, the Canadian Park and Recreation Association plays a similar role in promoting professionalism, helping to influence legislation and government policy, and sponsoring research and special leisure-service projects. In both countries, state and provincial recreation and park societies sponsor annual conferences, continuing education programs, and varied forms of technical assistance, both to improve the standards of professional practice and to encourage fuller public support for recreation and parks as an organized field.

Table 1-1. Growth in Annual Personal Expenditures on Recreation (in Billions)

Type of Product or Service	1970	1980	1985	1990	1993
Total recreation expenditures	91.3	149.1	195.5	261.9	304.1
Percent of total personal consumption	5.0	6.1	6.8	8.0	8.8
Books and maps	10.5	10.2	11.4	15.3	16.6
Magazines, newspapers, and sheet music	13.2	18.4	17.9	20.9	20.4
Nondurable toys and sports supplies	9.5	17.4	22.3	28.7	32.2
Wheel goods, sports and photographic equipment	10.3	20.2	24.4	28.3	28.1
Video and audio products, computer equipment, and musical instruments	8.8	17.5	29.7	54.1	83.7
Radio and television repair	2.7	3.5	3.3	3.4	3.1
Flowers, seeds, and potted plants	4.0	5.9	7.0	9.7	10.5
Admissions to specified spectator amusements	8.2	9.9	10.2	11.5	12.5
Motion picture theaters	4.2	3.8	3.6	3.8	4.2
Legitimate theaters, opera, and entertainments of nonprofit institutions	1.3	2.7	2.8	3.7	4.1
Spectator sports	2.8	3.4	3.7	4.0	4.2
Clubs and fraternal organizations except insurance	3.8	4.0	6.3	7.5	7.9
Pari-mutuel net receipts	2.8	3.6	3.2	3.2	2.9
Commercial participant amusements	6.3	12.5	16.1	20.3	22.0
Other	11.3	25.8	43.5	58.9	64.2

Source: Statistical Abstract of the United States. 1995. Washington, D.C., U.S. Government Printing Office.

In addition to such major organizations that address the overall recreation, park, and leisure-service field, there are numerous other organizations that promote specialized aspects of recreation, such as armed forces recreation, therapeutic recreation, resort management, fitness spa management, college and university programming, employee services departments, sports management, and travel and tourism.

Societal Trends Affecting Recreation

Certainly, the progress that has been made in this field has been remarkable, and has contributed significantly to the quality of life and to social and economic advancement in the United States and Canada. At the same time, a number of major shifts are occurring throughout the industrialized world that impose new challenges for leisure-service managers in U.S. and Canadian agencies. Nine of these critical areas of social change are described in the pages that follow.

1. *Shifts in Living Patterns*

It was reported in the early 1990s that more than half of the population of the United States was living in metropolitan areas of a million or more people, following decades of movement from small towns and farms to urban and suburban communities. Despite the widespread perception that older cities have lost many residents, nine of the nation's ten largest metropolitan areas gained in population over the past two decades, with population growth most marked in Florida and the American Southwest. In both the United States and Canada, smaller communities and rural settlements in Western and Midwestern regions tended to lose residents.

This trend reflects the shift of growing numbers of retirees to more favorable climates or to lower cost-of-living areas, as well as the consolidation of available jobs in favored areas and the lifestyle attractions of metropolitan regions.

2. *Changing Family Structures*

A second major shift in U.S. and Canadian populations has involved the steady decline of traditional two-parent families in which one parent, usually the father, was employed, while the other fulfilled homemaker and child-care responsibilities.

Following World War II, as growing numbers of women entered the workforce, seeking fuller economic and social independence, many children in families with both parents employed began to receive inadequate parental care and supervision. This trend has been affected by the rise in the number of divorces and births to single parents, resulting in greater numbers of single-parent households and "latch-key" children.

Increasingly reported instances of physical and sexual abuse of children, growing numbers of homeless individuals and families, and the isolation of many elderly individuals have become significant problems of the 1980s and 1990s. As a consequence, many public, nonprofit, armed forces, and other leisure-service agencies have identified the provision of family-directed programming as a critical priority.

3. *Social and Moral Values*

Closely linked to the problem of changing family patterns has been the widely publicized issue of declining social and moral values. This issue involves a number of major concerns:

1. The ready acceptance of gambling as a form of popular and even family-oriented entertainment, with many cities and states now relying on lotteries, gambling casinos and riverboats, pari-mutuel betting, and other games of chance to provide a partial solution to their economic problems.
2. The use of narcotics by increasing numbers of young people, as well as the reliance on alcohol as a form of recreation.
3. A pattern of sexual promiscuity on the part of many young people, resulting in the spread of deadly, often incurable forms of sexually transmitted diseases.
4. The growth of violence and physical abuse within families and in neighborhood settings, often involving assaults by teenagers or even preadolescent children.

One may question whether such forms of antisocial or self-destructive behavior should be considered examples of recreation. Nevertheless, they often represent a search for excitement or pleasure and, as such, clearly are part of the overall leisure spectrum.

4. *Gender-Related Issues*

As women have assumed fuller economic and social independence, and have moved rapidly into areas of the business, professional, and political worlds that formally were closed to them, they also have begun to challenge the restrictions limiting their recreational lives.

Girls and women were traditionally discouraged from participation in school, college, and community sports. As a result of legislation such as Title IX in the United States and on a wave of favorable court decisions, many more girls and women today take part in organized athletics. Many more serve as television or radio sports commentators, and in management roles in academic and professional settings.

Women have begun to be accepted as jockeys and race-car drivers. Their increasing participation in high-risk or strenuous outdoor pursuits is important symbolically in overcoming stereotypes of women as physically and emotionally fragile creatures.

Clearly, then, there has been a pronounced decline in the number of gender-based barriers against girls and women in leisure activities. A related shift has occurred in youth-serving organizations, such as Boys' and Girls' Clubs and Campfire Girls, which were formerly segregated by sex and now serve joint memberships. Linked to this trend has been the continuing struggle of gay and lesbian individuals to overcome both legal and social forms of discrimination. It has also involved the fuller acceptance of women as professional leaders or managers within the various specialized sectors of the leisure-service field, and at the highest levels of responsibility.

5. *The Impact of Multiculturalism on Leisure*

A fifth major area of change in the United States and Canada involves multiculturalism, the recognition that North American communities, historically dominated by white, Anglo-Saxon, Protestant power structures and cultural models, have changed dramatically in recent years.

Past racial or ethnic-based discrimination meant that Americans of African, Hispanic, Asian, or Native American descent often had sharply limited opportunities in education, employment, housing, and other social areas. Until the post-World War II era, members of racial minorities were systematically barred from recreation, parks, and other leisure settings, by law in the southern states and by tactic community custom in many white-dominated neighborhoods or organizations in border states and the North.

As a result of the Civil Rights movement and resulting legislation and court decisions, most of these barriers have been removed, although lawsuits continue to identify continuing practices of racial discrimination in places of public accommodation. There is general agreement today that the United States must accept and value its identity as a multicultural society. In many cities, recreation and park agencies are striving to promote fuller understanding of varied ethnic and national backgrounds, and to celebrate multicultural folk customs and traditions through community festivals and other events.

In Canada, while the racial issue has not been as major a concern as it has been in the United States, there has long been a rift between the English-speaking majority and those of French ancestry in the eastern provinces. Separate school systems and recreation programs have reflected this division, although many Canadian recreation and park agencies have sponsored heritage programs to promote the traditional cultures of European origin, as well as native Eskimo or Indian populations.

6. *Recreation for Persons with Disabilities*

Another important concern for leisure-service programmers stems from the growing need to provide expanded leisure opportunities for persons with physical or mental disabilities.

Historically, such individuals were frequently hidden or over-protected by parents, kept in custodial institutions, or barred from normal community leisure settings. However, since World War II, there has been a growing trend toward promoting their independence and making mainstream recreation opportunities available to these persons. Recreation experiences increasingly are used as a form of psychosocial clinical treatment, to promote recovery from illness or trauma, and to facilitate integration into the community. In non-treatment settings, recreation is provided for people with disabilities simply to meet their leisure needs and to facilitate mainstreaming into community life.

Major places of legislation have been passed since the 1970s to ensure that people with disabilities are provided with the fullest possible opportunities in terms of education, family life, employment, and leisure. In both the United States and Canada, professional societies, public and voluntary recreation agencies, and other special groups have initiated major projects to meet needs of people with disabilities.

7. *Technology's Influence on Leisure*

An inescapable development of the late twentieth century has been domination of many forms of leisure by new technological developments. The new high-tech world has transformed outdoor recreation: (1) in the air, through hang-gliding, sky-diving, and ultra-lite aircraft; (2) in the water, with scuba diving, water-skiing, para-sailing, the use of jet-skis and similar pursuits; and (3) on land, with off-road vehicles and innovative hunting and climbing equipment.

With the widespread popularity of indoor forms of technologically-based play and entertainment, such as video games, videocassettes, and other electronic amusements, much public leisure is dominated by powerful business conglomerates (see Figure 1-1). Through the sophisticated design of recreational goods and services, promoted by well-funded advertising and public relations image-building campaigns, the public is drawn to leisure products of all kinds, ranging from popular music and sports memorabilia to video games, toys, vacation cruises, and home entertainment systems.

Radio and Television Broadcasting Ventures
  Cable Networks: MTV, Showtime, The Movie Channel, Nickelodeon/Nick at Nite
  Cable Systems: In California, Pacific Northwest and Midwest
  Television Syndication: The Cosby Show, I Love Lucy, Roseanne
  Television Programs: Frasier, Wings, Entertainment Tonight, Arsenio Hall Show
  Broadcasting Units: Seven TV stations, 14 radio stations, Paramont Television Network, part of USA Network

Film and Music Operations
  Paramount Pictures: "The Firm," "Wayne's World 2," etc.
  Film Distribution and Production: Part-owner, Spelling Entertainment Group and Republic Pictures Corp.
  Video: More than 3,500 Blockbuster home video stores
  Music: Sound Warehouse, Music Plus, Super Club

Miscellaneous Enterprises
  Entertainment Facilities: Part-owner, Discovery Zone FunCenters
  Publishing: Simon and Schuster, Prentice-Hall, Macmillan
  Sports Companies: Madison Square Garden and MSG Network, New York Knicks, New York Rangers
  Five Regional Theme Parks

Figure 1-1. Example of entertainment conglomerate: Viacom/Paramount/Blockbuster Takeover/Merger, with $21 Billion Market Value.

Source: Time, *January 17, 1994, p. 42.*

Two chief concerns arise from this trend. The first is that the public may come to believe that recreation and leisure needs can best be met by *buying* products or services, rather than by engaging in real-life experiences that involve challenge, new forms of awareness, human interaction, or creative growth.

The second concern is that many commercially sponsored forms of entertainment nurture values of questionable worth.

Indeed, there is considerable evidence that growth of violence among children and youth may be influenced by the images and values portrayed in combative and gory video games, and by the often racist or sexist themes of much popular contemporary music.

8. *Recreation's Environmental Impact*

In both the United States and Canada, there has been growing concern about the relationship between outdoor recreation and the natural environment. While the major recreation and park professional societies have done much to promote positive ecological values and assist environmental legislation, the reality is that many outdoor pursuits pose a serious threat to the environment. The building of roads and resorts in wilderness areas, the use of offroad vehicles, and the use of the outdoors by boaters, hunters, campers, and climbers often threatens the natural ecology by polluting lakes, damaging vegetation, and destroying wildlife habitats. As a consequence, outdoor recreation educators and authorities have begun to recognize the need for a sound environmental ethic to govern the planning and maintenance of wilderness areas.

Similarly, urban environments constitute an important priority for leisure-service planners and programmers. Many older cities suffer from abandoned factories and railroad yards, degraded housing, and deteriorated waterfront areas. More and more, urban planners are rehabilitating such sites, creating appealing new housing opportunities linked to waterfront, sports, and performing-arts complexes to serve residents, attract tourists, and provide employment opportunities.

9. *Era of Austerity: Fiscal Cutbacks*

At the same time that public spending on leisure goods and services has increased each year, local, state, and provincial governments in many parts of the United States and Canada have experienced severe economic problems since the 1970s, due to growing costs of welfare, health care, crime prevention, and aging infrastructures, linked to declining tax revenue. As a consequence, many local governments have been forced to slash their budgets, particularly for social services and cultural programs that are not viewed to be as critical as police and fire departments.

Leisure "Haves" and "Have-Nots." Wealthier towns and suburban communities generally have been able to impose new or increased fees for recreation participation, thus helping to support their programs and justify the creation of new or innovative facilities and programs. In addition, many upper-socioeconomic class families have moved into real estate developments that provide their own private recreation opportunities, such as golf courses, tennis courts, fitness centers, marinas, and riding facilities. However, both in inner-city areas and in rural regions populated by residents at the lower end of the socioeconomic scale, it has not been possible to resort to such marketing-oriented means of gaining fiscal support. Particularly in ghetto neighborhoods, with ravaged parks and playgrounds, and recreation centers with only the most basic programs, commercial recreation attractions and nonprofit youth agencies also tend to be lacking.

This situation has created a have/have-not dichotomy in many urban areas—what some recreation and park educators have described as "recreation apartheid"—with a severe disparity in programs serving many members of racial and ethnic minority populations.

New Emphases in Recreation Programming

The challenge for U.S. and Canadian recreation, park, and leisure-service programmers is to provide leisure experiences that improve the quality of life of all community residents, and contribute to the development of their emotional, physical, social, and cognitive lives.

At the same time, leisure-service planners need to be aware of special societal needs related to race and ethnicity, sex and gender roles, disability, age, and related factors, with emphasis on recreation's important role as a health-related form of experience and social service. Ecological concerns and the need to protect both wilderness areas and improve crowded, depressed urban environments also represent a key set of priorities.

All this means that many recreation programmers have moved sharply away from their earlier, traditional functions in carrying out simple after-school or summertime activities within a narrow range of age-related programs in day camping, sports and games, arts and crafts, swimming, and nature studies.

Instead, programmers are responsible for serving a much broader range of participants in activities involving more innovative programs relating to special interests, personality development and living skills, health and fitness, family and gender-related concerns, travel and tourism, adventure and "risk" activities, performing arts, and special services for those with physical, mental, and social disabilities.

Such efforts must be carried on within a context of intelligent and efficient fiscal planning, and with input from community representatives, neighborhood councils, and other advisory groups. Although recreation is essentially a human experience, it is an economic enterprise as well. It requires money to pay for ball fields, tennis courts, swimming pools, and marinas, for arts and crafts instructors, therapeutic recreation specialists, theater directors, and all related expenses. This money may come from tax funds, gifts and grants, bond issues, fees and charges for participation, membership dues, and a host of other sources. It may also involve partnerships or joint program sponsorships with other organizations or businesses.

Today's recreation, park, and leisure-service programmers have the dual role of providing a valued social service and operating as business-oriented professionals within a marketing-based and entrepreneurial perspective. The specific challenges facing these individuals are presented in fuller detail throughout this text, along with the strategies and practical methods that are used to plan and operate successful recreation programs today.

Summary

This chapter presents a conceptual and historical introduction to the process of recreation, park, and leisure-service programming. It defines three basic terms—recreation, play and leisure—and then outlines the past development of recreation as an important social concern and governmental responsibility in the United States and Canada. The development of several specialized areas of recreation delivery systems is described, along with the expanding commercialization of recreation that has led to the current view of leisure as an industry. Linked to the expansion of recreation and park agencies, the emergence of specialized programs of higher education and professional societies is also examined.

The final section of Chapter 1 deals with nine important social trends that affect North American recreation and leisure-service programming today. These range from shifting living patterns and demographic changes, to environmental and economic concerns that represent serious challenges for the field.

Summing up, the chapter stresses that recreation and park agency programs should no longer be viewed simply as a means of providing fun or satisfying the pleasure-seeking needs of the public at large. Instead, recreation must be recognized as a health-related field addressing significant societal needs and meeting the concerns of varied population groups with respect to age, gender, ethnic background, disabilities, and socioeconomic level. At the same time, successful recreation programming must also meet participants' needs for exciting, challenging, and enjoyable pastimes, within a sound and efficiently managed fiscal framework.

Suggested Questions for Class Discussion

1. Briefly define the similarities and differences among recreation, play, and leisure. Have class members illustrate each term with examples from their own family lives or experiences.

2. What were several key trends or factors in the historical expansion of recreation, park, and leisure-service agencies that responded to widespread social concerns?

3. The chapter identifies nine different trends in contemporary society that will pose challenges for recreation programmers in the years ahead. As a class, discuss three or four that seem the most significant. Why do they represent important challenges, and what policies might recreation and park managers and program planners adopt to meet them successfully?

References

1. Christopher K. Jarvi, "Leaders Who Meet Today's Changing Needs," *Parks and Recreation,* March 1993, p. 62.

2. Mark S. Searle and Russell E. Brayley, *Leisure Services in Canada: An Introduction* (State College, PA: Venture Publishing, 1993), pp. 16-17.

3. U.S. Department of Commerce, *Statistical Abstract of the United States* (Washington, D.C.: U.S. Government Printing Office, 1995), p. 253.

4. Daniel J. Stynes, "Leisure: The New Center of the Economy?" in *Issue Papers* (State College, PA and College Station, TX: Academy of Leisure Sciences, 1993), pp. 11–17.

Chapter *2*

The Programming Process

Broadly defined, programming is the process of conceptualizing leisure services as well as determining the elements necessary for successful service provision. Programming is at the core of leisure-service delivery and requires a broad array of knowledge and skills to adequately attract and affect constituents. . . .

Our profession must develop new and creative approaches to programming that result in the improvement of the efficiency and effectiveness of service delivery. Tremendous opportunities exist to advance programming for professionals who are flexible and willing to take the steps necessary to benefit from innovative change. It requires, however, the involvement and commitment of every level of management, production, and marketing.[1]

This chapter is concerned with the basic concepts and practical steps that underlie successful recreation, park, and leisure-service programming. It defines the term *program* and shows its critical importance within the overall leisure-service field. The chapter then outlines the critical elements of programming, and shows how program plans may encompass a wide range of possibilities—from the total recreation opportunities offered by a complex agency over a sustained period of time, to a single brief event or participant experience.

A number of different approaches advanced by leisure-service leaders over the past several decades are presented, along with a simplified model of the programming process as it is generally carried out today. In this chapter, the topics presented address the following undergraduate curriculum accreditation objectives established by the NRPA/AALR Council on Accreditation:

Knowledge of the role and content of leisure programs and services. (8.15)

Ability to organize and conduct leisure programs and services. (8.16)

Understanding of and the ability to facilitate the concept of leisure lifestyle for continued individual development and expression throughout the human life span. (8.17)

Ability to apply programming concepts, including conceptualization, planning, implementation, and evaluation of comprehensive and specific therapeutic recreation services. (9D.13)

Recreation Programs Defined

A dictionary definition of *program* suggests that it may be any of the following:

A public proclamation, manifesto, and official bulletin . . . a prospectus: a catalogue of projected proceedings or features . . .

A brief outline or explanation of the order to be pursued, or the subjects embraced, in any public exercise, performance or entertainment; usually a printed or written list of the acts, scenes, selections, or other features composing a . . . performance.

A plan of future procedures; as, one's program for the day; the party program . . . [2]

J. Robert Rossman describes the term program as an elastic concept used to embrace a variety of different operations carried on by leisure-service agencies, including activities, events, and services engaged in by participants who seek certain personal outcomes from their leisure involvement.[3] Other authorities refer to programmed recreation chiefly as organized and purposeful activities, designed in an orderly and systematic way to bring about desired individual and group outcomes.

In this text, *recreation program* refers to the full range of organized and structured leisure experiences offered by an agency, as well as the unstructured or unsupervised use of play areas, sports facilities, and other indoor or outdoor recreation settings. It may refer to activities carried on throughout the year, during a specific season, for a limited term, or on a single occasion.

Recreation Program Functions

Most public leisure-service agencies have three distinct program-related functions:

1. The *direct delivery of services,* such as organized sports leagues, special-interest groups, day camps, organized classes, clubs, outings, or special events conducted under supervision or leadership;

2. The *provision and maintenance of facilities* for play that is largely self-directed, such as the use of golf courses, tennis courts, beaches, picnic grounds, or hiking trails, in which there may be a degree of supervision but little structured leadership; and

3. The *facilitation or coordination of programs in the community at large,* through assistance in scheduling, staff training, sharing of facilities, consultation, joint program sponsorship, or other cooperative efforts.

Program functions may also include activities and services that are not recreational as such. For example, in many corporate-sponsored, armed forces, or voluntary agencies, programs may include such services as substance-abuse counseling, weight-loss workshops, stress-management and assertiveness training, day-care programs for children, discount buying programs, and charter travel arrangements.

Recognition of Programming's Importance

In the past, in many recreation and park agencies, programming tended to be viewed as a responsibility of lesser importance than such administrative functions as facility construction and maintenance, personnel management, and fiscal operations.

As recreation, park, and leisure-service agencies have become large-scale, immensely diversified enterprises over the past three decades, and as the social trends described in Chapter 1 became more evident and pressing, programming has gained fuller recognition as the hub around which all agency operations must revolve. Today, all personnel must be deeply concerned with the task of service delivery and with the provision of high-quality program experiences that successfully meet the leisure-related needs and interests of participants.

APRS Recreation Program Division

To illustrate this growth in the recognition of programming's importance, in the mid-1990s, the American Parks and Recreation Society, a major branch of the National Recreation and Park Association, established a Recreation Programmers Division with the following general purpose:

To create a well-informed public concerning the values of quality recreation programs for an individual as well as the community, and also to expand the knowledge of practitioners who have the opportunity to directly influence the general population by providing strong leadership through facilitating quality programs and services.

Among the specific functions assigned to this new division are:

Information exchange: mailing lists, agency brochures, program ideas, educational materials.

Prepare and compile educational materials. Conduct educational sessions at national, regional, and state conferences and workshops.

Pursue opportunities for networking and/or establishing positive relationships with national organizations and initiatives.

Enhance the parks and recreation profession through the legislative process.[4]

Key Elements in Recreation Programming

Five key elements influence and provide input to the recreation, park, and leisure-service programming process:

1. The *sponsoring agency,* with its guiding philosophy or mission, history, tradition, fiscal and physical resources, and staffing capability, all of which influence the kinds of programs it can and should provide.

2. *Participants,* or potential participants. These may consist of all community residents, in the case of a public department, or such special groups as patients in a hospital, members of a YWCA, service personnel on an armed forces base, or any other target audience determined by demographic characteristics or special needs.

3. *Activities and Services.* Depending on the agency's fundamental mission and the characteristics of participants, activities, and services may be drawn from a broad range of pursuits. In addition to activities that are clearly recreational—sports, games, or crafts, for example—they may also include other kinds of educational, remedial, or enrichment experiences.

4. *Areas and Facilities.* Beyond the traditional provision of parks, playgrounds, sports fields, and other special facilities, leisure-service agencies may utilize varied innovative centers, including fitness complexes, marinas and water-play parks, environmental education sites, and family amusement centers.

5. *Leadership.* In the past, recreation leaders tended to be full-time, year-round generalists responsible for directing face-to-face activities or the supervision of playgrounds, centers, or other traditional program areas. Today, program activities increasingly are led by part-time specialists, seasonal employees, or volunteers, while full-time employees tend to be assigned to management or supervisory responsibilities.

These five critical elements in recreation programming are illustrated in Figure 2-1, which shows how they might appear in four typical agency settings. They are then discussed in much fuller detail in later chapters of this text.

Sponsoring Agency	Participants	Activities and Services	Areas and Facilities	Leadership
Neighborhood senior center, sponsored by public recreation and park department	Elderly men and women, residents in neighborhood	Social activities, arts and crafts, cards, trips, lunch program, other social services	Multi-purpose rooms in local recreation center, church parish building, or similar facility	Coordinator assigned by department, plus community volunteers, aides and club members serving on committees
Campus recreation program, sponsored by athletic department or office of student life or campus association	Students, faculty and staff members, both residents and commuters, on college or university campus	Sports and games, such as flag football, softball or basketball, in club or intramural competition*	Indoor and outdoor sports and aquatic facilities operated by athletic or physical education department	Physical education faculty members or staff of athletic department, with graduate student aides and other student volunteers
Physical rehabilitation or recreation therapy unit in hospital or special physical medicine treatment unit	Resident in-patients or out-patients in several treatment categories, such as orthopedic trauma, brain injury, etc.	Modified sports, games, hobbies, self-care activities and trips to community events, to promote independent living skills	Gyms, exercise rooms, aquatic areas, and varied community-based settings (stadiums, theaters, etc.) for trips	Professionally qualified therapeutic recreation specialists, working with medical personnel and other activity therapists
Cruise ships that operate through the year, visiting Caribbean islands and Mexican beach resorts.	Mix of young, middle-aged and elderly persons, both married and single, including family groups	Entertainment shows, games and stunts, fitness and poolside events; gambling casino, island tours with snorkeling and sightseeing	Pool and fitness center, lounges and nightclubs, casinos, on-board shops, movie theater, skeet-shooting area, land-based attractions	Professional staff: social director and band, singers, dancers, games leaders, casino staff, tour guides

Figure 2-1.   Example of key elements in four types of leisure-service programs.

*This program focuses on physical recreation, and might also include outdoor events, such as camping, ski, or scuba trips. A more comprehensive campus recreation program would also include cultural and social activities

Traditional Approaches to Recreation Programming

One familiar model of the recreation programming process assumes that programming is based on a sequence of four steps—*philosophy, principles, policies,* and *procedures,* sometimes referred to as the Four Ps.

1. *Philosophy* represents the *broad framework of goals and values* that help to shape the mission of recreation and leisure-service agencies in general, as well as those of specific agencies. Typically, it incorporates a belief in the values of positive leisure experiences in terms of meeting the significant human needs of participants, in helping to bring about worthwhile personal benefits and societal outcomes. Beyond this, a specific agency's mission statement might be based on its assigned role in community life—for example, as a youth-serving organization, a health-care facility, a religious body, or a profit-seeking business.

2. *Principles* represent a *more detailed statement of an agency's beliefs* regarding the goals it seeks to achieve, its responsibilities in community life, its convictions about the role of recreation, inclusion or exclusion of participants, relations with other organizations, and related issues. Principles may include basic tenets with respect to environmental concerns, fiscal support, input from community groups, and other matters with impact on program decision-making.

3. *Policies* represent *specific action-oriented guidelines* that translate principles into statements of agency priorities or day-by-day operational rules. Policies deal with such practical realities as planning activities and program schedules, assigning and supervising personnel, and setting fees for program participation.

4. *Procedures* consist of concrete, detailed statements of *how varied aspects of program operations are to be carried out,* with respect to staff assignments, safety rules, facility maintenance, public relations, handling of fees, the conduct of trips and outings, and dozens of other program tasks.

Guidelines for Program Planning

A second traditional approach to recreation, park, and leisure-service programming is based on a set of guidelines that represent widely held professional beliefs or principles. While these guidelines apply most directly to public, tax-supported recreation and park agencies, many of their elements would also apply to other types of leisure-service organizations.

1. *Community recreation should serve all elements in the community without discrimination based on sex, age, race, religion, sexual orientation, or disability.*

Clearly, different community groups have varying leisure needs or interests, and some groups may be more dependent than others on publicly provided programs and facilities. The principle suggests that all groups must be served, but that this may be done in differentiated ways. It raises questions related to serving groups with special interests based on ethnic identification, individuals with disabilities, or those who are economically disadvantaged and cannot pay fees or charges.

2. *Community recreation should be couched within a framework of democratic social values and should provide positive leisure opportunities that meet significant community needs.*

If this guideline is to be meaningful, rather than an ineffectual platitude, each element of program service should be carefully scrutinized by asking the following kinds of questions:

In Phoenix, Arizona, the Parks, Recreation and
Library Department schedules many community
celebrations. These include an annual Victorian
Holiday Costume and Doll Show, a 4th of July
Fireworks display, and a Cinco de Mayo Festival
featuring Mexican folk dancing.

Does this activity promote healthful behavior and self-concepts, and healthful intergroup relationships? Does it embody constructive or negative uses of leisure? Does it clearly contribute to the physical, social, and emotional well-being of participants, and to family and neighborhood cohesion?

3. *Community recreation should provide a varied range of activities, and both diversity and balance in leisure opportunities.*

Program activities should emphasize not only physical recreation such as games and sports, but also mental, creative, cultural, and social forms of participation. Activities also should be offered at various levels of intensity or skill and, whenever possible, should lead to culminating events such as tournaments or festivals that heighten motivation and support positive public relations.

4. *Recreation programs should involve community residents or organization members in setting policies, and planning and conducting activities.*

This guideline is based on two points: (1) recreation should be used to promote democratic values, with program planning giving neighborhood residents or organization members meaningful input that provides a sense of civic pride and responsibility; and (2) programs will be more favorably accepted if they are based on systematic needs assessments that identify consumers' real desires.

5. *Community groups with special needs should be adequately served with meaningful social programs and services.*

Many public recreation and park departments and voluntary agencies have accepted responsibility for serving individuals of all ages with varied forms of physical or mental disability. In other communities, leisure-service agencies provide special services for delinquent or at-risk youth, including drug-abuse, sex education, and counseling programs, and services for the homeless and families on public assistance.

6. *Recreation activities should be designed to meet significant personal needs of individuals, based on age, gender, and related factors.*

Program activities should be selected to meet basic human needs, such as the need for social acceptance and friendship, discovery of one's creative or aesthetic potential, challenge and achievement, and physical and cognitive growth. Recognizing the principle of individual differences, program choices should be attuned to the special needs of children, youth, adults, and the elderly.

7. *Recreation programs should be flexibly scheduled to meet the work-related or other time commitments of potential participants.*

In the past, many recreation programs were rigidly scheduled, with fixed seasonal, weekly, or daily activity schedules, and few alternative opportunities for participation. Scheduling was often unresponsive to the real needs of many residents. In some cities recreation centers were closed on holidays, as other municipal offices were, despite the fact that holidays were the times when the greatest number of youth and adults would wish to use

The arts play an important role in community recreation. Adults enjoy painting and sculpture hobbies at the Vero Beach, Florida, Center for the Arts, and children take part in a stage make-up workshop in the city's Children's Theater. Ballet and creative dance are popular activities in Montgomery County, Maryland.

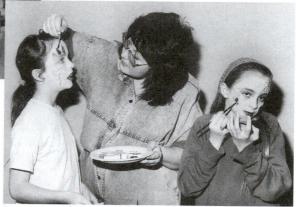

recreation facilities. Today, the need to program activities more flexibly is recognized. Daytime programs for nonworking individuals, such as elderly persons, those with disabilities, homemakers with young children, or those with nighttime jobs, are supplemented by evening and weekend events for those who work or attend school during the day.

8. *Recreation programs should make the fullest possible use of available community facilities and should adhere to a sound environmental ethic.*

Although most municipal recreation and park departments have excellent outdoor areas and facilities, many have insufficient indoor resources to meet community needs. Therefore, maximum use should be made of facilities owned by schools, churches, Ys, and other agencies, either through joint sponsorship arrangements or on an exchange-of-services basis.

9. *Recreation programs should be supervised and administered by qualified professionals.*

With a substantial number of colleges and universities today providing higher education in recreation, parks, and leisure services, all leadership and management positions involving full-time, professional-level functions should be filled by qualified personnel. Increasingly, certification based on initial and continuing education, experience, and/or performance on examinations is being used to identify professional personnel. At the same time, many leisure-service agencies make extensive use of nonprofessional leaders with specialized program skills, or paraprofessional leaders or volunteers under careful supervision and direction.

10. *Recreation programs should be systematically evaluated to determine whether they are meeting appropriate standards, achieving stated goals, and satisfying community needs.*

This evaluation may be accomplished through periodic program reports, reviews by department supervisors, surveying participants, or program appraisal by consultant teams. Evaluation has two key goals: (1) measuring whether the agency and its programs meet standards established by recognized professional societies; and (2) determining the extent to which program objectives have been realized.

11. *Community recreation programs should be meaningfully interpreted to the public through communications media, advisory councils, or other channels for two-way contact.*

Varied forms of communication, such as radio, television, newspapers, fliers, special reports, and town meetings or recreation councils should ensure that the public is given an accurate, constructive picture of the recreation program, including the problems it faces and the strategies it is using to solve them. Beyond this, strenuous efforts should be made to develop favorable community relations, through joint planning, program cosponsorship, or other forms of input or mutual assistance.

12. *Dynamism and creativity should be an essential part of programming.*

Leisure-service programs should be exciting and innovative. Presenting surprisingly new program elements, locations, and leadership approaches, as well as varying schedules and activity formats, stimulates public interest and participation.

Program Planning Approaches

In addition to such general guidelines, a number of leisure-service authors have identified recreation program planning models representing different approaches for leisure-service agencies to adopt. Howard Danford identified four such models: (1) the *traditional* approach, which relies heavily on activities that were successful in the past; (2) the *current-practices* model, which is influenced by trends in other agencies, as reported in the literature or at professional meetings; (3) the *expressed desires* model, which bases programming decisions on the expressed needs and interests of community residents; and (4) the *authoritarian* approach, in which decisions are made based on the planner's own knowledge and values.[5]

Elsewhere, the author of this text suggested a planning model termed the *sociopolitical* approach, in which changing social conditions and special-interest group pressures were seen as instrumental in shaping programming decisions. Later, James Murphy identified two other program-planning models: (1) the *cafeteria* approach, in which members of the public simply select from an extensive menu of varied program activities the activities that appeal to them; and (2) the *prescriptive* approach, in which recreation is used as a means of achieving social change, through intervention or active therapy.[6]

More recently, Edginton, Compton, and Hanson suggested several other program-planning theories, based on psychosocial foundations, which emphasized gathering and interpreting demographic data, identifying consumer needs, and developing a hierarchy of social values and functions. Edginton and his co-authors described recreation programming as analogous to a huge tree, with tap and feeder roots that contribute to or influence the process, consisting of eight factors: educational, geographical, historical/anthropological, psychological, sociological, biological, economic, and political.[7]

Other Contemporary Models

Some recreation programming authors, such as Carpenter and Howe, have drawn heavily on the behavioral sciences to design leisure programs that meet the developmental needs of participants at each stage of the life-cycle.[8]

Illustrating the trend toward developing highly complex or abstract approaches to program planning, Sandra Little presented a number of diagrammatic models dealing with leisure experiences and the programming process, in a recent issue of the *Journal of Physical Education, Recreation and Dance*.[9] One of these models is shown in Figure 2-2.

In another approach J. Robert Rossman has proposed that leisure-service program planners use "imaging"—that is, visualizing through one's internal imagination—to develop

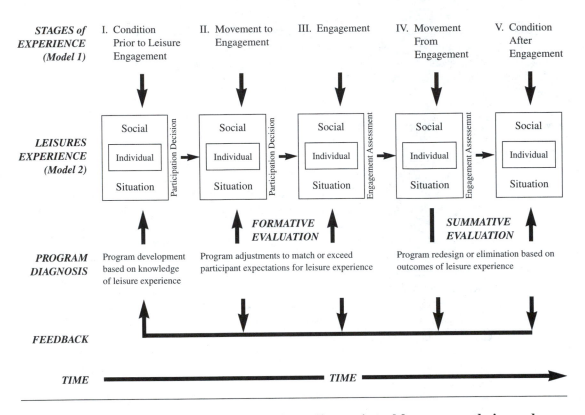

Figure 2-2.   Model of leisure experience used as a diagnostic tool for program design and evaluation (Little).

multiple forecasts of interaction scenarios as a means of anticipating possible errors in a program.[10]

While such innovative approaches clearly contribute to creative program planning in recreation, park, and leisure-service systems, one might ask whether pragmatic agency managers are likely to accept overly complex or theoretical approaches to programming.

Three Influential Approaches Today

Recognizing this, it is helpful to identify the most influential recreation program planning approaches today, in terms that are as simple and realistic as possible.

Three fundamental orientations dominate contemporary program planning. These are the *quality-of-life, human-service,* and *marketing* models of leisure-service programming.

Quality-of-Life Approach

This view holds that recreation represents a critical element in happy living, contributing broadly to relaxation and health, personal pleasure, family togetherness, and neighborhood solidarity. Recreation and leisure are seen as ends in themselves rather than as means to other ends.

Human-Service Approach

The human- or social-service approach to recreation and leisure regards recreation as not only a significant form of human experience but also a tool for achieving important social outcomes in the modern community, such as improving health and fitness, or reducing juvenile delinquency.

Marketing Approach

In contrast to the first two models, the marketing approach to recreation, parks, and leisure-services programming represents a business-like view of recreation as a commodity that should be designed and presented to the public at large or to target audiences using the same methods that business entrepreneurs use in delivering other products or services.

All organized recreation programs today reflect one or more of these influences, described more fully in Chapter 4. In some agencies, one or two approaches tend to dominate; in others, all three are at work. Obviously, in nonprofit organizations such as local public recreation and park agencies or youth-serving voluntary agencies, human-service needs must have a high priority. In contrast, commercial businesses and private-membership organizations must necessarily place greater emphasis on marketing goals and methods.

A Combined Approach: The Benefits-Driven Model

In an effort to synthesize the key features of each of the preceding three approaches to recreation-program planning, a growing number of professionals and educators have begun to present a *benefits-driven* model of programming. Detailed in Chapter 4, this approach emphasizes the need to define clearly the goals, purposes, and positive outcomes of programs, to focus sharply on achieving these benefits, and to systematically measure the degree to which they have been achieved. While this is a relatively new approach, it has been widely featured at professional conferences and in publications, and it seems probable that it will be adopted more widely in the years ahead.

The Program Development Cycle

Numerous authorities have identified the successive steps involved in recreation programming, which range from identifying agency goals and objectives, to conducting program activities and evaluating their outcomes, as shown in Figure 2-3.

In actual practice, these steps may overlap, or two or more tasks may be carried out at the same time. It would be rare for any leisure-service agency to follow the sequence shown in a consistent, uniform way. For example, a large municipal recreation and park department would be likely to have numerous different program elements, some of which continue year-round, some of which are seasonal, and others which have a brief program life. Each is likely to require different planning or implementation actions at different

1. Establish agency's philosophical base, or mission statement

2. Assess participant and community needs and interests, and agency's capabilities and resources

3. Identify specific recreation program goals and objectives

4. Explore full range of program possibilities and alternative activity/service formats

5. Formulate detailed program plan, including schedules, staff and facility assignments, and fiscal projections

6. Implement program, including publicity, registration, and ongoing supervision

7. Evaluate program, with continuing feedback for program modifications, and recommendations for future action

Figure 2-3.   Steps of recreation programming cycle.

points during the year. A typical recreation center director might simultaneously be meeting with community groups to plan a spring festival, overseeing a sports tournament currently under way and preparing a report on adult workshops in the arts that took place the previous fall.

Each of the seven steps in the recreation programming cycle is briefly described, to provide a preliminary understanding of the sequence.

1. *Establish Agency's Mission or Philosophical Base*

Before it is possible to make meaningful program planning decisions, it is necessary to identify the agency's mission or philosophical base. In many cases, the mission is made explicit in a constitution or set of bylaws, charter, enabling legislation, or other formal statement of purpose. In other cases, it may evolve over time through self-study task-force reports, or be influenced by goals statements or long-range planning reports of national boards or other sources of authority.

2. *Assess Participant and Community Needs and Interests*

A key preliminary step in program planning involves conducting a systematic assessment of participant needs, not only of those who have already been involved in agency activities, but also of other potential patrons. This assessment may be done through a variety of techniques that examine the views and leisure-related wishes of community residents or organization members.

From a broader perspective, this step may involve carrying out environmental scans, or audits. These involve studying the external environment within which the agency functions, including social and economic conditions, demographic trends, and the programs of other agencies. The agency's internal scan should include a detailed assessment of its past and present programming offerings, in terms of their relation to its overall mission, and also in terms of attendance, fiscal costs and returns, demonstrated benefits, and related elements.

3. *Identify Specific Program Goals and Objectives*

Having undertaken the preceding steps, an agency is now ready to identify the goals and objectives that it should strive to meet in its program offerings. Like environmental scans, goals are generally of two types: (1) *external,* representing the outcomes that the agency seeks to achieve for participants, or for the community at large; and (2) *internal,* which relate to operational efficiency, achieving public support and fiscal solvency, attendance or membership, and related organizational concerns.

In general, goals are broad statements of purpose, while objectives are concrete, short-term, measurable statements of projected accomplishments or program outcomes. In some cases, the agency's goals and objectives may be determined through its staff's independent decision-making process. Often, however, they are subject to higher authority, such as the national council of an organization, a recreation and park board or commission, or the commanding officer of an armed forces base.

4. *Explore Full Range of Program Possibilities*

As later chapters show, the range of program possibilities for leisure-service agencies is immense. It may include dozens of different types of sports and games, outdoor recreation pursuits, cultural arts, and social programs and hobbies, in a host of varied formats, such as instructional classes, special-interest groups, and competitive settings.

In considering each possible offering, program planners must ask these questions: Will this activity be of interest to community residents or organization members? Is it keyed to our agency goals and objectives? Does it meet the needs of women and girls, racial and ethnic minorities, the elderly, and people with disabilities? Are other agencies already offering such activities? If so, is there a need for us to do so?

5. *Formulate Detailed Program Plan*

Following the stage of identifying and considering all program options, it is necessary to make hard choices and outline a detailed program structure. Decision-making may be done in a number of ways, ranging from authoritarian action to a shared participative approach.

The plan itself should contain the following elements: (1) a listing of major program activities, with a designation of their locations, schedules, formats, and the populations to be served; (2) a time frame or flow chart, which outlines the sequence of publicizing events, registration, the activities themselves, and program evaluation and/or reports; (3) designated staff assignments for specific activities; and (4) budget breakdowns that itemize the anticipated costs of overall and separate program operations, along with the revenues expected from fees, rentals, and other charges.

6. *Program Implementation*

This is the action-oriented, service-delivery phase of the programming process. At the outset, it includes varied forms of direct publicity to promote and sustain public interest, attendance, and support. Public relations efforts may also be designed to inform and influence the power structure that ultimately controls the leisure-service enterprise, such as city officials, hospital medical directors, and other administrative heads.

A second important task in implementing programs involves registration. Many leisure-service agencies conduct organized programs such as classes, leagues, workshops, and series of events or performances that require the initial payment of fees during preliminary sign-up periods. As Chapter 10 will show, registration procedures have become increasingly efficient through the use of phone-in or credit-card registration, and through the use of computer software packages.

As programs get under way, careful supervision is required to ensure that activities are carried on with a maximum degree of participant satisfaction. Supervisors must maintain open lines of communication, so problems are dealt with properly, assistance is given to program directors when necessary, and conflicts are resolved promptly.

Emphasis must be placed on careful risk management and the enforcement of sound safety and accident-prevention practices. Strict attention must be paid to the environmental impact of program activities, and to compliance with legislative and court-mandated guidelines governing discrimination against program participants and staff.

7. *Program Monitoring and Evaluation*

Evaluation—the systematic, objective measurement of program quality and outcomes—represents the final phase of the leisure-service program development process.

Evaluation is often viewed narrowly as the effort at the conclusion of the activity, to judge whether it has been successful. Typically, program participants and perhaps staff members may be asked to fill out a rating sheet at the end of an event indicating their overall appraisal of it. Such a review is essential in determining whether a given offering should be continued in future programs, or whether its format or method of presentation should be changed.

However, evaluation should also be carried on *throughout* a program's operation, in order to gather feedback that may be used at any point to change leadership methods or make other needed modifications in service delivery. Both forms of evaluation contribute to the agency's total management information system. Having comprehensive data on all program aspects, including attendance, costs and revenues, use of facilities, and staff performance, is critical to managerial effectiveness. Having access to computer systems that store, analyze, and transmit quantitative data of this type is an important ingredient in the evaluation process.

To illustrate the ways in which computer software systems may be used to plan, monitor, and evaluate programs, Figure 2-4 lists a number of the specific applications of computers in program registration procedures, and Figure 2-5 shows how a computer spreadsheet provides instant, comprehensive information regarding participant reservations in several activity areas.

While such computerized tracking systems are invaluable in planning, implementing, and evaluating programs, not all kinds of important information can be effectively expressed through numbers. Therefore, comprehensive evaluative procedures should also include qualitative judgments that involve observation and anecdotal materials, and that take account of the human factor in leisure-service programming.

Household and Family Members:

Household information includes ID No. assigned automatically or manually, names, addresses, and telephone numbers for two guardians, as well as resident/non-resident, insurance data, and optional activity interests and groupings and gender, birthday, school grade, social security number, optional medical record, etc.

Activities and Sections:

Provides for multiple activities and sections with optional sales tax. Tracks waiting lists, current and past enrollments, pre-registration, and activity income and expense, cancellations and refund processing, and all fee and payment data.

Instructors:

Instructors can have multiple pay rates and can be paid on an hourly, percent, or flat fee basis. Includes tracking of job descriptions, special hiring information, job performance data, and termination reasons. Each activity can be assigned a primary instructor, and secondary instructors.

Reports and Forms:

Activity listings, rosters, status reports; attendance worksheets; below minimum enrollment reports, waiting list reports, registration receipts, mailing labels, user codes reports, instructor evaluations, instructor comments report, family member comments report, etc.

Figure 2-4.   Example of computer software functions in program registration.

```
RecTrac! Demo Data Base                          RecTrac                              Page  1
Run Date: 11/02/94                        FACILITY SCHEDULE BY DATE
Run Time: 13:29:30                        10/01/94 THROUGH 10/12/94                    User ZZZ

Rsv No   Date     Beg Tm End Tm  Src      Lookup Name      Home Phone    Work Phone      Type   Loc'n Facil Maint  Cnt Stat
------   ----     ------ ------  ---      -----------      ----------    ----------      ----   ----- ----- -----  --- ----
   508  10/01/94  10:00A11:00A   L/S      Soccer League 8 and Und  N/A    N/A            SOCCR  HS    1             0 Firm
   508  10/01/94  11:00A12:00P   L/S      Soccer League 8 and Und  N/A    N/A            SOCCR  HS    1             0 Firm
   508  10/01/94  12:00P01:00P   L/S      Soccer League 8 and Und  N/A    N/A            SOCCR  HS    1             0 Firm
-----  RESERVATION COUNT FOR ABOVE DATE ------)    3 -----------------------------------------------------------------
   455  10/02/94  02:00P04:00P   F/R      Special Olympics        (802)879-3432 (802)878-5532  GYM   HS   GYM  HOOP 110 Firm
                                          CONTACT ==) John Edwards
-----  RESERVATION COUNT FOR ABOVE DATE ------)    1 -----------------------------------------------------------------
   477  10/03/94  07:00P09:00P   A/R      25081-A Photography     N/A    N/A            ROOM   CENTR ROOM1          0 Intl
                                          CONTACT ==) Giles Willey
   503  10/03/94  09:00A10:00A   F/R      Babe Ruth League        (802)878-9343 (802)654-5833  BASEB HS   D1         0 Firm
                                          CONTACT ==) Randy Jones
   474  10/03/94  06:00P09:00P   A/R      22011-C Coed Volleybal  N/A    N/A            GYM    HS    GYM           0 Intl
                                          CONTACT ==) Don Trombley
-----  RESERVATION COUNT FOR ABOVE DATE ------)    3 -----------------------------------------------------------------
   477  10/05/94  07:00P09:00P   A/R      25081-A Photography     N/A    N/A            ROOM   CENTR ROOM1          0 Intl
                                          CONTACT ==) Giles Willey
   503  10/05/94  09:00A10:00A   F/R      Babe Ruth League        (802)878-9343 (802)654-5833  BASEB HS   D1         0 Firm
                                          CONTACT ==) Randy Jones
   474  10/05/94  06:00P09:00P   A/R      22011-C Coed Volleybal  N/A    N/A            GYM    HS    GYM           0 Intl
                                          CONTACT ==) Don Trombley
-----  RESERVATION COUNT FOR ABOVE DATE ------)    3 -----------------------------------------------------------------
   508  10/06/94  05:30P06:30P   L/S      Soccer League 8 and Und  N/A    N/A            SOCCR  HS    1             0 Firm
-----  RESERVATION COUNT FOR ABOVE DATE ------)    1 -----------------------------------------------------------------
   508  10/08/94  10:00A11:00A   L/S      Soccer League 8 and Und  N/A    N/A            SOCCR  HS    1             0 Firm
   508  10/08/94  11:00A12:00P   L/S      Soccer League 8 and Und  N/A    N/A            SOCCR  HS    1             0 Firm
   508  10/08/94  12:00P01:00P   L/S      Soccer League 8 and Und  N/A    N/A            SOCCR  HS    1             0 Firm
-----  RESERVATION COUNT FOR ABOVE DATE ------)    3 -----------------------------------------------------------------
```

Figure 2-5.   Example of computer spreadsheet tracking activity registrations.

Source: Rec Trac! (Vermont Systems, Inc.)

Other Factors in Program Development

Beyond the basic concepts and programming processes that have been described in this chapter, there are a number of other important forces at work in the planning and implementation of recreation, park, and leisure-service programs.

These include such factors as developing an adequate fiscal framework for the funding of recreation programs, balancing marketing against human-service needs, and reconciling the conflicting needs and interests of different groups of residents, organization members, or potential participants. Each of these factors is discussed at greater length in the following chapters of this text.

Summary

Beginning with an overview of general principles and guidelines for recreation program planning, this chapter describes a number of traditional and contemporary theories of program development. It then stresses three major orientations that influence leisure-service agencies today: the *quality-of-life, human-service,* and *marketing* perspectives. Also discussed is a fourth approach, the *benefits-driven* model, which many programmers are adopting today.

A seven-step sequence of the process of recreation program development is presented, including: (1) establishing the agency's philosophical base, or mission; (2) assessing participant and community needs and conducting internal and external environmental scans; (3) identifying specific program goals and objectives; (4) exploring the full range of program possibilities; (5) formulating an overall program plan; (6) implementing the program, with emphasis on such steps as publicity, registration, ongoing supervision, and risk management; and (7) carrying out systematic evaluation and monitoring procedures, both during program operations and at their end.

Suggested Questions for Class Discussion

1. Clarify the meaning of the terms *program* and *programming.* Give examples of each of the three kinds of program functions carried out by public leisure-service agencies: providing organized program activities under leadership; providing places and special facilities for largely self-directed recreation; and facilitating or coordinating recreation programs in the community at large.
2. Individuals or small groups of students could review and analyze the programs of community leisure-service agencies with which they are familiar, or agencies that they may visit as a class assignment, in terms of:

a. Determining the extent to which the agencies adhere to the programming guidelines presented on pages 24–29; or
b. Examining the agencies' overall approaches to program development, in terms of the models formulated by Danford, Murphy, Edginton, and others, or in terms of the quality-of-life, human-service, and marketing approaches detailed in the chapter.

References

1. James A. Busser, "Leisure Programming: The State of the Art," *Journal of Physical Education, Recreation and Dance (Leisure Today),* Oct. 1993, p. 1.
2. *Webster's New International Dictionary of the English Language* (Springfield, MA: Merriam Publishers, 1956), p. 1977.
3. J. Robert Rossman, *Recreation Programming: Designing Leisure Experiences* (Champaign, IL: Sagamore Publishing, 1989), p. 3.
4. "NRPA/APRS Adopts Recreation Programmers Division," in *Bulletin of NRPA Northeast Service Center,* Rocky Hill, CT: Mar. 1994.
5. Howard Danford, *Creative Leadership in Recreation* (Boston, MA: Allyn and Bacon, 1964).
6. James F. Murphy, *Recreation and Leisure: A Humanistic Perspective* (Dubuque, IA: Wm. C. Brown Publishers, 1989). p. 1
7. Christopher R. Edginton, David M. Compton, and Carole J. Hanson, *Recreation and Leisure Programming: A Guide for the Professional* (Dubuque, IA: Wm. C. Brown Publishers, 1989), p. 16.
8. Christine Z. Howe and Gaylene M. Carpenter, *Programming Leisure Experiences* (Englewood Cliffs, NJ: Prentice-Hall, Inc., 1985).
9. Sandra L. Little, "Leisure Program Design and Evaluation," *Journal of Physical Education, Recreation and Dance,* Oct. 1993, pp. 27–28.
10. J. Robert Rossman, "Program Design Through Imagery," *Journal of Physical Education, Recreation and Dance,* Oct. 1993, pp. 30–32.

Chapter 3

Setting the Stage:
The Leisure-Service System

When asked if they are in the "recreation industry," many [commercial recreation managers] deny that they are. Instead, they say that they are in the business of selling hotel rooms, meals, airline seats, tennis memberships, and so forth. Whereas recreation professionals believe that they are in the business of facilitating a total leisure experience, traditional commercial managers often see themselves merely as sellers of a specific product.[1]

This chapter presents an overview of the eight major types of leisure-service agencies. It describes these agencies' organizational structure or legal authorization, their philosophy and program emphases, the populations they serve, and related types of information. While many recreation, park, and leisure-studies students may have been exposed to such information in other courses, for those who are beginning study in this field, this orientation to the overall leisure-service system is essential.

Following the descriptions of the separate agency categories, the chapter discusses the similarities and differences of the eight groups of leisure-service sponsors. It shows both how they tend to compete with each other and how they cooperate in co-sponsorship arrangements and resource sharing. Throughout, examples of program practices of agencies throughout the United States and Canada are presented.

The topics presented in this chapter relate to the following undergraduate curriculum objectives established by the NRPA/AALR Council on Accreditation:

Understanding of the roles and interrelationships of diverse leisure-service delivery systems, including such specialties as the therapeutic recreation and the business enterprise system. (8.12)

Understanding of the concept and use of leisure resources to facilitate participant involvement. (8.19)

Knowledge of the legal foundations and responsibilities of leisure-service agencies, and of the legislative process and the impact of policy formation on leisure behaviors and service, in all levels of government, community organizations, and business enterprise. (8.36)

Understanding the Leisure-Service System

Why is it important to have an in-depth understanding of the eight different types of agencies that provide organized recreation and park programs?

First, there is the obvious point that recreation and leisure sponsors do not operate in a vacuum. Different organizations often share similar goals and methods, and, as this chapter will show, both compete and cooperate with each other in joint programming efforts. Therefore a narrow focus on a single type of recreation agency would not provide recreation and park students with an adequate understanding of the overall leisure-service field, or prepare them to operate effectively in joint partnership program ventures.

Beyond this, although many leisure-studies students may have a strong initial interest in a specialized area of service—such as public recreation and park management, or therapeutic recreation service—the reality is that leisure studies is an immensely diversified field in which professionals may move from one specialization to another as they pursue their careers. Obviously, a basic understanding of the overall recreation, park, and leisure-service field, and the varying program emphases of different types of agencies, will be helpful at an early stage of professional development.

The term *system* has been widely used in the social sciences and in business management studies in recent years. Generally, it is used to refer to any institution, social process, or other phenomenon that has a number of separate parts that in some way relate to or are connected to each other.

Thus, one may refer to the health-care system, the educational system, the transportation system, or the leisure-service system of a nation. Clearly, organized recreation service is *not* a system in the sense of being a fully integrated or coordinated structure, having differentiated functions and logically determined assignment of responsibilities. However, it *is* a system in the sense that its different parts interact with each other and, taken as a whole, provide an immense body of varied leisure programs for the population.

In the United States and Canada today, there are eight different types of agencies that provide recreation and leisure programs and services. They are: (1) public, governmental recreation and park departments; (2) voluntary, nonprofit organizations; (3) commercial recreation businesses; (4) private-membership organizations; (5) therapeutic recreation services; (6) armed forces recreation units; (7) employee recreation programs; and (8) college- and university-sponsored programs.

---

1. Governmental Recreation and Park Agencies

The type of organization that chiefly is responsible for meeting the overall recreation needs of the public at large is the local, governmentally-sponsored recreation and park agency.

In most U.S. and Canadian communities, local government has assigned a public, tax-supported department, bureau, or office of recreation and parks the function of providing constructive leisure-service opportunities in the form of organized activities or physical facilities for play. Such agencies may be found on any of several levels: city, town, village, special district, or county. In many cases, school districts also provide independent or cooperative recreation programming for youth and adults. Other community agencies, such as housing authorities, youth-service boards, libraries, and offices concerned with cultural development or environmental protection, may also offer tax-supported or subsidized recreation programs.

The rationale for local government's sponsoring public recreation and park programs and areas was expressed several decades ago by George Butler:

Municipal government offers many individuals their primary or only opportunity for wholesome recreational involvement, particularly among poorer people in large cities.

Only through government can adequate funds be acquired for playgrounds, parks, and other outdoor recreation areas.

Municipal recreation is "democratic and inclusive"; it serves all ages, races, and creeds, and places the burden of support upon the entire community.

Municipal recreation is comparatively inexpensive, when compared with private expenditure for recreation; yet, by spreading the cost of development over the entire population, municipal recreation can provide a full range of facilities and services.

People demand public recreation and are willing to be taxed for it, as evidenced by steady growth of programs, passage of referenda and bond issues, and overall support of recreation through the years.[2]

Today, the authority and functions of municipal recreation and park agencies are defined in state-enabling legislation and in local ordinances, charters, educational codes, and other legal documents. Typically, local governmental recreation and park agencies are administered by a director, superintendent, or general manager appointed by the mayor, city council, or public recreation and park board or commission. Other professional staff members, such as program specialists, full-time leaders, and maintenance and construction personnel are usually part of the civil service structure.

Funding of public recreation and park departments has traditionally been supplied by general tax funds, with land acquisition and facility development costs often met by special bond issues. Today, growing numbers of more affluent communities and suburban areas rely heavily on fees and charges to support their operational budgets.

MACPARS Report. In a major mid-1980s study of municipal and county recreation and park departments in the United States carried out by the University of Georgia, in cooperation with the United States Forest Service, detailed information was gathered from over 1,240 small, medium, and large communities.[3] Small and medium-sized recreation and park operations were generally found to be carried on under municipal jurisdictions, while larger communities were more often served through county agencies. In many cases, departments cooperated with school systems in providing indoor and outdoor programs.

Most departments operated extensive sports fields and courts, as well as pools, gymnasiums, and recreation centers. Many also provided natural-resource-oriented facilities, such as campsites, lakes, and trails for hiking or biking. Programs serving persons with physical or mental disabilities were provided in about half of the communities studied, with special programs for elderly persons being offered by about two-thirds of the departments.

Examples of Programs and Services

Many large municipal and county departments offer extensive and varied ranges of classes, workshops, special events, and competitive programs. To illustrate, the Department of Recreation of Montgomery County, Maryland, recently sponsored the following fall programs:

Senior Adult Bowling Tournament
Co-Recreational Fall Softball
Special Interest Car Meet
Fall County-Wide Classes in Fine
    Arts, Crafts, Dance, Fitness
Senior Adult Track Meet, Golf
    Tourney, Tennis Clinic, and
    Senior Olympics
Germantown Oktoberfest
Hallowe'en Party, Parade, and
    Games

Creative Carousel Pre-School Program
Senior Adult Sports Fest
Men's Fall Softball, Touch Football, and
    Men's and Women's Soccer
Eastern Area Swap Meet
Ethnic Heritage Festival
Maryland Professional Baseball School
Learn-to-Swim Program
Therapeutic Recreation Fall Program
Senior Adult Tea Dance
Annual Rubber Bridge Tournament

Administrative Program Structures

Most municipal and county leisure-service agencies structure their year-round programs under three types of headings or administrative divisions: (1) categories of participants; (2) major groups of activities; and (3) geographical locations, such as districts or major facilities.

Categories of Participants.   For example, the municipal Department of Recreation and Culture in Ottawa, Canada, has six such administrative subdivisions: Preschool Programs, Children's Programs, Youth Programs, Adult Programs, Senior Adult Programs, and Programs for Persons with Disabilities.

Programming by Groups of Activities and Services.   Typically, the Long Beach, California, Department of Parks, Recreation and Marine offers hundreds of classes, workshops, leagues, events, and free-play opportunities grouped under such program units as Arts and Crafts, Beauty and Self-Improvement; Dance; Fitness; Music; Special Interests and Hobby Groups.

Program Organization by Facilities.   In this third approach to program organization, many large recreation and park departments offer groups of activities at such facilities as sports or fitness centers; cultural or performing arts centers; youth and senior centers; nature centers; skating rinks; historical sites; and other facilities serving specialized leisure interests.

Beyond their major role of providing recreational programs and related leisure opportunities, many public departments also serve the important function of promoting leisure awareness as a social concern. Typically, they may assist other agencies with leadership training, scheduling and publicity, the use of facilities, and related management concerns.

Government Functions on Other Levels

In both the United States and Canada, government provides tax-supported recreation programs and facilities on other levels, such as state, provincial, and federal agencies. The National Park Service, the U.S. Forest Service, and the Bureau of Land Management in the United States, and Parks Canada, are federal departments with huge networks of forests, parks, historic sites, reservoirs and lakes, and other sites for outdoor recreation. Other federal agencies provide assistance to leisure-related arts programs, tourism and commerce, services for the elderly and people with disabilities, and research or technical assistance related to various forms of recreation.

Similarly, state and provincial agencies provide varied forms of outdoor and wilderness recreation, along with programs concerned with multicultural and national heritage, special populations, and other social and cultural needs. States and provinces maintain a network of hospitals and other institutions serving persons with mental illness or developmental disability, dependent aging persons, and other special populations.

2. *Voluntary, Nonprofit Community Organizations*

A second major type of leisure-service agency in the United States and Canada is the community-based, nonprofit organization that serves the public with a wide range of leisure programs and services. These agencies are nongovernmental and therefore are not tax-supported, although some receive support in the form of special government grants or contracts.

Such organizations operate under administrative policies that usually are set by boards of unpaid private citizens, hence the term *voluntary*. Despite the voluntary nature of these agencies' boards, many have extensive staffs of paid professionals in addition to volunteers. In the past they were often referred to as "youth-serving" or "character-building" organizations. Today, many serve a broader age range, with programs designed to meet the needs of members for varied experiences that contribute to healthy physical, social, emotional, and intellectual growth.

Types of Nonprofit Agencies

Such organizations are generally of two types, from an administrative perspective: (1) those that operate as part of a large-scale national structure, federation, or governing body, with local units that provide direct services; and (2) independent, local organizations that have their own trustees or boards. Most such agencies are incorporated under state laws governing charitable or nonprofit educational and religious associations.

Such nonprofit groups rely on membership fees, gifts, and fund-raising drives for financial support. As quasi-public organizations, they are able to be more actively involved in community or social issues than tax-supported public agencies. In some cases, they may have a degree of relationship with government, as in the case of the Police Athletic League, which often has police officers in administrative or leadership roles.

Nonprofit, leisure-related groups are of three general types in terms of sponsorship and program focus: (1) *nonsectarian* youth-serving agencies; (2) youth-serving organizations *linked to a specific denomination* or religious institution; and (3) *special-interest organizations* that tend to serve a broader age range, and that focus on a specific area of social need or recreational involvement.

Nonsectarian Youth-Serving Agencies

There are thousands of such organizations throughout the United States and Canada. This chapter presents brief descriptions of three of the largest and most influential such organizations today.

Girl Scouts.   Girl Scouts of the U.S.A. is the largest nonprofit organization for girls in the world, with approximately 3.5 million girl and adult members in eighty countries. Members subscribe to the ideals stated in the Girl Scout Promise and Law, and take part in diverse programs for different age-level groupings. These programs include recreational, educational, citizenship, and cross-cultural activities and projects with a special focus on the challenges facing girls and women in modern society.

Police Athletic League.   This is a recreation-oriented, juvenile-crime-prevention program that relies heavily on athletics and recreational activities to improve relations between police officers and children and youth, particularly in high-risk inner-city neighborhoods. Affiliated with the National Association of Police Athletic Leagues, Inc., and numerous other organizations, it serves over three million boys and girls in over eight hundred cities and towns in the United States and its territories, and in Canada. It offers over one hundred different recreational, cultural, and educational programs, including team sports, boxing, drum and bugle corps, hobbies, crafts, and computer clubs. In addition, it sponsors numerous citizenship and leadership development programs and projects.

Boys' and Girls' Clubs.   The Boys' Clubs of America began as an all-male program, with a separate Girls' Club movement in many communities. Both had the goal of reaching children and youth living in neighborhoods threatened by poverty, gangs, and varied forms of social pathology. Today, the two groups have merged in joint Boys' and Girls' Clubs that serve one million boys and three-hundred thousand girls. Clubs offer a variety of recreational pursuits, along with tutoring and employment projects; special programs in housing developments, schools, and churches; teen travel programs, National Youth of the Year competitions, and related ventures.

Religious-Sponsored Youth-Serving Agencies

A second major category of nonprofit youth-serving organizations is groups that are affiliated with or directly sponsored by religious denominations or institutions. Millions of young people in the United States and Canada are involved with such groups and their programs, which often include important recreational elements.

Religious-sponsored youth organizations, which may be independent or may be part of national federations or movements, have several purposes: (1) to promote specific religious values through such experiences as camping, discussion groups or clubs, sports and the arts, and leadership and volunteer projects; (2) to provide a positive counterpart to the many negative influences on young people; and (3) to serve as a means of involving young people in the overall work of the church, temple, or other religious institution, or as a means of enriching their sense of affiliation.

Each of the major religious denominations in the United States and Canada provides varied forms of recreation and related education and social programs for its members, particularly children and youth.

Protestant.   Most Protestant sects, such as Methodist, Baptist, and Lutheran, sponsor national youth organizations that promote religious education, recreation, and other social services. In addition, individual churches or networks of churches of the same denomination within a city or metropolitan region often sponsor sports, clubs, camping, social events, and leadership training activities, along with religious education and Bible study.

College students hold job internships in armed forces recreation programs, on a canoe trip in Fort Wainright, Alaska, and learning office management skills in Camp Zama, Japan. In voluntary youth organizations like the Boys and Girls Clubs of America, sports play an important role, and well-known entertainment stars like Denzel Washington often serve as national spokespersons.

Catholic. Within the Roman Catholic Church, the National Federation for Catholic Youth Ministry works to foster the personal and spiritual growth of young people.

A key force in this effort is the Catholic Youth Organization, which sponsors extensive programs coordinated at diocesan levels and supplemented in individual churches and parishes. Sports in particular are viewed as a means of leading young people to "Christ-centered" lifestyles. One diocesan CYO states that the purpose of its athletic program is to

> . . . *provide not only for the development of particular physical skills, but also social interaction, emotional stability, affirmation and spiritual strength. . . . The coach's challenge is to take those teachable moments of victory or loss and give witness to Christian values by the manner in which he/she mentors the young people. CYO sports are committed to the acceptance of and love for people of all nationalities and races. Through our CYO program, we build community and a bond of unity. . . . CYO sports are different from secular athletic programs.*[4]

Camping and environmental education represent major program areas in a number of large metropolitan areas. In Cleveland, for example, the Catholic Youth Organization operates several day and overnight camping sites, including Camp Christopher, an extensive facility that houses eight week-long sessions for children and youth, with special sessions for individuals of all ages with disabilities.

Jewish. In a third major category of religious sponsorship, the Jewish Community Center Association comprises 275 Jewish community centers, Young Men's and Young Women's Hebrew Associations and camps in North America, with over a million participants taking part in diverse program opportunities.

Typically, Jewish community centers offer sports and fitness, music, drama and dance, arts and crafts, lectures, holiday celebrations, and social programs for all ages. Teen leadership conferences include workshops on AIDS, anti-Semitism, family relationships, and maintaining Jewish identity. Within such programs, recreational activities serve the purpose of being "threshold" attractions that encourage young people to join temples or synagogues and maintain religious affiliations.

Beyond those organizations that are affiliated with particular denominations, other major leisure-service agencies have religious connections. For example, the Young Men's Christian Association and Young Women's Christian Association traditionally were linked to Protestantism and had strong Bible studies components, although these organizations have now de-emphasized their spiritual program content. Today, the YWCA describes itself in the following terms:

> *The YWCA works for the empowerment of women through advocacy on public issues that affect and concern women and the lives they touch. Men can join as associate members with all membership benefits except voting rights. The YWCA's goals encompass the struggle for peace, justice, freedom and dignity for all people and the elimination of racism wherever it exists . . .*[5]

The YWCA works toward these goals by sponsoring literacy centers, alternative high school programs for young mothers and counseling for young fathers, day care programs, networking projects for disabled women and girls, employment programs for displaced homemakers, and related projects. At the same time, recreation is a major part of the YWCA's offering, including numerous classes, clubs, and events in sports and fitness, the arts, hobbies, and areas of personal and professional growth.

Special-Interest Organizations

In addition to the type of agencies just described, a third form of nonprofit organization is characterized by having a special interest, in terms of either promoting a particular activity, or meeting a special social need.

Sports-Related Groups

In the United States and Canada, there are varied nonprofit organizations concerned with the operation of amateur and professional sports on every level. Usually, they direct themselves to the promotion of a single sport.

Leading examples of such groups include Little League and Babe Ruth Baseball, which sponsor or sanction competitive leagues for different age groups on a local level, leading to national and international championships. The United States Tennis Association promotes and governs tennis play on various levels, sponsoring such special projects as the USTA National Junior Tennis League, the USTA Schools Program, and numerous similar ventures. Similarly, the American Bowling Congress sponsors major tournaments, publishes magazines, sets rules for competition and equipment inspection, and has over twenty separate departments that promote and market bowling as a popular form of recreation.

Finally, organizations such as the National Association of Youth Leagues and the National Youth Sports Coaches Association conduct varied activities that range from leadership training and coaching certification, to parent education, volunteer coaching award programs, and programs that deal with sports management concerns such as equipment purchasing, insurance, and legal services.

Environmental and Outdoor Recreation Groups

Another major category of nonprofit organizations consists of groups such as the Sierra Club and the Appalachian Mountain Club, which are concerned with environmental issues and outdoor recreation.

For example, the National Outdoor Leadership School in Lander, Wyoming, is directly concerned with sponsoring courses in wilderness skills, conservation, and leadership in mountaineering, wilderness exploration, and water-based skills such as kayaking and canoeing. Each year, the school conducts dozens of such courses, including such specialties as horsepacking, skiing and dogsledding, glacier mountaineering, and whitewater rafting in settings throughout the world.

The organizations described here represent only a tiny segment of the full range of nonprofit membership groups that promote forms of special recreational interests. Hundreds of other groups serve leisure needs in areas of cultural or creative involvement, such as amateur theater, music, and dance; arts and crafts; hobbies and collecting pastimes; and chess and card games.

3. *Commercial Recreation Businesses*

A third major type of recreation-sponsoring organization consists of commercial recreation businesses. These are businesses or companies that provide recreation programs, services, products, or equipment to the public at large, on a for-profit basis.

Broadly viewed, commercial recreation encompasses the fields of travel and tourism, entertainment or professional sports, fitness centers, private instruction in recreational activities, and the manufacture of leisure-related supplies, vehicles, clothing, and equipment. Examples are theme parks, resorts, cruise ships, private camps, dance studios, bowling centers, racquet sports clubs, health spas, sports stadiums, and places combining entertainment and socializing, including night clubs, bars and taverns, movie houses, gambling casinos, and dinner theaters.

Commercial recreation businesses fall under three categories of ownership: (1) *sole proprietorship,* in which one individual owns the business fully and is in total charge of its operation; (2) *partnership,* in which two or more persons own and operate a business with shared financial responsibilities and management powers; and (3) *corporation,* which is a legal entity, typically owned by shareholders (either publicly or privately) and represented by a board of directors who oversee the corporation's goals and policies, and hire the management team that runs the operation.

Commercial recreation managers often have a limited background in recreational programming or philosophy, and tend to see themselves chiefly as entrepreneurs who are selling a product or service. However, they are becoming increasingly aware of the value of intelligently planned program activities and special events that draw customers and satisfy their leisure needs and interests. In many cases, commercial recreation managers sponsor programs jointly with public or other leisure-service agencies, or involve recreation professionals in their planning. In addition, they now participate widely in major recreation and park conferences and training programs, advertise in professional journals, and see themselves as more closely involved in the overall leisure enterprise.

For example, Crossley describes a chain of sports retailers in Colorado and Utah whose stores are known as Sports Castles:

> . . . . *they have basketball courts, tennis courts, ski ramps, golf cages, casting pools and other facilities where patrons can try out the equipment. They offer instructional classes, sell sports travel and ski area passes, and sponsor a variety of community events.*[6]

Examples of Innovative Commercial Ventures

Beyond such expanded marketing efforts, commercial recreation sponsors are often quick to develop new enterprises based on emerging public trends. For example, when travelers brought back word of bungee-jumping in Australia, numerous jump centers were established around the United States (some legal and some covert), with people paying substantial fees to jump attached to long rubber cables from bridges, cliffs, or giant cranes.

Similarly, when games of make-believe stalking and assassination became popular on college campuses and in other settings, some entrepreneurs began to devise commercial forms of warlike or murder-centered play, including special equipment and team structures. Figure 3-1 illustrates one such venture, using air guns and paint balls, in rural Pennsylvania.

Another trend involves commercially operated family-fun, gymnastic, and martial arts centers designed primarily for children's recreation. These centers operate in many communities today (see Figures 3-2 and 3-3).

Figure 3-1.   Example of innovative programming: brochure for new stalking sport.

Figure 3-2, 3-3. Examples of advertisements for children's gymnastics and family-play centers.

Other commercial recreation sponsors take what traditionally were fairly simple pursuits, and expand them into complex and expensive forms of play. Hunting now represents a major business, as illustrated by Canadian outfitters in Quebec's sub-Arctic territory, who package trips to shoot moose, black bear, caribou, snow geese, and other game, with elaborate arrangements for flying hunters into remote locations, providing accommodations and guide service, obtaining permits, and transporting meat or trophies. Charges range in the thousands of dollars.

4. *Private-Membership Organizations*

A fourth type of sponsor of recreation programs is private-membership organizations. These include country clubs, yacht clubs, golf clubs, tennis clubs, and hunting and fishing clubs that customarily own and operate their own facilities, serving only their own members and their guests. Other examples of private-membership organizations include fraternal and service clubs, and condominium, vacation, and retirement communities with extensive play facilities and programs designed to serve only their own residents.

Such organizations are usually constituted in one of two ways: (1) as *membership associations* formed by private citizens who maintain control over them through elected officers and committees; or (2) as *organizations that are commercially owned and operated*, within the general format of private-membership groups. Often, they have highly selective admission policies requiring careful screening by membership committees.

Although they serve only a limited segment of the population, private-membership organizations provide a significant segment of leisure opportunity, particularly in terms of outdoor recreation, sports, and social programming. Some social scientists have pointed out that as the quality of public recreation and park facilities and services has declined in many metropolitan areas, wealthier families have tended to retreat behind the walls of these private-membership associations and clubs.

A useful example of private-membership recreation programming linked to residential development is found in Sun City, Arizona, the nation's largest retirement community. To accommodate the interests of its more than 45,000 members, the Recreation Centers of Sun City, a nonprofit corporation serving residents and their guests, sponsors 150 different chartered clubs offering an immense range of sports, hobbies, social, and creative pastimes, in seven large recreation centers.

Residence-Based Programs

In many residential complexes, for example, swimming pools, fitness centers, and tennis courts are routine parts of the builder's appeal to potential buyers or renters. One such residential complex is Starrett at Spring Creek, a twenty-thousand resident, middle-income, ethnically diverse community in Brooklyn, New York. This forty-six building apartment complex is virtually a self-contained city, with its own shopping center, newspaper, television studio, schools, medical/dental center, and recreational facilities that include:

Football and baseball fields, handball and basketball courts, outdoor playground, sitting area, walkways and bicycle paths. A 8,500 square-foot center houses a state-of-the-art facility for health and fitness. . . . It has year-round Olympic and children's swimming pools, and a year-round tennis facility with 10 indoor-outdoor courts and *organized instruction and competitive leagues. Numerous cultural, social and entertainment programs and trips, including artists-in-residence, performance, concerts and exhibitions enrich the program.[7]*

5. Therapeutic Recreation Service

The fifth important category of organized leisure-service programming is therapeutic recreation service, defined in the mid-1990s as follows:

> *Practiced in clinical, residential, and community settings, the profession of therapeutic recreation uses treatment, education, and recreation services to help people with illnesses, disabilities, and other conditions to develop and use their leisure in ways that enhance their health, independence, and well-being.[8]*

Illustrating the increased recognition of recreation as a health-related field, therapeutic recreation consists of leisure programs and services designed to meet the needs of persons with varied types of physical, mental, and social disabilities and illnesses. When intended as a form of treatment or rehabilitation, therapeutic recreation may be offered in hospitals, nursing homes, physical rehabilitation and mental health centers, where activities are provided within a medically directed clinical framework to achieve specific treatment objectives.

When provided in community settings, special recreation programs are often very similar to those serving nondisabled persons, except that it may be necessary to modify equipment, rules, or other aspects of participation, to ensure successful performance and satisfaction for persons with disabilities. Following national trends toward deinstitutionalization and the effort to mainstream persons with disabilities into various aspects of community life, the policy today is to provide leisure opportunities in integrated settings whenever possible.

Therapeutic recreation may be sponsored by many different kinds of organizations, including numerous nonprofit groups and service clubs, and public recreation and park departments, as shown in Figure 3-4. Many such organizations have established special centers with modified equipment and staff members who have formal training in this field.

6. Recreation in the Armed Forces

The sixth separate category of organized leisure service consists of program serving populations on military bases. Historically, the purpose of military recreation has been to contribute

Individuals with physical disabilities take part today in a wide range of sports and outdoor activities. Wheelchair athletes (top left) compete in racing in Kamloops, British Columbia, and in skiing outings using modified equipment, in New England's Northeast Passage outdoor recreation program. Wheelchair tennis (bottom) has become an increasingly popular sport for many participants.

SOMETHING TO THINK ABOUT

Do you have a child with a disability?

Would you like him/her to enjoy a summer camp experience with other children from your community?

MCDR encourages parents to **consider MAINSTREAMING** (participation in community summer camp programs) as an opportunity for fun and growth for disabled children. Accommodations to ensure successful participation in summer camps are provided upon request as follows:

Interpreter • Financial Assistance
Adapted Equipment • Companion*

*A minimum of 4 weeks is needed to arrange for companions and interpreters. Although every effort will be made to provide companions, they cannot be guaranteed.

Summer brochures will be available in each area office by the end of February. Register immediately if mainstreaming interests you as space is limited.

For more information on how to arrange for accommodations, please call a mainstreaming facilitator at 217-6890/ TDD 217-6891.

VOLUNTEER OPPORTUNITIES are available to teens interested in working as a companion for a child with a disability. Call the Volunteer Coordinator at 217-6890.

Montgomery County Recreation

Figure 3-4. Information brochure on programs serving children with disabilities: Montgomery County, Maryland, Department of Recreation, Therapeutic Section.

significantly to the physical fitness and emotional well-being of participants, including service men and women and their families, and civilian employees of the military. Competitive sports in particular are believed to build *esprit de corps* and pride. In isolated settings, military recreation helps to prevent boredom and burnout, and in dangerous settings it provides relaxation and release from stress.

In today's armed forces, with society's high rate of divorce, promoting family stability is especially important, since the conditions of military living often make normal family life difficult and contribute to poor morale and performance on the part of armed forces personnel. Military recreation should therefore provide many of the leisure-related benefits and opportunities that are normally available in civilian life. Appealing social and creative programs are also intended to reduce problems of alcohol and drug abuse, which affect many military personnel on all levels. Pat Harden sums up the mission of military recreation:

> *Readiness is the cornerstone of this administration. A ready-to-fight force is linked intrinsically to the morale, sense of well-being, commitment and pride in the mission of each Service and family member. Our Morale, Welfare and Recreation (MWR) programs play a direct role in developing and maintaining these characteristics within our force and are more important than ever during this time of transition, when profound changes relating to reduction of armed forces are having a powerful impact on Service members and their families.*[9]

Facilities and programs vary greatly in armed forces units around the world, ranging from elaborate athletic facilities, libraries, recreation centers, craft shops, social programs, hobby groups, and sports competition on various levels, to very minimal programs on smaller bases or ships. Many MWR programs also include social-service elements, such as stress management, substance abuse, day care, and related forms of assistance, along with trip planning, ticket purchasing, and equipment rental services.

Fiscal support of military programs is provided by both *appropriated* funding (money allocated by Congress to the Department of Defense for general support of the armed forces) and *nonappropriated* funding (money raised from post-exchange profits, vending machines, liquor sales in service clubs, and fees for participation in programs).

---

7. Employee Recreation Programs

The seventh important category of leisure-service sponsorship in the United States and Canada consists of programs designed to serve employees of companies or other large institutions such as governmental or health-care agencies. Known originally as "industrial recreation," such programs were begun as early as the nineteenth century as an example of paternalistic business management policies, and to reduce anti-social uses of leisure that were seen as detrimental to productivity.

In the early 1950s, the *Wall Street Journal* estimated that expenditures by business and industry for employee recreation amounted to $800 million annually, and by the mid-1970s the *New York Times* reported that fifty thousand private companies were spending a total of $2 billion a year on recreation-related programs. Recent reports indicate that today four thousand businesses are corporate members of the National Employee Services and Recreation Association (founded in 1941 as the National Industrial Recreation Association). A substantial number of businesses also belong to the Association for Worksite Health Promotion, which illustrates the strong connection between organized recreation and health and fitness concerns, and the need for many companies to reduce health-care costs.

Today, the major goals of employee recreation programs include the following: (1) promoting employee fitness, health, and efficiency; (2) improving employer-employee relations; and (3) upgrading company image, recruitment appeal, and personnel retention. Program activities fit under several headings:

Fitness and Sports Activities, including softball, bowling, golf, basketball, volleyball, tennis, and varied aerobic exercise and conditioning services, often conducted under medical guidance or directed by sports-medicine or sports-physiology experts;

Social and Cultural Programs, including holiday and award parties, banquets, company picnics, dinner/theater outings, charter travel tours, non-job-related adult education, hobby clubs, and varied music, drama, and dance activities; and

Service Programs, such as discount ticket services for concerts and theater events, United Fund drives and blood donation drives, discount sales, first aid and CPR training, employee assistance programs related to weight loss, stress management, and alcohol and drug abuse, smoking cessation groups, family counseling, and other activities.

Substantial numbers of company sponsors—insurance companies, banks, airlines, hospitals, government agencies, and manufacturing companies—operate recreation facilities including ball fields, camps, parks, fitness trails, hunting and fishing properties, and separate recreation buildings.

Funding patterns vary in employee recreation programs. In many companies, programs that are directly concerned with promoting health and fitness and improving the job performance of employees are fully paid for by management, while other activities of a social or clearly recreational nature must be paid for, at least in part, by participants.

Many employee services and recreation programs also provide programs for workers with non-traditional work schedules, including the estimated one in five men and one in six women with shifts other than normal day shifts.

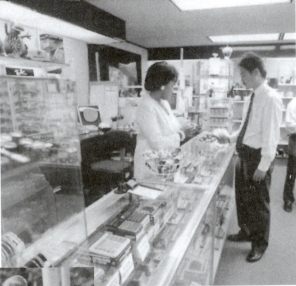

Many companies provide recreation for their own employees, or sponsor events for the community at large. The Conoco Co., Houston, Texas, operates a snack bar, the "Fuel Stop," and the Parsons Corporation in Pasadena, California, manages a company store, as examples of diversified employee services. Below, the CoreStates Financial Corporation in Philadelphia sponsors a major bike race annually.

8. *College- and University-Sponsored Programs*

A final major category of recreation sponsorship consists of programs provided to meet the leisure needs of students, chiefly in colleges and universities, but also in co-curricular activities in elementary and secondary schools. Examples of campus recreation programs are intramural sports associations, sports clubs, outing clubs (such as ski or scuba clubs), cultural arts series, and social programs and events such as concerts, dances, holiday celebrations, and other recreational activities carried on under the direct sponsorship or supervision of the college, university, or school administration.

Recreation programs on college and university campuses may be administered by a dean of student life or student affairs who is responsible for student personnel services that are not of a strictly academic nature. Often the administrative control of the programs is determined by the nature of their content, with sports, fitness, and outing activities falling under the management of a recreation or athletic director, or a department or school of physical education, and social and cultural programs being supervised by a student life or campus activities office.

Today, campus recreation is generally viewed as an important element in the full spectrum of student services that includes housing, health care, counseling, and academic advice. Recreation is recognized as part of a full life, contributing to a student's rich academic experience. Indeed, many co-curricular leisure programs are carried out in cooperation with academic departments and help to extend the real-life experience of students in areas involving student leadership, political activity, journalism and publications, business management, and the creative arts.

The largest single area of campus recreation activity often consists of sports and fitness activities. This field is represented by the National Intramural and Recreational Sports Association (NIRSA), a nonprofit professional organization committed to the development of high-quality recreational sports programs and services. NIRSA is an umbrella organization with membership drawn from over two thousand universities, colleges, military installations, health clubs, recreation and park departments, YMCAs and YWCAs, and corporations throughout the United States and Canada. It sponsors workshops, conferences, and training programs, and publishes training materials and periodicals.

Leisure Service as a System

What conclusions about leisure service as a system can be drawn from these descriptions of the eight different types of recreation sponsors?

First, it is obvious that the overall field of recreation and leisure services is immensely diverse, in terms of the different kinds of agencies that provide programs and facilities, with their range of goals, philosophies, populations served, and program content. Indeed, each of the eight categories of sponsors is relatively independent of the other types. Several have their own professional societies, training programs, or systems of personnel certification. There are relatively few attempts to coordinate the efforts of these wide-ranging agencies, to develop common statements of purpose, or to apply standards of effective practices or codes of ethics.

Competition Among Sponsors

Far from having a common identity, leisure-service sponsors often are highly competitive with one another. This is particularly evident in the gambling sector of the commercial recreation field, where different types of gambling attractions battle for an increased share of the recreational bettor's dollar.

Competition is also evident in the health and fitness field. During the 1970s and 1980s, thousands of organizations—commercial, nonprofit, private-membership, and academic—built fitness centers outfitted with expensive equipment layouts. However, with a decline of adult interest and participation in fitness programs during the late 1980s and early 1990s, many of these ventures, facing reduced revenues, became increasingly competitive with each other.

In some cases, legal or tax-related challenges have been made to voluntary agencies in direct competition with commercial recreation businesses, threatening those agencies' nonprofit status.

Growth of Cooperative Relationships

At the same time, there has been a pronounced trend toward cooperation and cosponsorship among some segments of the leisure-service system.

For example, within any major area of recreational activity, one type of agency may serve a specialized role that benefits other types of agencies. In boating, government provides regulations, waterways, marinas, and ramps, and conducts rescue operations when needed. Voluntary agencies teach boating skills, sponsor organized boating camps, and certify boating instructors. Commercial businesses manufacture, sell, and repair boats and boating equipment, and operate commercial marinas and boating centers. Armed forces bases frequently have sailing, water-skiing, and other aquatic sports as part of their programs of activity. Colleges may feature sailing or scuba courses, and private-membership organizations frequently own marinas or sailboating complexes. These varying functions of different types of agencies often lend themselves to cooperative networking and mutual assistance, to promote recreational boating.

Cooperation among leisure-service sponsors has taken several different forms:

1. Joint planning, financing, and construction of major recreational facilities by public, private, commercial, and other sponsors;
2. Privatization of public recreation and park facilities and programs, through subcontracting of management responsibilities, leases, or concessions with private or commercial operators;
3. Corporations providing direct assistance to recreation programs and projects, including park rehabilitation or maintenance; and

4. Cooperative sponsorship of varied programs by public, voluntary, and business organizations.

Over the past two decades numerous major sports stadiums, multi-purpose auditoriums and exposition centers, boating complexes and marinas, and other facilities have been constructed with shared sponsorship and funding by states, municipalities, the owners of professional sports teams, and other recreation entrepreneurs.

The readiness of taxpayers to support such arrangements is based on the view that association with highly visible sports teams or other leisure attractions contributes to a community's positive image and to its economic health.

Examples of Partnerships

Cooperative construction agreements may be used to develop socially oriented programs and facilities. For example, the Long Center in Clearwater, Florida, a youth-oriented recreational complex, was financed through an intricate partnership among governmental and nonprofit agencies, accompanied by foundation grants, tax-incentive decisions of Florida's Department of Community Affairs, business contributions, and a Pepsi/Pick Quik promotion.[10] The center's extensive facilities, including pools, fitness rooms, classrooms, and spaces for sheltered workshops and rehabilitation, are shared by several different public and private agencies, who also share maintenance responsibilities.

Since the 1970s, a number of businesses have "adopted" nearby parks, providing volunteer leaders or planners, assigning maintenance staff, or establishing foundations to assist in the operations of the parks. Some companies have funded special community programs serving disadvantaged youth or those with disabilities. Others have supported arts festivals or ethnic heritage series. On a larger scale, many major sports events or teams in international competition are funded by large corporations.

In other cases, universities and armed forces units have worked together. The Department of Recreation and Parks Management of California State University at Chico has operated a ten-week summer day-camp program for children of U.S. Navy personnel and civilian employees in Japan. The program, known as Willie Wildcat Summer Day Camp, was organized with assistance from the U.S. Naval Training Unit at Patuxent River, Maryland, and provided Chico students with valuable field experience in a military recreation setting.[11]

A final example of growing cooperation among different branches of the overall leisure-service system involves alliances among schools, public authorities, and groups of volunteer citizens, to operate joint school-and-community multi-service centers. In several Canadian provinces, there is a long tradition of citizen's councils or committees taking responsibility for such programs, with public and private groups joining together with school boards in so-called "social marketing" alliances. To illustrate, a number of Ontario municipalities have recently completed joint construction of school-community centers. In the city of Etobicoke, the multi-service center includes an elementary school, a recreation and day-care center, and a library and natural interpretive area, with shared staff and joint operation of programming by school, municipal recreation, and other authorities.

Summary

This chapter serves two purposes. First, it helps readers aware of only a limited sector of the overall leisure-service field to become familiar with a broader view of the organization, structure, goals, and program elements of the eight different kinds of agencies that constitute this field.

By providing this cross-section, this chapter makes these points: (1) many agencies whose primary function is recreational also provide activities and services that meet other important human or social needs; and (2) many organizations whose major purpose is *not* to sponsor recreation programs do so in a secondary way, in order to achieve their overall missions more effectively.

The second purpose of this chapter is to examine recreation, park, and leisure-service agencies *as a system,* showing that while the field is highly diversified and lacks joint planning or coordination as a whole, there is nevertheless a substantial degree of interaction among its separate components as they deliver program services to the public at large. The chapter should therefore serve to widen the perspectives of students in this field, both in terms of how they envision it and in terms of their own career plans.

Class Projects and Assignments

1. As an individual or small-group project, students can gather materials illustrating the organization and program elements of two or more of the different types of leisure-service agencies described in this chapter. Then, as an in-class exercise, they can present their findings and compare these different agencies, using verbal presentations, audiovisual materials, and display of brochures, reports, or other descriptive materials.

2. An alternative approach would be to invite representatives of different types of agencies (armed forces, therapeutic, commercial, etc.) to present descriptions of their organizations before the class.

3. A more ambitious assignment, extending over a major portion of the semester, would be for a team of students to do a community survey within a town, county, or other metropolitan area, to identify and describe as many examples as possible of the eight different types of program sponsors, showing how they both cooperate and compete with each other, and contrasting their goals and program emphases.

References

1. John Crossley, "Multi-Tier Programming in Commercial Recreation," *Parks and Recreation,* Mar. 1990, p. 69.

2. George D. Butler, *Introduction to Community Recreation* (New York: McGraw-Hill, 1976), pp. 58–62.

3. *Local Opportunities for Americans: Municipal and County Park and Recreation Study (MACPARS)* (Alexandria, VA: National Recreation and Park Association, University of Georgia, and U.S. Forest Service, 1988).

4. *Diocesan CYO Athletic Philosophy* (Cleveland, OH: Catholic Charities, CYO and Young Adult Agency, 1995).

5. *Membership in the YWCA* (New York: Young Womens' Christian Association Program Brochure, 1994), p. 2.

6. Crossley, *op. cit.,* p. 70.

7. *Fact Sheet: Starrett at Spring Creek* (Brooklyn, NY: Public Affairs Office, 1995).

8. *Definition of Therapeutic Recreation* (Approved by National Therapeutic Recreation Society Board of Directors, Feb. 1994).

9. Pat Harden, "Armed Forces Recreation Services: Our Hallowed Ground Raison D'Etre," *Parks and Recreation,* Dec. 1994, p. 24.

10. Mark Abdo, "Financing Recreation Complexes in the Future," *Parks and Recreation,* Dec. 1992, pp. 27–29.

11. Al Jackson, "Willie Wildcat's Day Camp in Japan," *Parks and Recreation,* Oct. 1992, pp. 51–53.

Chapter *4*

Programming's Philosophical Base: The Benefits-Driven Approach

One of the characteristics of a profession is that it has a social mandate. That mandate is grounded in meeting a fundamental need of society, whether it be a concern for its health, system of justice, literacy, or quality of life. Without a mandate, there is no soul, no sense of purpose, no sustaining will, which attracts people to the cause. . . . [1]

Marketing is imbedded in the minds of most parks and recreation practitioners. We have embraced marketing management techniques from the world of private business, and many of us believe that any increase in the popularity of our services is due to the marketing mindset that we have built into our practices.[2]

As an area of social service, business enterprise, and governmental responsibility affecting all communities and citizens, the field of recreation, park, and leisure services must be defined by a clearly understood sense of purpose.

As shown in Chapter 2, three major orientations have influenced programming in the recreation, park, and leisure-service field over the past several decades. These approaches are (1) *quality-of-life;* (2) *human-service* or *social-service;* and (3) *marketing.* This chapter examines these three orientations in detail, and shows how they influence the recreation and leisure-service programming process. It concludes with a description of the *benefits-driven* approach, which has become a strong thrust in recreation and park management during the 1990s.

The topics presented in this chapter relate to the following undergraduate curriculum objectives established by the NRPA/AALR Council on Accreditation:

> Understanding of the significance of play, recreation, and leisure throughout the life cycle relative to the individual's attitudes, values, behaviors, and use of resources. (8.04)
>
> Knowledge of the responsibility of the leisure-service profession to make available opportunities for leisure experiences for all populations, including those with special needs and disabilities. (8.13)
>
> Ability to promote, advocate, interpret, and articulate the concerns of leisure-service systems for all populations and services. (8.14)
>
> Understanding of people within diverse social groups and the relationship of such groups. (7C.05)
>
> Knowledge of marketing techniques and strategies. (8.28)
>
> Understanding of the relationship of business, society, and the economy, including the role of the entrepreneur. (7A.03)
>
> Understanding of and ability to utilize current technology for the management of leisure services, including organizing, marketing, implementing, and monitoring these services. (9A.02).

Purposes of Organized Recreation Service

Today, with a greater than ever need to justify community support for organized recreation services, it is essential to define the purposes and positive outcomes of this field. This is particularly true because most individuals, if they were asked why they engaged in recreation, would be likely to reply "for fun" or "for relaxation." If pressed further, they might cite motivations related to health and fitness, sociability and companionship, or the pleasure, creativity, or excitement found in varied forms of play.

However, compelling as they may be in personal terms, such responses tend not to be very convincing as an argument for supporting recreation and park agencies, particularly when measured against the priorities of other community services such as police, fire health, and education. In an effort to clarify the fundamental thrust of leisure programming, three models—quality-of-life, human-service, and marketing—have been promoted over the past few decades. Each of these approaches is discussed below in terms of its past development and present-day impact. An analysis of a newer approach to leisure programming—the benefits-driven model—follows the discussion of those older models.

The Quality-of-Life Approach

Although a number of philosophers, educators, and recreation and park pioneers had developed convincing arguments for the value of organized play in community life, the predominant public view of recreation during the early decades of the twentieth century was that it was a source of personal pleasure. Play for fun was a keynote of North American life at this time, and formal definitions stressed that recreation was activity carried on voluntarily in one's free time, without extrinsic purpose. Two sociologists, Martin and Esther Neumeyer, described recreation as:

> . . . *any activity pursued during leisure, either individual or collective, that is free and pleasurable, having its own immediate appeal not impelled by a delayed reward beyond itself or by any immediate necessity.*[3]

The image of organized recreation as contributing to the quality of life is vividly illustrated in a program brochure published by the public recreation and park department in Kamloops, British Columbia, Canada (Figure 4-1).

Strikingly, although leisure-service program planners obviously recognize the need for recreation activities to provide pleasure to participants, educators and researchers generally have given fun little weight as a motivation. Sociologist Walter Podilchak points out that the term *fun* is often used synonymously with *leisure,* but that the scholarly literature in the field does not reflect this association.[4]

Remember when:

- You helped your baby to swim,
- You hit your first home run,
- Your kids weren't bored in July and August because of Summer Sunshine,
- You learned a wok was a good way to cook Chinese food,
- You discovered dancing with your partner could be fun,
- You scored your first goal in hockey,
- Wednesday night was fun when you joined mixed volleyball,
- You fit into your clothes because of fitness classes,
- Your preschooler presented you with a work of art from preschool class,
- You did your first clown trick from Clown College,
- You painted your first water colour painting,
- You attended your first preschool class without Mom or Dad,
- You learned to glide on skates,
- You attended the senior's picnic and enjoyed your lunch despite the liquid sunshine.

Figure 4-1.   Motivational message: Kamloops Recreation brochure.

Recently, however, some researchers have begun to explore the importance of enjoyment for its own sake in recreational involvement. Leonard Wankel, for example, points out that fun and enjoyment are the most important self-reported reasons for participating in youth sports.[5] Columnist John Leo cites a number of examples of researchers who have documented the value of fun—including elements of humor, laughter, and sociability—in reducing stress and contributing to a longer life span.[6]

Realistically, most participants in varied leisure pursuits probably do not consciously think of such values or outcomes. Instead, they make recreational choices or commitments largely because of the motivations suggested earlier—for pleasure, challenge, sociability, or creative expression—and, ultimately, as part of the search for happiness and a critical element in one's quality of life.

The Human-Services Approach

However, from the very beginning of the recreation and park movement in the United States and Canada, there was also a clearly articulated belief that organized play contributed significantly to community life.

Historians tell us that a major purpose of the first city playgrounds was to combat juvenile delinquency in crowded streets where there were no other opportunities for safe, healthy play. Youth organizations and sports were valued because of their assumed contribution to good citizenship, and camping and other outdoor pursuits were promoted because they encouraged respect for the outdoors and recalled the wilderness experiences of early settlers.

Government support of organized recreation was expanded during the Great Depression of the 1930s, when millions of unemployed men and women needed constructive leisure outlets to maintain morale. With federal funding in the United States, thousands of recreation facilities and park areas were constructed or improved to meet such needs. In addition, hundreds of thousands of men and women were employed as recreation leaders, or in community centers, arts programs, or performing units that enriched the national culture.

During the 1960s and early 1970s, crash programs of recreation were provided in inner-city neighborhoods in response to the destructive summer riots that had paralyzed numerous communities. In the late 1960s, the President's Commission on Civil Disorder identified the lack of adequate recreation opportunity as a key factor leading to these riots.

Social Functions of Organized Recreation Service

So, at the same time that recreation was viewed by many as chiefly a matter of personal pleasure or release, educators and researchers began to identify its important social functions. While these functions obviously differed from community to community, it was generally agreed that they included the following elements:

1. Enriching the quality of life by providing emotional satisfaction, sociability, and release from stress;

Many public recreation and park agencies organize historical or cultural festivals. In Kamloops, British Columbia, traditional themes of Western Canada are shown in colorful Indian dance demonstrations, reenactment of voyageurs exploring new territories, or performances by drill teams of the Royal Canadian Northwest Mounted Police.

2. Contributing to personal development in physical, emotional, and social terms throughout the life span;

3. Making the community a more attractive place to live, through the provision of parks, open spaces, and other appealing environments;

4. Helping prevent the antisocial uses of leisure by providing positive, alternative forms of play and promoting constructive social values;

5. Strengthening neighborhood and community ties as residents take part in volunteer service programs and help organize their own programs;

6. Improving intergroup and intergenerational relations by sharing backgrounds and encouraging participation among varied residents;

7. Meeting the needs of special populations, such as those with physical or mental disabilities;

8. Promoting economic health and community stability, by producing revenues and jobs, and by attracting new businesses and residents;

9. Enriching community cultural life, particularly through programs and institutions in the performing and fine arts;

10. Promoting community health and safety through sports and fitness programs, and through regulation of high-risk activities; and

11. Providing constructive outlets for ritual, ceremony, and aggressive drives, which have characterized all societies throughout history.[7]

In the mid-1970s, David Gray and Seymour Greben summed up the far-reaching idealistic views of many recreation, park, and leisure-service educators and practitioners who were convinced that the human-service model should represent the primary thrust of this field. Gray and Greben urged the recreation and park profession to pursue the following goals:

To adopt a humanistic ethic as the central value system of the recreation profession;

To develop and act on a social conscience that focuses park and recreation services on the great social problems of our time and develop programs designed to contribute to the amelioration of those problems;

To develop a set of guidelines for programs that emphasize human welfare, human development, and social action; and

To establish common cause with the environmentalists and other social movements that embrace a value system similar to our own.[8]

Realistically, however, such goals have not been embraced by many professionals, who instead have been concerned primarily with ensuring the financial and political stability of their agencies. In a 1982 study of urban recreation and park directors throughout the United States, Christopher Edginton and Larry Neal found that these municipal leisure-service managers gave the highest priority to securing fees and charges, receiving a fair share of the local tax dollar, and maintaining a high level of political and public support. In contrast, managers indicated relatively little concern with such goals as helping participants achieve personal goals, promoting physical fitness, strengthening community cohesiveness, or nurturing the family unit.[9]

Despite such reservations, many recreation and park professionals continue to support the human-service approach to leisure-service programming. Increasingly, they urge the provision of significant, goal-oriented recreation programs in urban, poverty-stricken neighborhoods. They argue for the use of recreation to help in the prevention and treatment of delinquency and crime, promoting mid-night basketball leagues and other big-city social programs for at-risk youth. Indeed, in the early 1990s, many therapeutic recreation specialists in particular explored the extension of special programs to serve such population groups as the growing number of homeless individuals and families, victims of sexual abuse, HIV and AIDS-infected individuals, and gay and lesbian youth.

Based on such convictions, many practitioners in the public and nonprofit sectors of recreation and leisure-service programming continue to adhere to the human-service models. However, the influence of these practitioners has been sharply undercut by the widespread adoption of the marketing approach to agency operations.

Marketing Model of Leisure Service

As Chapter 1 points out, the era of austerity that began in many communities in the late 1970s and early 1980s compelled harsh cutbacks in fiscal support for many governmental and nonprofit organizations. In response, public recreation and park agencies on all levels began to place increasing reliance on varied revenue sources to support their facilities and programs, and to compensate for reduced tax-based support.

This trend was transformed rapidly into a full-fledged acceptance of principles and operational methods that were found in business environments and that were commonly referred to as marketing approaches. This shift was not unique to the leisure-service field. Many other professionals—doctors and lawyers, and managers of cultural institutions such as museums, libraries, orchestras, and opera and ballet companies—all began to develop sophisticated ways of gaining support and gathering needed revenues.

Entrepreneurial Strategies

The shift toward a marketing orientation in recreation, parks, and leisure services was perceived as a necessity in the face of rapidly changing social and economic conditions that demanded innovative and creative management strategies in all fields.

For example, Gray pointed out that many public and voluntary organizations tended to be bureaucratic, with fixed goals and routines, and a general outlook that feared surprises, discouraged new initiatives, and punished failure. He argued that in an era of growing social problems and challenges to leisure-service agencies, a new approach was necessary:

> *Entrepreneurial organizations support reasonable risk-taking, learn from failure, and reward success. . . . They realize that change creates opportunity and maintain an environmental scan to assess where [it] exists. . . . They tolerate ambiguity, encourage intuitive path-findings. They plan by working backward from a preferred future.*[10]

Leisure Seen as an Industry

Beyond adopting an entrepreneurial leadership style, many leaders in the field argued that recreation and leisure needed to be recognized as an industry and operated as a business, rather than as a form of public or social service. For example, in the mid-1980s, the American Association for Leisure and Recreation began to use the term *recreation industry* to describe the leisure-service field. Similarly, *Trends,* published by the National Park Service and the National Recreation and Park Association, concluded that public recreation and park managers were essentially the same as their commercial counterparts:

> *Managed recreation is a profession that provides services to consumers of all demographic stripes and shades. Under this designation, a public park superintendent is in the same business as a resort owner, as are a theme park operator and the fitness director of a YMCA. . . . There are many changes overtaking the industry . . . [and it is becoming] more competitive, more complex and more in need of a high degree of professionalism to manage these changes.[11]*

Increasingly, managers in nonprofit recreation agencies were urged to see themselves as part of the total spectrum of business-sponsored entertainment and play. Their principles and methods, it was implied, should be the same as those of motion-picture and music recording companies, professional sports teams and stadium owners, and theme-park and cruise-line operators.

Adoption of Marketing Principles

In a leading recreation and park management text, Howard and Crompton defined marketing as

> *the analysis, planning, implementation and control of carefully formulated programs designed to bring about voluntary exchanges with target markets for the purpose of achieving agency objectives. It relies heavily upon designing offerings consistent with clients' wants, and on using effective pricing, communication and distribution to inform, motivate, and service the markets.[12]*

Crompton stressed that the role of public recreation and park managers had changed from being administrators concerned with the responsible allocation of government money, to being entrepreneurs who functioned in the public sector with minimal support from tax funds. Thus, nonprofit leisure-service managers must aggressively seek out resources with which their agencies can serve the public most effectively. Expanded revenue generation strategies may yield benefits, Crompton points out, that go far beyond simply providing funds to support programs. These include the following:

1. Increased fiscal resources that can be used to support projects or program elements that would otherwise not be funded;
2. Increased respect from municipal officials, because the need for tax support is reduced, and programs may be improved without tax increases;

3. Enlarged citizen and political constituency support, which may assist in developing new programs and projects that will yield increased revenues;
4. Enhanced reputation of the department as an innovator in government services;
5. Increased incentive to agency staff to offer high-quality, needed services, with pricing policy that promotes accountability, since the public will not pay for inferior programs or services; and
6. Challenge to staff members that encourages an atmosphere of creativity, energy, excitement, and commitment to agency goals.[13]

As later chapters will show, the marketing approach involves considerably more than simply attempting to "sell" a product, through high-pressure advertising, or clearing a substantial profit. Instead, the marketing process includes the following elements: (1) market research to identify appropriate target audiences or consumer needs; (2) design of product for maximum appeal, productivity, and sales; (3) determining appropriate price for product or service, and method of delivery; (4) promoting product through packaging, publicity, or advertising; (5) monitoring the delivery of the product or service (in this case, the operation of the recreation program or use of the facility by the public) to ensure maximum quality and customer satisfaction; and (6) assessing the program's degree of success and its potential for being repeated or continued.

Other Marketing Elements

At the heart of the marketing approach is the principle that program quality must be at the highest level possible, and that satisfaction must be made the keynote of management activity. All stages of programming should ensure that registering and taking part in activities are as convenient and painless as possible. Maintenance must be thorough and efficient to guarantee an attractive environment for play, and all leisure opportunities should be tailored to suit the needs, interests, and schedule choices of participants.

While effective public relations and advertising efforts, along with appealing programming packages, may succeed in drawing new participants, it is also essential to retain those already enrolled. In describing the marketing approach used by the Park Authority in Fairfax County, Virginia, Lynn Tadlock cites the findings of a technical assistance research study showing that it costs, on average, five times as much money to gain a new customer as it does to retain an existing one.

Having a comprehensive information data base that provides timely, accurate facts and figures, is critical. Tadlock writes:

> *Sound marketing strategy is also based to a great extent on internal market information [including] operational records, such as admissions, program registration data, usage patterns, fees collected and sales receipts . . . recreation center visitation and memberships. . . . Within the next year we anticipate installing a more ambitious computerized site information system with key features such as automation of point-of-sale operations, site entry and class registration data. With this tool, we'll be able to analyze attendance patterns or the results of our latest advertising campaign almost simultaneously.[14]*

Patrons Seen as Customers

Underlying the marketing approach is the conviction that the primary emphasis in recreation and park management should be on serving individuals who are essentially customers or consumers—that is, people who can pay their way.

In many cases, when a public agency itself cannot profitably operate a facility, such as a golf course, marina, or other complex, it is now likely to subcontract to a private commercial operator through a lease or concession agreement. This arrangement frequently results in a higher level of fees being charged to patrons of the facility.

Inevitably, the needs of groups within the community that do not have financial resources, such as the unemployed or welfare-dependent family, individuals with serious physical or mental disabilities, at-risk youth, and economically disadvantaged elderly persons, are given a lower priority than the well-to-do in program planning.

A number of leading recreation and park professionals and educators have expressed concern about the degree to which the marketing model has come to dominate the leisure-service field, with the risk that the other important goals of publicly sponsored programs will be increasingly ignored. Ronald Riggins writes that the public department

> *is charged with the responsibility to consider more than the economic attraction of an activity, the size and "purchasing power" of the group seeking participation, or the social, political and economic status of the persons in that group. This obligation lies at the root of the public parks and recreation movement.*[15]

Reconciling Human-Service and Marketing Emphases

Given that the two approaches that have just been described constitute powerful influences that affect not only public but also voluntary nonprofit and other types of leisure-service agencies, how can their different value systems be reconciled?

First, it is apparent that the marketing approach has been very widely adopted in different types of recreation programs, and has helped many agencies gain in public support, financial stability, and the ability to provide a diversified and rich assortment of recreation programs since the 1970s.

At the same time, some departments have been able to develop administrative arrangements that have made important program elements available to poorer or special-population groups. For example, fees for admission to skating rinks, pools, and other recreation resources may be applied in one neighborhood or district of a city, but not in others. In other cases, fees may be waived for disadvantaged families on welfare, or other arrangements may be made to permit free use of facilities at given times.

In some communities, foundations, companies, or private individuals may provide grants to help subsidize special programs to meet human-service needs. In other cases, when fees are set for given program elements, such as summer day camps or trip programs, it may be possible to set fees for the economically capable that provide a degree of revenue beyond per-individual costs and make it feasible to offer reduced rates, or free admission or registration, for economically disadvantaged participants.

Thus, even in recreation, park, and leisure-service agencies that have essentially adopted a marketing orientation, efforts can be made to meet other important social needs of organized recreation programs.

Benefits-Driven Approach

In addition to employing such strategies, a growing number of leisure-service agencies today have begun to employ a relatively new approach to program planning and implementation: the benefits-driven model.

The benefits-based approach implies a strong shift to identifying and documenting recreation "outputs," or beneficial outcomes, for visitors to federal, state, or provincial parks, and other outdoor settings. However, it has not been limited to such settings. At a number of professional meetings in the United States and Canada during the mid-1900s, directed by Prof. Lawrence Allen of Clemson University, it has been made clear that the benefits-based approach applies to all types of recreation, park, and leisure-service agencies and programs.

Beyond this, the benefits-based approach also can be used to strengthen the quality-of-life, human-service, and marketing models of program delivery. In terms of program planning, it has had three applications: (1) identifying the key personal and social outcomes or benefits of organized recreation programs; (2) designing and conducting programs to achieve such outcomes and benefits; and (3) evaluating programs systematically to measure success in achieving these benefits, and making known to communities or the public at large the findings of proven leisure-service outcomes.

This approach to program delivery is related to a larger thrust called the Benefits Approach to Leisure (BAL). BAL has been used to guide recreation policy planning and management, advance leisure theory and research, and contribute to agency operations. B.L. Driver and associates point out that the BAL model has been widely applied to outdoor recreation and resource management by the Forest Service and other recreation and park agencies in the United States, and in Canada, Australia, and several other countries. They write:

When applied to management [this] approach is called Benefits-Based Management (BBM). Advantages of BBM include providing more objective justification for allocations of public funds to leisure, clarifying visitor demands and needs, promoting sound resource allocation decisions, optimizing management by clarifying outputs, enabling consumers to exercise greater sovereignty in their leisure decision making, facilitating closer working relationships among a variety of recreation-tourism partners, and promoting the profession.[16]

Identifying Recreation Outcomes

Since the 1980s, there has been a marked increase in the number and quality of research and evaluation studies designed to identify and document the values and benefits of organized leisure programs.

Numerous reports summarize the physical, emotional, social, and cognitive outcomes of recreational experiences, both in general terms and in specific leisure settings and programs. A major study supported by the National Institute on Disability and Rehabilitation Research of the U.S. Department of Education compiled the findings of hundreds of reports of the impact of therapeutic recreation, from a medical perspective.[17]

The Ontario Parks and Recreation Federation published a similar comprehensive report, summing up several major categories of the benefits of recreation and park programs, from a community perspective.[18] In another detailed text, Driver, Brown, and Peterson outlined the overall benefits of organized leisure services.[19]

In the mid-1990s, a task force working in conjunction with the National Recreation and Park Association set out to document the effectiveness of organized recreation in dealing with a range of serious social problems.[20]

These and similar efforts are helping to demonstrate the value of recreation, park, and leisure services, and to provide directions for agency professionals in planning and carrying out leisure programs. When the benefits emphasis becomes a shaping force in the planning and operation of recreation programs, it becomes more than simply a theoretical rationale. Instead, it constitutes a powerful engine that drives all elements of the leisure-service operation. Under such circumstances, programs become benefits-driven.

Designing Benefits-Driven Programs

Based on a fuller understanding of the potential benefits of organized recreation, leisure-service planners are now setting more specific, positive goals intended to lead to desired outcomes. Within a benefits-driven framework, they are identifying critical priorities or needs of their agencies, and then designing programs aimed at meeting these priorities or needs.

For example, the Bureau of Naval Personnel of the U.S. Navy has developed extensive training materials designed to help its Morale, Welfare and Recreation management personnel use the benefits-driven approach in developing programs and services. First, planners developed a comprehensive statement of MWR's primary goals within the nation's armed forces. These included these needs: (1) to effectively enhance the capability of Navy personnel to achieve their fullest work potential; (2) to be more responsive to training and deployment requirements; (3) to help reduce health and personal problems; (4) to promote unit *esprit de corps* and cohesion; (5) to enable Navy personnel to withstand stress; (6) to create a climate of support for Navy families and reciprocal support of the Navy by families; (7) to result in greater satisfaction with the military lifestyle; and (8) most importantly, to strengthen officers' and sailors' commitment to the mission of the Navy.

These overall goals are succinctly stated in a model showing Morale, Welfare and Recreation's mission-support objectives and contributions to Navy operations (Figure 4-2).

Evaluating Outcomes and Disseminating Findings

The third stage of the benefits-driven process requires that all programs be thoroughly and systematically analyzed. Findings should be applied to improve programs while they are

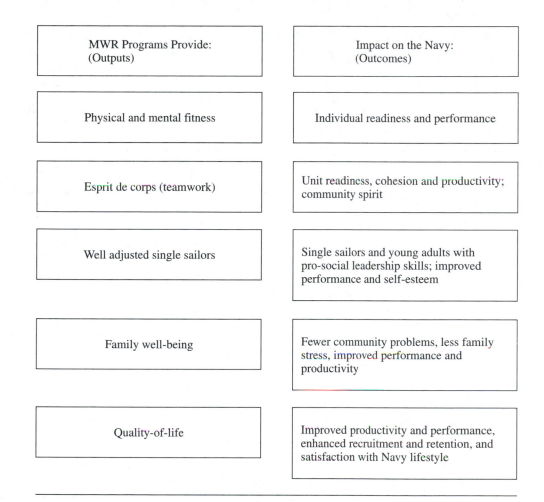

Figure 4-2. MWR mission statement support output/outcome statement.

Source: MWR Directors' Seminar Discussion Paper, John "Pat" Harden, Patuxent River, MD, Bureau of Naval Personnel, Navy MWR Training Unit.

being carried on and in future program operations. Numerous examples of program evaluation in action are provided in later chapters of this text.

Role of Professional Societies

In some cases, professional societies may play a leading role in using the benefits-driven approach to promote public understanding and support for recreation and park programs. One example is found in the Essential Benefits of Recreation project that has been carried out by the Canadian Parks/Recreation Association. Using materials developed by the Parks and Recreation Federation of Ontario, this project incorporated a Speakers' Bureau concept, with the following goals:

1. To establish a clear understanding and awareness that recreation is an essential element in the quality of life of our people and communities.
2. To provide potential advocates with the tools and the confidence to speak boldly about the individual, social, economic, and environmental benefits of recreation services.
3. To motivate the practitioners and volunteers that guide recreation decisions to invest time, energy, and dollars in the process of helping the recreation field live up to its potential.
4. To provide information and insight on the first steps that might be taken to reposition recreation solidly on the social, economic, and environmental agendas of the 1990s.[21]

Throughout Canada, the benefits-driven approach has had a growing impact on recreation and park management program planning. *Recreation Canada* concludes:

> *As a result of this shift in focus toward delivering personal, social, economic and environmental benefits—not just services and programs—new visions are being articulated, goals and objectives are being analyzed, structures are being assessed, staff are being oriented, new criteria for evaluation are being developed, new program and service priorities are being identified, strategic alliances are being formed, and marketing strategies are evolving.*[22]

It has been increasingly clear that the overall purpose of leisure-service agencies of all kinds must be not only to achieve specific personal or social benefits for participants, but also to reinforce and redirect public values and behavior generally, that have an impact on leisure lifestyles.

Need for Broader Vision of Goals

Many of the problems of contemporary society stem from negative uses of leisure, or self-destructive involvement in pleasure-seeking behavior. Statistics show that the number of unmarried pregnant teens has doubled since the 1970s and the number of teenage suicides has tripled. The average teenager spends 1.8 hours per week reading; 5.6 hours on homework, and 21 hours watching television.

Despite the documented contribution of physical activity to wellness and despite the apparent fitness craze of the past two decades, fewer than ten percent of American adults are now reported to engage in regular physical activity at recommended levels, while nearly forty percent report no leisure-time physical activity. Walking for exercise and working out at health clubs both declined markedly by the early 1990s.

The mission of recreation, park, and leisure-service professionals and programmers must therefore be not only to achieve positive outcomes for participants, but also to enrich participants' understanding of leisure and its benefits, linked to other constructive social and personal values.

A Standard of Goodness

In its essence, this mission must rest on a philosophical position that values human life and dignity, and that sees leisure as a critical force in modern society in terms of both people and the environment. Dustin, McAvoy, and Schultz make the point strongly that, while recreation is an area of life that is based on personal freedom, ideally it should also involve the obligation to do "the right thing." They refer to the "hedonist error," which suggests that pleasure is the primary or only goal of leisure. Realistically, the search for pleasure may be associated with many self-destructive activities or with recreation experiences that seriously damage the natural environment.

From this perspective, Dustin, McAvoy, and Schultz argue that recreational pastimes that preserve life, promote life, and help life achieve its highest destiny, are morally superior to those that do not. Recreation programmers must therefore resist the temptation to provide leisure experiences that may be popular but nevertheless consume limited non-renewable resources, are destructive of other life forms, or in some way contribute to personal or social problems. They conclude:

> *The standard of goodness must be applied in each case. To what extent does this activity contribute to the physical and mental health, the sense of being loved and loving, the feelings of belonging and self-esteem, and the growth and development of life in its entirety? To what extent does it detract? . . . To what extent, then, is this recreation activity morally good or bad?*[23]

Ultimately, then, the benefits-driven approach is concerned with the total role and perception of leisure in society, and with its constructive impact on personal wellness, positive family values, social relationships, and economic well-being.

At the same time, it must be recognized that recreation and parks not only are forms of human and social service, but also are fiscally based enterprises that are most likely to flourish when they embody sound marketing principles and strategies. The chapters that follow show how these perspectives may be combined effectively within a benefits-based management approach to the programming process.

Summary

This chapter describes the initial step of recreation, park, and leisure-service programs: the need to establish a sound philosophical base and to formulate an overall mission statement that can be used in defining an agency's program goals.

It discusses the three key approaches that have influenced the leisure-service field in recent decades: *quality-of-life, human-service,* and *marketing.* These differing approaches are not necessarily exclusive, and may exist side-by-side in any agency's program, as the agency seeks to meet a variety of community needs. At the same time, there is an inevitable conflict between the human-service and marketing orientations, when the latter gives primary emphasis to gathering revenues by serving the more affluent population groups in a community, while providing the poor or other groups with special needs with only the barest minimum of leisure services.

The chapter concludes with a description of a fourth approach that is rapidly gaining acceptance, the *benefits-driven* model, which emphasizes the need to identify the significant personal, social, and economic outcomes to be achieved by recreation programs, and to design programs to achieve these benefits. Such benefits have been widely documented in the literature, suggesting that this approach offers a unique way of combining the best elements of the quality-of-life, human-service, and marketing emphases within a combined planning strategy. The ultimate criterion, however, should be the application of a "standard of goodness" ensuring that constructive social values and positive outcomes result from recreation and leisure-service programming.

Class Assignments and Projects

1. Hold a class debate in which students argue for and against each of the three approaches to organized recreation service (quality-of-life, human service, and marketing), citing the strengths and weaknesses of each. To prepare for this session, students should do additional research in the current literature.

2. As an extension of the first assignment, students should identify the specific impact of the marketing approach (with its emphasis on fees and charges, fiscal self-sufficiency of programs, and privatization of major facilities) on the problem of leisure "haves" and "have-nots." (see pp. 14–15, 74–75).

3. What is the essential thrust of the benefits-driven approach to recreation and park management and programming? Students should review the benefits reports cited in this chapter, and should summarize their major findings.

References

1. H. Douglas Sessoms, "Lessons from the Past," *Parks and Recreation,* Feb. 1992, p. 47.

2. Kevin Tisshaw, "Leadership, Principles and the Marketing Mindset," Recreation Canada, Vol. 51, No. 2, 1993, p. 16.

3. Martin H. Neumeyer and Esther Neumeyer, *Leisure and Recreation* (New York: Ronald Press, 1958), p. 22.

4. Walter Podilchak, "Establishing the Fun in Leisure," *Leisure Sciences,* Vol. 13, No. 2, 1991, pp. 123–124.

5. Leonard Wankel, "Personal and Situational Factors Affecting Exercise Involvement: The Importance of Enjoyment," *Research Quarterly for Exercise and Sport,* Vol. 56, No. 3, 1985, pp. 275–282.

6. John Leo, "One Laugh = 3 tbsp. Oat Bran," *U.S. News and World Report,* Jan. 23, 1989, p. 55.

7. Richard Kraus, *Recreation and Leisure in Modern Society* (New York: Addison Wesley Longman, Inc., 1997), pp. 136–158.

8. David Gray and Seymour Greben, "Future Perspectives," *Parks and Recreation,* July 1976, p. 49.

9. Christopher Edginton and Larry Neal, "Ordering Organizational Goals," *California Parks and Recreation,* June/July 1982, p. 12.

10. David Gray, "Managing Our Way to a Preferred Future," *Parks and Recreation,* May 1984, p. 48.

11. J. Zenger, "Leadership: Management's Better Half," *Trends,* Vol. 4, No. 3, 1987.

12. Dennis R. Howard and John L. Crompton, *Financing, Managing and Marketing Recreation and Park Resources* (Dubuque, IA: Wm. C. Brown Co., 1980). p. 320.

13. John L. Crompton, *Doing More with Less in the Delivery of Recreation and Park Services: A Book*

of Case Studies (State College, PA: Venture Publishing, 1987), p. 5.

14. Lynn S. Tadlock, 'Marketing Starts with Information," *Parks and Recreation,* May 1993, p. 50.

15. Ronald Riggins, "Social Responsibility and the Public Sector Entrepreneur," *Journal of Physical Education, Recreation and Dance (Leisure Today),* Oct. 1988, p. 60.

16. B.L. Driver *et al.,* "Pilot Tests for Implementing Benefits-Based Management," Fort Collins, Col.: *Presentation at Fifth International Symposium on Society and Resource Management,* June 1994.

17. Catherine P. Coyle, W.B. Kinney, Bob Riley and John W. Shank, *Benefits of Therapeutic Recreation: A Consensus View* (Philadelphia, PA: Temple University and National Institute on Disability and Rehabilitation Research, 1994).

18. *The Benefits of Parks and Recreation* (Ottawa, Can: Parks and Recreation Federation of Ontario, Canada, Ontario Ministry of Tourism and Recreation, Canada Fitness and Amateur Sport, 1993).

19. B.L. Driver, Perry J. Brown, and George L. Peterson, eds., *Benefits of Leisure* (State College, PA: Venture Publishing, 1991).

20. *Research Round Table: Validation of the Impact of Recreation on Social Problems* (Minneapolis, MN: NRPA Congress Work Session and Continuing Project, Oct. 1994).

21. "Benefits: Get the Message Out," *Recreation Canada,* Vol. 51, No. 2, 1993, p. 8.

22. "Benefits," *Recreation Canada,* Vol. 51, No. 5, 1993, p. 8.

23. Daniel Dustin, Leo McAvoy, and John Schultz, "Recreation Rightly Understood," in Thomas Goodale and Peter Witt, eds., *Recreation and Leisure: Issues in an Era of Change* (State College, PA: Venture Publishing, 1990), p. 102.

Chapter 5

Establishing Program Goals and Objectives

Program development is the organization and administration of leisure experiences through systematic planning. When planning, you as a programmer must anticipate, coordinate, and implement. . . . Planning functions are carried out within the confines of the organization in which you work. The unique philosophy and organizational structure of leisure-service agencies determine the exact procedures, under which they operate and offer programs to their constituents.[1]

It is . . . crucial that the needs assessment process adopted by our department provides detailed information about the various leisure participation patterns and interests of the many interest groups in our community. Leisure-service delivery agencies must be able to clearly articulate who they are providing services for, what they are trying to accomplish, and to what extent they have been able to meet these goals.[2]

The beginning steps of the program development process are to establish the agency's philosophical base, assess participant and community needs and interests, and formulate appropriate goals and objectives. This chapter describes these tasks, with emphasis on conducting environmental scans and carrying out needs assessment surveys. It highlights the need to ensure that program objectives are consonant with the agency's mission, and that they respond both to human-service needs and to fiscal realities. Only when the intended positive outcomes of programs—both for the individual participant and for the community at large or the sponsoring organization—are clearly defined at the outset, can the benefits-driven programming approach be effective.

The topics presented in this chapter address the following undergraduate curriculum objectives established by the NRPA/AALR Council on Accreditation:

Understanding of and the ability to analyze programs, services, and resources in relationship to participation requirements. (8.20)

Understanding of procedures and techniques for assessment of leisure needs. (8.21)

Knowledge of principles and procedures for designing leisure services, resources, areas, and facilities. (8.23)

Understanding of the principles and practices basic to the effective management of recreation users in natural resources settings. (9B.04)

Understanding of the role and function of health care and human service systems, including therapeutic recreation's contribution to each. (9D.08)

The Role of Mission Statements

Each recreation, park, and leisure-service organization should have a clearly defined philosophy or mission statement, which is periodically reviewed in the light of changing conditions, needs, and agency capabilities.

A mission statement is essentially a summary of an agency's philosophy, in terms of its purpose or social role. Often it consists of a number of long-term goals that define the organization's function in community life. Customarily, mission statements are formulated by administrators, approved by policy-making boards or advisory groups, and printed in formal agency documents. Usually, it is assumed that they will be operative over a period of several years, and that they will provide a framework for program planning, policy development, and other agency functions. Customarily, mission statements appear in printed form in bylaws, preambles to constitutions, charters, authorizing legislation, or similar documents. They may also be presented, often in simplified form, in descriptive brochures about the department or agency.

One such mission statement, for armed forces recreation, was presented in Chapter 4. Three others follow, illustrating the purposes and social roles, in turn, of nonprofit, voluntary agencies, a community-based therapeutic recreation organization, and a public recreation and park department.

Mission Statement of Police Athletic League

The mission of the National Association of Police Athletic Leagues, which coordinates, promotes, and assists the Police Athletic League movement, is described in the following statement:

> *The National Association of Police Athletic Leagues is a non-profit charitable organization established to provide and maintain a means and method for the exchange of ideas, experiences and information on youth problems; their causes and treatment; and to study methods and procedures necessary to develop a constructive program [to solve] youth problems; to promote competition in the advancement of sportsmanship and citizenship; to be a constructive force locally and nationally in the interest of youth and the promotion of friendly and cooperative relationships between members of the association.*[3]

Individual Police Athletic Leagues in cities throughout North America are likely to have their own mission statements that stress their particular program emphases in terms of preventing juvenile crime, improving relationships with law enforcement agencies, and promoting youth citizenship and leadership values.

Therapeutic Recreation: Mission of RCH, Inc.

The mission of RCH, Inc. (formerly known as the San Francisco Recreation Center for the Handicapped) is defined in the following statement:

Our programs are designed with the goals of stimulating the development of self-esteem, social interaction, leisure skills and interests, health and physical fitness, and creative expression. It is our belief that men, women, and children with disabilities are entitled to participate in community-based programs, and that they have a fundamental right to inclusion in every aspect of community life. Our Mission embodies the following objectives.

1. To provide programs in recreation and leisure, vocational rehabilitation and supported employment, adult development, children's services, and respite care services for individuals of all ages who have all types of disabilities;
2. To promote the development of the recreation and social skills appropriate and necessary for successful participation in community life;
3. To promote the development of vocational training skills needed for successful community-based employment;
4. To create and provide programs designed to give people with disabilities the opportunity to live and work safely in the least restrictive environment; and
5. To educate the community by serving as advocates for the rights of persons with disabilities, and by training professionals in methods to meet the community's changing needs.[4]

Other mission statements of therapeutic recreation or activity therapy departments in hospitals or rehabilitation centers tend to focus on specific goals of treatment concerned with the effective psychomotor, cognitive, and affective functioning of patients or clients, and with their developing meaningful and independent leisure lifestyles.

Combined Mission and Goals Statements: Knoxville, Tennessee Recreation Bureau

Mission statements tend to express broad philosophical values or intentions but may also take the form of long-range goals of leisure-service organizations. For example, J. Robert Rossman cites a set of three-to-five-year planning goals adopted by the Knoxville, Tennessee, Bureau of Recreation, which include the following:

> To enhance the quality of life for all citizens of Knoxville through the provisions of public recreation services;
>
> To employ a professionally trained staff and to provide staff an environment fostering personal and professional growth;
>
> To improve the efficiency and effectiveness of maintenance operations;
>
> To increase revenue production and to implement a budget process at the operational level in the Bureau; and
>
> To act as a facilitator or catalyst for the provision of recreation programs by other public or private organizations.[5]

Environmental Scans

It is essential to review mission or goal statements periodically to determine whether they are still relevant, or whether they need to be revised in the light of changing conditions. When periodic review is undertaken as part of the program planning process, it is accomplished through external and internal environmental scans.

External Environmental Scans

The external environmental scan consists of a comprehensive, timely examination of external factors within a community that affect or influence an agency's leisure-service role.

These factors may include any or all of the following:

1. *Social or demographic changes* in the community's population or in the membership of the organization being served, in terms of age, gender, race or ethnicity, socioeconomic status, disability, and similar factors that may influence participants' need for certain recreation opportunities, or that may constrain participants' involvement.

2. The *programs offered by other agencies* within the community, such as nonprofit, commercial, therapeutic, and private-membership groups, in terms of their filling certain needs or possibly offering the opportunity for partnerships or jointly sponsored programs.

3. Similarly, the *facilities provided by other governmental agencies,* such as state or adjacent county recreation and park departments, which may be readily available to citizens of the community, given their ability to travel and to pay possible fees.

4. *Emerging social problems* in such areas as youth crime and gang violence, drug and alcohol abuse, growing numbers of latch-key children, and dependent elderly persons, in which organized recreation may play a role, along with other social services.

5. *Physical changes in the community,* such as the constriction of open space, decline of industrial or waterfront areas, new transportation patterns, neighborhood changes, and other environmental concerns with implications for leisure services.

Information Gathering and Analysis

Such factors may be explored in several ways. First, information may be gathered from community or neighborhood councils, associations of social agencies, or municipal or county planning boards.

Program trends in other leisure-service agencies may be examined through direct contact with their staffs, or by examination of their brochures, annual reports, or interchange of visits.

Emerging social problems generally are publicized in the press, are explored in Parent-Teacher Association or other group meetings, or may be examined in meetings with the police, educational authorities, health officials, or similar groups.

Ecologically involved groups and individuals are usually good sources for information about environmental issues, and employment/unemployment trends may be documented through municipal offices or civic associations concerned with business development.

The purpose of the external scan is to identify major trends or problems that should be considered in planning recreation programs and services. As a simple example, if the external environmental scan showed that several community organizations, including Ys and a community college, offered superior, low-cost health and physical fitness programs, a public recreation and park department might well decide that programs of this nature should not represent a high priority for its own program planning. On the other hand, if the external scan showed that there was an increasing level of unemployment in one area of the city, the department might conclude that it should offer enriched daytime programming for adults in neighborhood centers in that area, supplemented by job counseling services and possibly fundamental vocational education courses as well.

Need to Limit Scope of Scans

Some authorities suggest that a very wide range of detailed information be gathered within all the social, demographic, health-related, political, economic, and other aspects of community life, as part of the external environmental scan. For example, Rossman indicates the questions that should be asked in examining a community's economic status:

> *What is the basis of the local economy? Is it diversified and therefore likely to remain stable? Is it an economy based on a single industry? What is the current economic stability of this industry? How much annual income do the majority of*

patrons have? How much discretionary income do the patrons have? What percentage of the leisure-service market share does the agency currently have? Is this likely to increase, resulting in increased income? Are there additional competitors who are likely to cut into the agency's market share? If so, what are the financial implications of this? What is the current tax base and tax rate? Is either of these likely to increase or decrease? If so, what are the programming implications?[6]

However, many of these questions ask for data that might not be readily available to recreation programmers, and that would require a considerable amount of time and effort to investigate. Other points call for sophisticated analysis, or could only be answered through speculation. Realistically, then, programmers should limit their investigation to the more *relevant* and *accessible* elements in the community environment that clearly would be useful in making recreation programming decisions.

Internal Environmental Scan

The internal scan consists of a similar examination of varied factors *within* the leisure-service agency that have implications for program planning. The examination might consist of the following:

1. A thorough review of all recent program offerings, classes, sports leagues, pool programs, day camps, special events, and other varied activities and services. The health of these programs would be assessed, in terms of both attendance trends and cost-benefit analysis, and their place on the program life cycle (see page 183).
2. Assuming that the needed information is available or can be readily obtained, participation statistics should be analyzed with respect to the profiles of different centers or districts of the community, or of different groups of participants.
3. The internal scan should also systematically examine all agency facilities, analyzing their degree of usage, physical condition and maintenance, staffing patterns, and adequacy to meet program needs.
4. The community relations aspect of programming should be reviewed, including the use of volunteers, center advisory committees, neighborhood councils, and cooperative programs with other public, nonprofit, or private agencies.

The internal data-gathering process should rely heavily on the examination of program reports and evaluation recommendations submitted throughout the year. It may also involve special meetings and planning sessions with advisory committees or councils, block associations, focus groups of representative residents brought together to consider specific issues, or other community relations sources.

Combined External and Internal Scans

In some cases, data-gathering procedures may collect both external and internal information. For example, the Leisure Services Department of the City of Sunnyvale, California, conducts a market activity survey that examines both external and internal elements of its

Competition:

    What activities are being offered by other agencies or private businesses that seem to be competing with your own?

    Are our costs/fees competitive?

    Is a partnership a consideration? Have you approached competition with the idea of a partnership? What was the result? If negative, why?

Profitability:

    What activity areas are most/least profitable for you?

    What activity areas seem to be declining?

    What areas have had unusual, prohibitive, or unexpected expenses occur?

    What activities have the highest/lowest expense/participant ratio?

    Is staff time/participant ratio appropriate? Please explain.

Facilities:

    Are current facilities adequate to accommodate current/future activities?

    If not, how are they limiting activity programming capability?

    Are there unique facility options that have been successful?

Trends and Demand

    What activities are growing/declining in popularity?

    Are there activity ideas you expect to expand in the near future? Why?

    Is there activity demand not currently being satisfied?

    Are there activities offered by competitors that are in such demand that you are considering offering them also?

    Are you considering any type of partnerships with competitors or other providers?

Figure 5-1.   Sunnyvale, California's market activity survey: self-study questions.[7]

---

programs, as shown in Figure 5-1. Staff members on various levels are asked to review their programs regularly, asking the kinds of questions suggested in this survey form.

Systematic Needs Assessment

At this point, enough information may have been gathered to conduct a review of the agency's goals to determine how adequately they are being realized, and whether or not they need to be revised in the light of changing community conditions. As a second step, it is necessary to assess systematically the needs and interests of the agency's patrons or potential patrons.

Nature of Needs and Interests

On the face of it, the expression *needs and interests* would appear to represent a relatively simple concept. What kinds of recreational activities would people like to take part in? What kinds of participation would meet their needs?

However, the concept is *not* that simple. A teenager's needs, for example, might reflect: (1) his or her *self-defined* needs or wants; (2) those seen as important by his or her *parents;* (3) other needs representing the *sponsoring agency's view of its mission;* or (4) the *community's concern* about appropriate teenage experiences. A teenager's needs may also be defined by behavioral scientists or other researchers who have studied the lives of adolescents and have analyzed their developmental stages and needs.

The concept of need must therefore be approached broadly, recognizing that it actually incorporates several different factors, such as the immediate *experiential effects* of taking part in an activity, the element of *motivation,* and the *actual outcomes* to be gained from participation.

Experiential Effects.   These are the most obvious and recognizable evidence of an individual's need to take part in activities. They include such effects as fun, pleasure, excitement, challenge, relaxation, escape, a sense of sociability, companionship, and accomplishment, and other feelings or emotions.

Motivations.   These represent more conscious and purposeful aspects of one's need for leisure involvement. They may include such elements as wanting to maintain or improve one's health and fitness, wishing to make a contribution to one's community, exploring recreational pursuits that may enrich vocational skills, gaining social status, and related motivations.

Program Outcomes.   These include the actual results of recreational participation, which can be measured empirically, and which tend to fall under four headings: (1) physical or psychomotor; (2) emotional or affective; (3) social; and (4) cognitive. Numerous studies have documented the effects of children's play, for example, under each of these headings.[8]

Meaning of Interests

The concept of interests is somewhat simpler than the concept of needs. Interests usually refer to the specific activities that an individual expresses a preference for, or actually engages in. However, does an interest represent an activity that an individual has taken part in in the past? If so, how long ago, how frequently, and with what degree of satisfaction? If a person indicates that he or she would "like to" take part in an activity, how reliably does that predict his or her actually engaging in the pursuit, if it were to be made available? What barriers or constraints might have limited participation in the past, and might continue to do so?

Needs Assessment Methods

Recognizing these difficulties, it is necessary to determine the needs and interests of participants in a systematic and reliable way. This determination usually is referred to as *needs assessment* and may make use of any of the following procedures or sources of information:

1. *Leisure needs-and-interests surveys,* directed to community residents at large, members of an organization, samples of overall populations, or more narrowly defined target groups;

2. *Use of evaluation forms or scorecards* that measure satisfaction with past programs and explore participants' desires for possible future programs;

3. *Suggestion boxes, informal contacts,* or *interviews* with individuals or small groups, to explore their leisure needs and interests or specific reactions to possible program elements;

4. *Use of advisory councils* or *committees, focus groups,* or *membership meetings* to discuss neighborhood or community needs on a broader scale.

Questionnaire Surveys

Of these varied approaches, the most commonly used method involves questionnaire surveys. These may be distributed to a sample of residents in a community, members of an organization or employees in a company, owners of vacation homes in a given area, or other population groups. They may be sent out through the mails, conducted by telephone interviews, handed out at the front desk or in lockers of Ys or fitness clubs, or distributed to subjects at church or service club meetings, or similar settings.

Design of Survey Instruments

In designing a needs-and-interests questionnaire form, it is essential to have the study's purposes clearly in mind. Subjects may be asked to rank-order the activities they would like to take part in, or to classify them on a scale of personal interest, as shown in Figure 5-2.

If the questionnaire's purpose is to get a precise reading of whether participants would actually take part in certain activities if they were offered, it could ascertain this by adding more narrowly differentiated response categories such as *definitely yes, probably yes, not certain, probably no,* and *definitely no.*

Please indicate your degree of interest in the following recreation programs or activities, by checking the appropriate boxes.

Activities/Programs	Very High	High	Moderate	Little Interest
Volleyball Club	( )	( )	( )	( )
Cooking Lessons	( )	( )	( )	( )
Softball League	( )	( )	( )	( )
Scuba Diving Class	( )	( )	( )	( )
Adult "Singles" Group	( )	( )	( )	( )

Note: As an alternative rating method, respondents might also be asked to rate each activity on a scale of desirability from 10 (very high) to 1 (very low). Typically, instruments of this type would be used to measure potential interest in specific program elements, if offered.

Figure 5-2.   Rating scale of activity preferences.

Some surveys examine other aspects of recreational interests, such as the preferred format for involvement, the probable frequency of participation, the preferred time and location of scheduled activities, and related information.

Figure 5-3 shows how questions on frequency, time, or location of preferred participation might be presented. In some needs-assessment surveys, respondents may also be asked about the range of fees or charges that they would be willing to pay for given activities, services, or memberships. However, it should be recognized that including all of these elements in a survey form may be extremely cumbersome if they are asked about each activity. Instead, respondents might simply be queried about their overall time, place, or fee preferences.

In designing surveys of this type, it is usually better to use closed-end questions, in which the respondent simply checks a single item or provides a numbered rating to indicate a preference. When conducted as interviews, surveys can more readily make use of open-end questions. In addition to giving factual responses, subjects may give fuller information on their recreation interests or views of the agency's program. Similar open-end methods may be used with focus groups or other advisory groups that assist the department in program planning.

In some cases, needs-and-interest surveys may not only seek to learn what activities community residents would like to take part in, but also to gather a general picture of their overall recreational involvements. For example, Figure 5-4 shows a section of a community survey of adult residents in Lower Paxton Township, Pennsylvania.

Frequency: How often do you expect to participate in this activity? Check one box.

Daily (in season) (   )   Once a month (   )
Several times a week (   )   Occasionally during year (   )
Several times a month (   )

Preferred times: Please indicate your first, second and third choice of times for participation in a specific activity.

	Early Morning	Later Morning	Lunchtime	Early Afternoon	Later Afternoon	Evening
Monday	( )	( )	( )	( )	( )	( )
Tuesday	( )	( )	( )	( )	( )	( )
Wednesday	( )	( )	( )	( )	( )	( )
Thursday	( )	( )	( )	( )	( )	( )
Friday	( )	( )	( )	( )	( )	( )
Saturday	( )	( )	( )	( )	( )	( )
Sunday	( )	( )	( )	( )	( )	( )

Location: Please indicate your preferred location for participation in activity. Indicate first choice only.

Barker Center (   )   Hamilton Center (   )
Gonzalez School (   )   Carver Park (   )

Figure 5-3.   Examples of questions about preferred participation patterns.

Recreation Activities.   We are interested in how often adult members of your household participate in the following recreational activities. Please check each of the activities in the appropriate box.

Activity	Frequency of Participation			Check if You Would Like To Participate More
	Never	Infrequently	Frequently	
Acting	( )	( )	( )	( )
Aerobics/Fitness Classes	( )	( )	( )	( )
Auto Repair	( )	( )	( )	( )
Baseball	( )	( )	( )	( )
Basketball	( )	( )	( )	( )
Bicycling	( )	( )	( )	( )
Bowling	( )	( )	( )	( )
Camping	( )	( )	( )	( )
Canoeing	( )	( )	( )	( )
Ceramics	( )	( )	( )	( )

Note: The original survey form included 35 additional activities, with many social and cultural pursuits listed. It also had response sections for a second household adult. If it is felt that the "frequency of participation" choices given here might yield inaccurate findings, more specific choices like those shown in Figure 5-3 could be used.

Figure 5-4.   Section of Lower Paxton Township community survey.

Broader Community Surveys

Needs-and-interests surveys often ask for detailed demographic information about respondents. For example, in a needs-assessment survey conducted by the Leisure Services Department of Saskatoon, Saskatchewan, detailed information was gathered through a door-to-door interview process that studied both present and potential program participants. Questions were asked with respect to: (1) age; (2) household income; (3) ethnographic background; (4) disabilities; (5) family structure or makeup; (6) employment status; and (7) gender.[9]

Respondents were also queried about their reasons for participation in agency programs, their treatment by staff, barriers to participation, and satisfaction with program involvement. Study findings indicated levels of participation and satisfaction in major program areas, as shown in Table 5-1.

Use of Surveys in Target Marketing

Surveys may be used to define target groups of community residents or organization members, and to determine their preferred program choices and conditions of involvement. In some cases, a full range of services may be directly correlated with different groups of respondents, as shown in a comprehensive study of U.S. Navy Morale, Welfare and Recreation programs (Table 5-2).[10] This study showed how five different groups of Navy personnel regarded the varied program elements offered within the MWR operation.

Table 5-1. Saskatoon Community survey: patterns of participation and satisfaction in nine program areas.

Program Areas	Presently Participating & Satisfied	Presently Participating & Would More Often	Not Participating But Are Interested	Total Market
Health/Fitness	44%	7%	11%	62%
Heritage	32%	1%	4%	37%
Lifeskills	9%	1%	11%	21%
Literary Arts	49%	1%	2%	52%
Multicultural	20%	1%	8%	29%
Outdoor Recreation	68%	5%	3%	76%
Performing Arts	40%	4%	6%	50%
Sports/Games	47%	7%	8%	62%
Visual Arts	25%	2%	8%	35%

Table 5-2. Prioritization of program elements by Navy MWR patrons.

Program Category	Active Duty (N = 4108)	Spouses of Active Duty (N = 612)	Retirees (N = 672)	DOD Civilians (N = 1032)	All Patrons (N = 6424)
Gymnasium/Playing Courts/Fields	1 (67%)	(52%)	(37%)	(62%)	(62%)
Fitness Center	2 (65)	(59)	(32)	(57)	(60)
Information, Tickets and Tours	3 (60)	(59)	(62)	(60)	(60)
Automotive Hobby Shop	4 (45)	(25)	(32)	(28)	(39)
Outdoor Recreation Areas	5 (41)	(44)	(46)	(47)	(43)
Movie Theater	6 (36)	(43)	(44)	(31)	(37)
Child Development Services	7 (35)	(62)	(19)	(33)	(36)
Swimming	8 (35)	(47)	(32)	(32)	(35)
Travel Agency Services	9 (35)	(30)	(32)	(32)	(34)
Recreation Equipment Rental	10 (31)	(22)	(30)	(33)	(31)
Library Services	11 (29)	(39)	(36)	(41)	(33)
Bowling	12 (29)	(31)	(31)	(26)	(29)
Youth Recreation Program	13 (27)	(50)	(21)	(34)	(30)
Full Club Dining/Beverage Services	14 (22)	(23)	(55)	(37)	(20)
Local Intramural Sports	15 (21)	(8)	(8)	(15)	(17)

N = number of respondents. Number in parentheses is percentage of respondents choosing that program category as "very important."

Note: Other program elements not listed here included Golf, Club Entertainment or Beverage Lounge, Craft and Hobby Programs, Sports Above Intramural Level, and Recreation Centers/Special Events.

Formulating New Program Goals and Objectives

By assembling information gathered through the external and internal environmental scans, evaluation reports, and needs-assessment surveys, it is possible to formulate new program goals and objectives. These should reflect changing social and economic conditions, agency priorities, and the expressed needs and interests of participants.

The terms *goals* and *objectives* generally are used rather loosely, often interchangeably. More specifically, goals represent broad statements of purpose reflecting the basic philosophy or mission of an organization. They often are referred to as purposes, and appear as parts of agency mission statements.

In contrast to goals, objectives represent statements of intent that are much more specific and measurable. They describe in concise, often quantitative terms, the actions that an agency intends to carry out, and the outcomes that it seeks to achieve within a given period.

Program objectives are generally of two types: (1) those that serve as means to an end, and are usually called "input" or "implementation" objectives; and (2) those that represent ends, or desired outcomes or program results.

Examples of Input/Implementation Objectives

These usually involve actions that an agency intends to carry out as part of an overall program plan. The following objectives illustrate this:

1. To successfully establish four multiservice senior centers, each with an average membership of 150 men and women over the age of 60, in 4 districts of the city.
2. To expand Boys' and Girls' Clubs membership by 56 percent over a 5-year period, through an intensive campaign of recruitment and program enrichment.
3. To provide day-care programs serving a minimum of 200 children of service personnel on a military base, within the next 6 months.

Other implementation objectives might involve personnel assignments, fiscal arrangements, or other actions intended to promote agency efficiency or expand services, such as these objectives:

4. To review fees and charges for all youth and adult classes and sports leagues, with target of increasing agency revenues from such sources by 15 percent in the winter program period.
5. To implement policy to enable economically disadvantaged families to attend specific recreation programs or facilities (including swimming pools, skating rinks, and the public zoo) without charge, on selected weekdays.
6. To cooperate with community groups to rehabilitate 5 Little League ball fields, using department equipment and materials, and neighborhood volunteers, during months of March and April of the coming program year.

Examples of Outcome Objectives

These would include the intended results of program sponsorship, in terms of measurable social change within a community or other special setting, or in terms of participant-centered outcomes.

As an example of a social change objective, a large insurance company or manufacturing concern might initiate an employee counseling program on drug and alcohol substance abuse, with the objective of reducing the number of problem incidents reported each month from an average of seven to an average of three. In a large urban public-housing project with a high level of vandalism, juvenile delinquency, and gang activity, the objectives of a summer recreation program might be to reduce the overall statistics of these antisocial behaviors by a given percentage. Information could be provided by local police precincts, housing managers, and neighborhood business owners.

Participant-centered objectives involve desired changes in participants' knowledge, skills, values, or behaviors that are the target of specified program activities. In many cases, they simply have to do with the acquisition of competence in performing a particular activity, such as swimming or bicycle riding.

For example, Rossman cites the following objectives of a baseball clinic for children. He writes that at the end of the clinic:

> Participants will be able to answer 70 percent or more of written questions on baseball rules.
>
> Participants will be able to answer 70 percent or more of written questions on baseball strategy.
>
> Participants' batting averages will increase by 0.050 or more.
>
> Participants will indicate whether their skill at playing the position they chose increased significantly.[11]

In general, precise behavioral objectives designed to measure the effect of recreational involvement are found more frequently in therapeutic recreation programs, where treatment plans frequently specify the areas in which patients or clients need to grow or progress, and where they outline detailed examples of desired change.

Most knowledge- and skills-related objectives in therapeutic recreation are usually fairly simple to identify, and provide the basis for program leadership. Often, they may be placed within a time sequence, in which a participant is guided in a progression from skill to skill. As each learning objective is achieved, the overall program goal is finally reached.

Use of Treatment Protocols

Therapeutic recreation objectives are frequently stated in treatment plans, or *protocols,* which include such elements as (1) diagnostic information, including patient/client symptoms and problems requiring intervention; (2) assessment criteria, including specific areas to be assessed and measurement instruments to be used; (3) the specific nature and sequence of interventions; and (4) the outcome criteria, including the changes to be expected, and when and how they will be measured.

An example of such a treatment plan or protocol is shown in Figure 5-5, which presents treatment objectives, intervention methods, and outcome criteria for an adult psychiatric facility.

Individual Goals and Objectives

STAFF MEMBER _STEVE SUMPTER, M.S., C.T.R.S._   **DEPT.**_REHABILITATION_
PROBLEM NO_____DECREASED FUNCTIONAL. COPING SKILLS, AND SOCIAL SKILLS_
MANIFESTATIONS: SOCIAL ISOLATION, DIFFICULTY EXPRESSING FEELINGS, INABILITY TO
_____RELAX, MINIMAL RISK TAKING, LIMITED TASK COMPLETION, EASILY BORED,_
_____DECREASED SELF-ESTEEM, DISORGANIZED THINKING AND DECISION-MAKING._
STRENGTHS USED IN PLAN:_____

DISCHARGE CRITERIA/GOAL: _PATIENT WILL DEMONSTRATE HEALTHIER WAYS TO COPE._

DATE	PLAN OBJECTIVES	INTERVENTION APPROACH/ACTIONS	EVALUATE PROGRESS STATEMENT
	Pt. will participate in all Rehabilitation Groups on a daily basis by:	Orient patient to the Rehabilitation schedule, monitor attendance, and encourage participation in all ordered groups.	
	Pt will demonstrate improved ability to complete assigned tasks, take risks, self structure, and discuss anxieties related to participation in these groups by:	Assist patient in evaluating the therapeutic value of activities such as: Craft Workshop, Art Experience, Leisure Skills, Outings and Group Recreation for involvement in after discharge. Identify ways to enhance the value of leisure in developing improved leisure skills.	
	Pt. will discuss a D/C Plan and Leisure Time Plan using information from program participation by:	Meet with patients on 1:1 basis to assess their plan prior to discharge.	

Figure 5-5.   Patient-Care plan—Capistrano by the Sea Hospital, California.[12]

Other Program Planning Factors

A number of other factors play roles in reviewing agency goals and establishing new objectives within the program planning process. In terms of the agency's overall mission and general goals, each objective should be scrutinized to determine whether it is in accord with these guiding principles.

For example, from a marketing perspective, will input/implementation objectives justify themselves in terms of providing substantial revenues, or achieving a favorable cost-benefit balance? Will they help raise the status of the agency in the public's mind or in the view of civic officials? Will they incorporate cooperative relationships with other agencies or community groups, and will they result in attractive threshold activities that draw large numbers of participants into the program?

From the benefits-driven point of view, will the program elements incorporated in the new program objectives contribute directly to health, community pride, positive social relationships, family stability, good citizenship, and other important personal or civic outcomes? Will they meet needs identified in the external environmental scan?

Other important factors include the following:

1. The agency's policies and procedures as they affect program sponsorship capability;
2. Legal or social equity factors related to the agency's commitment to serve all segments of the community;
3. Concerns related to risk management, and participant and staff safety;
4. The analysis of program costs and projected revenues, balanced against the social value of program elements; and
5. Possible cosponsorship arrangements or sources of special funding for program activities and services.

Each of these factors is described briefly in the concluding section of this chapter, and is explained in fuller detail in later chapters.

Influence of Agency Policies and Procedures

Leisure-service organizations of all types normally have policy manuals, handbooks, or printed guidelines governing varied aspects of their programs. These may relate to such issues as providing services to special populations, the rental of department facilities, sponsorship of religious holidays or other sectarian programs or events, political or legislative activity of staff members, and related administrative matters.

Legal Factors and Social Equity Pressures

Public recreation and park departments, like other municipal or county agencies, must function within a framework of law, arising from charter requirements, state enabling legislation, civic ordinances, or judicial precedents that govern their operations.

These factors affect agencies' personnel and fiscal practices, property acquisition procedures, and numerous other elements. In terms of programming, they impose the need to provide services on a nondiscriminatory basis to all potential participants, avoiding restrictions based on race, ethnicity, age, or gender; the need to adhere to policies related to free speech and assembly; and other operational needs.

Another related concern is the increased awareness of sexual abuse of children by adults in leadership roles. Policies dealing with parental permission for children to take trips, or ensuring that staff members are not alone with children in automobiles or other private settings, as well as issues involving sexual harassment of other employees, are all considerations affecting program operations.

Risk Management and Accident Prevention

Concern about possible negligence lawsuits is paramount in public or commercial leisure-service agencies that operate active outdoor recreation or sports programs. Accidents and even fatalities in wilderness exploration, whitewater rafting, skiing, boating, and other outdoor pursuits, as well as injuries in team sports such as football and ice hockey or the use of playground equipment, occur all too frequently.

Even in the initial stages of program planning, such questions as these must be asked: "Is a given activity reasonably safe for program sponsorship, in terms of its foreseeable degree of risk? Will specific forms of protection against accident lawsuits, such as client waiver forms or insurance coverage, be effective protection against major loss?" Particularly in terms of aquatic recreation, or even unstructured activities such as skateboarding, in-line skating, sledding, and community celebrations or festivals, careful program planning early on must address issues of risk management, public safety, and security control.

Among the strategies used to control such threats to agency operations are: (1) developing risk management plans that incorporate systematic accident-reporting and record-keeping; (2) facilities inspection and hazard abatement; (3) safety briefing of participants and ongoing supervision; (4) staff training and risk-management goal-setting; and (5) properly designed and practiced emergency procedures.

Cost and Revenue Factors

A fourth important area of concern has to do with whether recreation activities that are being considered fit comfortably into the agency's overall fiscal picture, in terms of both cost-benefit analysis and potential for the activities to produce significant revenues through fees and charges.

Cost/Benefit Considerations.   A preliminary analysis of projected costs and revenues of program elements makes it possible to estimate the per-participant costs of involvement, the overall cost of a given activity, and the break-even point at which a given number of participants will cover expenses associated with an activity or event. Depending on the degree of social utility or value in the program activity, planners may decide that a given activity may be expected to be fully self-sufficient (that is, to pay for 100 percent of its cost), or that it may cover a lesser percentage or none at all.

In many cases, a popular activity that yields substantial revenue may be scheduled as a profit-making venture, in order to help subsidize other non-revenue activities. As a specific example, a summer day camp might be self-sustaining at a per-participant charge of $500 for a six-week program, based on a given number of children registering. However, the recreation and park department might then set the registration charge at $600, to provide a margin of profit to subsidize a number of scholarship registrants who would take part in the camp's program at a reduced charge or without cost. Pricing and fiscal planning, as they relate to programming, are discussed more fully in Chapter 9.

Potential Cosponsorship Arrangements

Linked to the issue of costs and revenues needed to support program elements under consideration, is the potential for cosponsorships or other forms of funding assistance involving other community agencies.

The cosponsorship arrangement itself may range from an outside agency's providing all or part of the funding needed for a special project, to providing guidance and expert leadership, needed facilities, public relations assistance, and volunteer labor for a given program feature. In many cases, community organizations such as service clubs, church groups, and youth-serving organizations may enlist their own memberships in environmental cleanup efforts, volunteer leadership with special populations, or other community-service ventures.

Such projects show the contribution that recreation, parks, and leisure services can make in promoting democratic citizenship values. When different groups of community residents learn to take action and work together to improve neighborhood living conditions and overcome social problems, recreation has an immense potential to build a sense of community well-being.

Other Considerations: Participants and Program Elements

At this point, having re-examined and confirmed goals, conducted external and internal scans, carried out needs-assessment studies, and developed an appropriate set of objectives, the leisure-service agency is almost ready to develop its overall program plan.

However, several other important elements must be considered before major planning decisions can be made. They involve the following:

1. The *needs of participants,* not simply in terms of their responses to needs-assessment studies, but also with respect to their personal or group characteristics, in terms of age and life-stage, family situation, gender, race and ethnicity, possible disability, and similar factors;

2. An examination of all possible *program activities,* including such traditional pursuits as games, sports, arts and crafts, and similar pastimes, as well as more innovative or unusual activities and services; and

3. The *agency's resources,* in terms of the *leadership* that provides direction and supervision to program activities, and the *areas and facilities* essential to a diversified range of successful leisure experiences.

These elements require careful analysis and pre-planning, before the program plan itself can be developed. They are described in detail in the three chapters that follow, with illustrations drawn from varied recreation, park, and leisure-service agencies throughout North America.

Summary

This chapter begins by examining the role of mission statements that provide a framework for developing agency goals and formulating program plans. Typical statements from three different types of leisure-service organizations—nonprofit/voluntary, therapeutic, and public—are presented. To ensure that agencies' mission statements are attuned to changing needs and opportunities, many agencies carry out two kinds of searches for information: (1) external and internal environmental scans; and (2) needs-and-interests surveys.

Environmental scans are used to obtain a realistic picture of social and economic conditions in the community at large, as well as the role of competing agencies and a detailed analysis of the leisure-service agency's past and current operations. Needs-assessment surveys provide valuable information about participants' recreational interests and involvements, along with their preferences for program formats, locations, costs, and related factors.

Based on these data-gathering methods, recreation agencies are able first to determine their long-term goals and revise them when necessary, and then to transform them into specific action-oriented objectives that guide ongoing program planning. These objectives are of two types—*input/implementation,* and *outcome-oriented*—and provide a basis for later evaluating a program's success.

Discussion Questions and Class Assignments

1. What are the key areas of information that should be explored through the external and internal environmental scans? What methods are used to gather such information accurately and systematically? Give several examples of how the information gained can contribute to the review of program goals and objectives.

2. As an individual or small-group project, develop a needs-and-interests questionnaire survey to be used in doing a needs assessment of a specific population, such as retirement community residents, employees of a manufacturing company, or service personnel on an armed forces base. In your preliminary survey plan, include the major areas of inquiry, examples of the kinds of questions or items to be included, and the method to be used to distribute or administer the questionnaire.

3. As another individual or small-group assignment, develop a goals statement for a recreation program designed to serve a specific agency population, such as a community-based sports program for disabled youth and adults, or an outdoor recreation program for college students. Based on these goals, identify several specific program objectives, making sure that they involve measurable outcomes or accomplishments, within a precise time frame.

Note that both this and the preceding assignment represent fairly complex tasks, requiring substantial research, time, and student effort, to be carried out meaningfully.

References

1. Christine Z. Howe and Gaylene M. Carpenter, *Programming Leisure Experiences* (Englewood Cliffs, NJ: Prentice-Hall, Inc., 1985), p. 109.

2. Rob Gilhuly, "Leisure Needs Assessment Surveys: The Saskatoon Experience," *Recreation Canada,* Vol. 51, No. 2, 1993, p. 31.

3. *Mission Statement of Police Athletic League* (North Palm Beach, FL: National Association of Police Athletic Leagues, 1995).

4. *Mission of RCH, Inc.* (San Francisco, CA: Policy Statement of San Francisco Recreation Center for the Handicapped, n.d.).

5. J. Robert Rossman, *Recreation Programming: Designing Leisure Experiences* (Champaign, IL: Sagamore Publishing, 1989), pp. 111–112.

6. *Ibid.,* p. 102.

7. *Tools for Surveying the Market* (Sunnyvale, CA: Leisure Services Department, 1993).

8. See Lynn A. Barnett, "Developmental Benefits of Play for Children," *Journal of Leisure Research,* Vol. 22, No. 2, 1990, pp. 138–153.

9. Gilhuly, *op. cit.*

10. *Leisure Needs (Smart Compass) Survey* (Washington, DC: Bureau of Naval Personnel MWR Management Tool Kit, 1992), pp. 3.4.1–3.4.3.

11. Rossman, *op. cit.,* p. 163.

12. For a fuller discussion of patient-care plans and protocols, see Richard Kraus and John Shank, *Therapeutic Recreation Service: Principles and Practices* (Dubuque, IA: Wm. C. Brown Publishers, 1992), pp. 106–110.

Chapter 6

Analyzing Program Participants: Demographic Factors

Contemporary community life is characterized by identification with others who share values, interests, and lifestyles. Participation based on shared interests . . . is voluntary and exists as long as individuals are motivated to participate, identify, and relate to others who are similarly involved. It is therefore crucial that the needs-assessment process adopted by our department provides detailed information about . . . the many interest groups in our community. . . .

Participants are asked about their age, ethnographic background, whether or not they have a disability, the type of family structure they live in, their employment status, household income, gender, and geographic location.[1]

We now turn to a consideration of several elements that play a role in the program-planning process. The first of these involves the participants themselves, seen from several perspectives, such as age, gender, ethnic identity, and possible degree of disability. This chapter's purpose is to help the reader see recreation participants not as a faceless mass, but as people who share certain common leisure drives and motivations, but who also vary greatly in terms of their recreational needs, interests, and capabilities.

The following learning objectives established for undergraduate programs in recreation, park resources, and leisure services by the NRPA/AALR Council on Accreditation, are addressed in this chapter:

Knowledge of the responsibility of the leisure service profession to make available opportunities for leisure experiences for all populations, including those with special needs and disabilities. (8.13)

Ability to promote, advocate, interpret, and articulate the concerns of leisure services systems for all populations and services. (8.14)

Understanding of and the ability to facilitate the concept of leisure lifestyle for continued individual development and expression throughout the human life span. (8.17)

Understanding of people within diverse social groups and the relationship of such groups. (7C.05)

Understanding of how and why people perceive and respond to given resources and management practices. (9B.08)

Understanding of the characteristics of illness and disability and their effects on functioning, including leisure behavior. (7D.04)

Focus on Participants: Why and How?

Why must the recreation program planner focus sharply on the people he or she hopes to serve? The answer should be obvious. Nothing is as important in the planning process as the participants themselves. If their needs, interests, and capabilities are not recognized, and if program opportunities are not appealing to them and do not contribute significantly to the quality of their lives, then everything else about the program runs the risk of failure.

While it is impossible to develop rigid recreational prescriptions for individuals based on such demographic characteristics as age, gender, or ethnicity, clearly such factors influence the leisure choices of participants in terms of their readiness to engage in different pursuits, as well as the kinds of opportunities that are offered for them. Chief among the demographic factors that influence recreation participation is the element of age.

Influence of Age on Leisure Needs and Choices

One's place in the life span is closely linked to one's recreational interests and behaviors. Many recreation, park, and leisure-service agencies block out entire groups of program

Creative Dramatics	5–8 yrs	$35

Bring your imagination and join us for an adventure in creative dramatics. Using a multi-media approach to theater, explore the stage through pantomime, dance, art, storytelling, clowning, music and more!

Supersitters	11 yrs and up	$30

American Red Cross course provides training for kids in babysitting. Includes characteristics of children, toys and games, how to supervise, accident prevention, handling emergencies, simple first aid, basic care and feeding of children, and how to select a babysitting job.

Junior Golf (Beg)	9–15 yrs	$20

Professional instruction consisting of swing techniques, putting, chipping, rules and etiquette. Bring 5 iron, 9 iron and putter; range balls and green fees not includes.

Baton Twirling	5–7 yrs	$30

Twirling develops hand-eye coordination, flexibility and self-confidence. Learn basic twirls, marching and dance twirl routines culminating in a show and parade. All levels do parade marching 4–4:30 p.m. Int. level must have completed two previous sessions.

Figure 6-1.   Examples of age-directed programming for children.

Source: Program Brochure of Long Beach, California, Department of Parks, Recreation and Marine.

activities for participants within specific age parameters; others assign differing age limits to individual activities (Figure 6-1). The use of age-related grouping is also shown in the membership policies of many youth organizations, which assign their members to age-based classes or sub-groups.

Such practices represent more than the need for administrative convenience. Instead, they acknowledge the reality that throughout the life span, people undergo developmental changes and challenges and are best served by recreational pursuits that help them make these changes and develop skills that are linked to growth needs at each stage.

Stages of the Human Life Cycle

Program-planning guidelines often make use of developmental models that outline the stages of the human life cycle as shown in Table 6–1. In addition to identifying each stage, they typically describe normative patterns of development, including physiological, psychological, environmental, and other influences on human growth.[2]

Other texts identify periods of human development in terms of the need of individuals to progress through a series of psychosocial tasks attached to each stage. Erik Erikson, for

Table 6-1.   Chronological stages of human development.

Life Stage	Age Approximations
I. Prenatal	
Conception	—
Zygote	7 to 10 days
Embryo	10 days to week 8
Fetus	Week 8 to birth
II. Infancy	
Neonate	First 2 weeks
Infant	To 2 years
III. Childhood	
Early	3 to 5 years
Middle	6 to 8 years
Late	9 to 11 years
IV. Adolescence	
Early	12 to 15 years
Middle-late	16 to 18 years
Emerging adulthood	19 to 21–23 years
V. Adulthood	
Early adulthood	23 to 40–45 years
Middle adulthood	43 to 60–65 years
Early old age	65 to 75–80 years
Late old age	80 and over

Source: George Kaluger and Meriem Fair Kaluger, *Human Development: The Span of Life* (St. Louis: Times Mirror/Mosby, 1984).

example, suggests eight such stages and identifies what he considers to be the key challenge or conflicts facing individuals at each point:

Infancy	Basic trust versus basic mistrust
Early childhood	Autonomy versus shame and doubt
Play age	Initiative versus guilt
School age	Industry versus infinity
Adolescence	Identity versus confusion
Young adulthood	Generativity versus stagnation
Old age	Integrity versus despair[3]

In other breakdowns of the human development process in the program-planning literature, background information is cited that goes far beyond the realistic needs of recreation practitioners who work with different age groups. For example, in one programming textbook, the physiological determinants of human development include "genetic," "neurological," "glandular," and "blood chemistry" elements.

Instead of such excessively detailed or theoretical approaches, analyses that describe typical growth stages of participants in simple, relevant terms are of greater value to recreation programmers. The following section of this chapter therefore presents analyses within four broad age-group categories: children, youth, adults, and the elderly.

Recreation Programming for Children

Childhood is generally considered to be the period from approximately age two or three to the beginning of puberty and adolescence at about twelve or thirteen. Although many leisure-service agencies may serve infants or toddlers, in day-care programs or such activities as simple gymnastic or exercise sessions, pre-swimming classes, or informal play activity, organized recreation programs generally begin during the preschool years and continue through early childhood and the middle and late elementary years. Farrell and Lundegren note the following characteristics of children during the preschool years:

> Children engage in self-centered, side-by-side play, marked by little interaction or cooperative activity.
>
> They have short attention spans, but seek immediate gratification and praise.
>
> They are dependent on supervision for structured play activities, enjoy big muscle activities, fantasy and make-believe play.
>
> They have a high degree of curiosity and welcome new challenges and varied activities.[4]

During the early and mid-childhood years, children continue to be individualistic ("I centered") but are learning to participate in group activities. Emotionally they are often immature in that they have a low tolerance for frustration and require adult encouragement and understanding. Their physical skills are developing rapidly in both big- and small-muscle activities, and they have a longer attention span than preschoolers have. In terms of play behavior, they are interested in a wide variety of pastimes and learn best through concrete kinds of tasks.

Eight-to-ten-year-olds have more fully developed small-muscle skills, and are ready for most complex eye-hand activity. Because of their longer attention span, they can sustain interest for longer periods of time in each activity. Though their energy level is high, they may tire easily and must be given frequent rest periods. Their interest in belonging to groups is stronger than younger children's, and club or team activities should be provided.

Throughout childhood, the focus on organized recreation should be on promoting rounded, healthy development in physical and emotional terms, and on encouraging positive socialization and intellectual growth. Typically, activities provided by public recreation and park departments and voluntary youth-serving organizations include the following:

- *Informal play,* in playgrounds or indoor settings, involving use of sandboxes for younger children, slides, swings, climbing equipment, or other structures or tools to encourage creative exploration and exercise.
- *Games* and *sports,* including active group games—often of the "lead-up" variety that teach basic physical skills—and both individual and team sports for the middle and later elementary-grade children. Through organized sports leagues, children beyond the age of seven or eight are often involved in organized competitive play.

- A full range of experience in *creative activities,* including drawing, painting, and varied crafts pursuits, music, dramatic play, and such dance forms as creative rhythms, folk, modern and jazz dance, and ballet.
- *Outdoor experiences,* including nature games, camping, and environmental studies, often linked to outings, craft activities, and other outdoor pursuits.

In addition to public and nonprofit voluntary agencies, a growing number of for-profit enterprises have entered the children's play field. For example, such commercial chains as Gymboree and Kidsports have expanded nationally and in some cases have established franchises in other nations around the world, offering well-equipped, secure environments for play. Varied martial arts classes are also sponsored commercially today, with children learning such skills as karate, judo, jujitsu, or aikido.

Special Needs of Children Today

It must be recognized that leisure outlets provided for children in North America vary widely, depending on a family's socioeconomic status. While children in middle-class or affluent families are often given a wide range of opportunities—including private instruction in a host of skills, as well as the opportunity to travel, attend camps, or enjoy cultural pursuits—children in poorer neighborhoods often suffer from a dramatic lack of healthy play programs.

Compounding the problem, childhood is no longer the relatively blissful, innocent period of life that it was once considered to be. Instead, problems of drug-addicted babies, children in broken homes or families where both parents work and they are given "latchkeys" to care for themselves for long hours of the day, or children subjected to physical or sexual abuse are all too common. Under the barrage of violence- and sex-iaden rock and rap music, video games, movies, and television, and with the decline in traditional family values, childhood today represents a difficult period of personal growth for millions of young people.

Increasingly, public and nonprofit youth-serving organizations are seeking to meet these challenges. As a single example, the Girl Scouts of the U.S.A. has developed programs designed to help its young members in terms of their personal needs with respect to health, fitness, nutrition and eating disorders, self-esteem and body image, sexuality, and social expectations and stereotypes affecting girls. To illustrate, they offer a "contemporary issues" series of learning experiences devoted to these themes:

Tune In to Well-Being, Say No to Drugs: Substance Abuse
Girls Are Great: Growing Up Female
Into the World of Today and Tomorrow: Leading Girls to Mathematics, Science and Technology
Reaching Out: Preventing Youth Suicide

Caring and Coping: Facing Family Crises
Earth Matters: A Challenge for Environmental Action
Developing Health and Fitness: Be Your Best![5]

Recreation, Leisure, and Adolescence

Adolescence, extending through the teenage years, represents the second major stage of the life cycle that is of special interest to recreation programmers. It is a period of life marked both by steady progress toward maturity and by rebellion against adult-imposed values and expectations. Adolescent boys and girls are torn between the dependencies of childhood and the desire to have the freedoms and prerogatives of adulthood.

For all teenagers, this tends to be a time for discovering and affirming their identity and independence. For many it is a time of powerful feelings, idealism about the world, and introspective self-searching.

Teenagers are often concerned about adjusting to their maturing bodies, their physical appearance, popularity, and their developing sexual roles. Increasingly, they seek support and approval from members of their peer groups and conform to peer standards.

Moods may change frequently, from defiance and rebelliousness to cooperation and responsibility. As they reach their middle teens, many adolescents begin to show a high degree of responsibility and goal-oriented behavior, while others withdraw into a state of alienation and antisocial behavior.

TeenAge Views of Leisure

Kleiber, Larson, and Csikszentmihalyi studied the leisure-related accounts of several thousand adolescents, and grouped their reported activities into three major categories: (1) *productive* such as class work, studying, jobs, or other work- or career-oriented tasks; (2) *maintenance,* meaning functions of daily living, such as sleep, eating, transportation, or medical care; and (3) *leisure,* including sports and games, socializing, television-watching, and similar free-time pursuits.[6]

In a breakdown of the last group, two kinds of leisure were reported: (1) *relaxed* pursuits such as reading, listening to music, or socializing, that provided pleasure and relaxation but demanded little effort; and (2) *transitional* activities that were structured and somewhat demanding, such as crafts, hobbies, sports, and games, or participation in formal youth programs. The researchers concluded that the latter type of involvement provides a bridge to the adult world and represents valuable learning or socializing experiences for adolescents.

In another study, Cardin reported the leisure involvements of approximately three thousand youth in Arizona schools, in upper-elementary and high-school grades.

As shown in Table 6-2, the activities reported consisted heavily of outdoor recreation and peer-group social activities in which survey respondents participated. However, this

Table 6-2.   Youth participation rates: Arizona school study.[7]

	Activity	%
1	Hanging out	88.0
2	Attending sports events	85.4
3	Basketball	83.3
4	Walking	78.1
5	Swimming in a private pool	77.1
6	Using a park playground	76.6
7	Attending a concert	76.6
8	Jogging	75.1
9	Bicycling	74.4
10	Baseball/Softball	74.1

study did not gather statistics regarding such popular pursuits as playing video games, watching television, or listening to youth-oriented popular music. Nor did it attempt to assess participation in such forms of leisure activity as gambling, and the use of drugs and alcohol.

Challenges to Youth Programmers

In a report of the findings of a national study of over forty-six thousand U.S. teenagers, Linda Caldwell point out that negative factors in the lives of adolescents included such elements as being alone at home, hedonistic values, television overexposure, drinking parties, physical and sexual abuse, and social isolation. She described a number of high-risk behaviors or indicators that were examined in the study, including:

> . . . alcohol use (frequent use and binge drinking), tobacco, illicit drugs, sexuality, depression/suicide, antisocial behavior and others. . . . Thirty-one percent of all students in grades nine to 12 reported drinking six or more drinks at one time in the last 30 days . . . ; 25 percent reported frequent depression and/or attempted suicide. Of all 12th graders, 60 percent were sexually active, and 53 percent of these did not use contraceptives. Even more striking is the finding that in a typical high school, 40 percent of all students in grades nine to 12 were at risk in three or more of eight at-risk areas.[8]

Caldwell concluded that because leisure provides a context for both positive and negative behavior, both aspects of leisure involvement by teenagers should be addressed by leisure researchers and recreation programmers. Many public and nonprofit recreation, park, and youth-service agencies throughout the United States and Canada today have developed special programs for youth, in an effort to prevent juvenile delinquency and promote the positive social development of adolescents. In some cities, they have focused directly on working with gangs, cooperating with the police and other authorities in this effort.

In addition to such creative recreational opportunities, many public and nonprofit youth-serving organizations have also initiated special programs involving drug-abuse prevention, tutoring, and vocational counseling, and efforts to reduce gang activity and delin-

Stampmania	16 yrs–adult	$18

All aspects of rubber stamping including layout and design, suppliers, stamps, glitters, paper, embossing and much more. A $5 supply fee (to be paid at class) includes all materials including 10 glossy cards and envelopes to be decorated in class.

Watercolors	16 yrs–adult	$40

Beginners and advanced learn to paint multi-watercolor techniques through lectures, demonstrations and hands-on activities.

Photography (Beg)	16 yrs–adult	$32

The ideal "first course" for owners of 35 mm single-lens reflex (SLR) cameras. Learn about camera functions, films and useful skills to make better photographs. Bring camera and owner's manual.

Figure 6-2.   Examples of activities linking youth and adults.

Source: Program Brochure of Long Beach, California, Department of Parks, Recreation and Marine.

quency. Religious agencies often promote volunteer and community-service projects for adolescents, and organizations such as the Police Athletic League and Boys' and Girls' Clubs of America often sponsor "teen government," "mayor for a day," and similar programs that promote citizenship values and leadership skills among adolescents.

In terms of general programming for youth, major emphasis is usually given to varied team sports, aquatics, outdoor recreation, and creative and cultural activities, along with other programs that promote citizenship and teen leadership skills. While these are usually conducted in age-specific groupings, teenagers are sometimes linked with adults, in terms of registration policies (see Figure 6-2).

Recreation Programming for Adults

Since there are major differences between the life-cycle needs and characteristics of those who are barely out of their adolescent years and those who are approaching retirement, it is helpful to divide the overall adult group into smaller segments. Edginton and his coauthors divide adults into three categories: *young adults, adults,* and *pre-retirement adults:*

Young Adult	20–29	Seeks meaningful relationships, makes commitments, career choices, and uses a variety of recreation activities in the courtship ritual, may pursue outdoor and risk activities to test competency.
Adult Years	30–49	Major productive years, child-rearing responsibilities and other social obligations. Looks to recreation for activity, diversion, status, and autonomy.

Pre-Retirement	50–64	Reduction of intensity of some needs, generally
Adult		secure, enjoys social outings, provides leadership in
		social-spiritual-civic and volunteer organizations.[9]

This breakdown describes a somewhat idealized and problem-free pattern of adult life. Many individuals within this overall age group do *not* carry out the "courtship ritual" in a traditional sense, are *not* involved in child-rearing, or do *not* reach a state of security or become involved in community organizations, in their pre-retirement years.

However, in general, most adults are in a busy and productive life stage. Both men and women today are likely to be heavily involved in the work world, with the majority maintaining family responsibilities as well. As a group, many adults are capable of meeting their leisure needs independently, without special assistance or guidance. They tend to be physically mobile and financially able to purchase equipment and satisfy their leisure needs in other ways. However, for such groups as disabled people, economically disadvantaged adults, or single parents, varied constraints and financial factors may make it difficult for them to satisfy their leisure needs without special programming services.

Young Adults

For adults in the younger age bracket, leisure provides a means of consolidating their individual personalities and affirming their independence, while at the same time reaching out to form bonds with others, whether as part of courtship or in other social terms. Many adolescent interests—such as popular music, sports, or other hobbies—are likely to continue, along with interests in fitness, travel, and other pursuits made possible by the greater financial capability of the early adult years.

College students often take part in recreation that centers around the institutions they are attending, in college union programs, fraternity or sorority parties, sports, entertainment, and cultural events. In many colleges, physical education programs now include an emphasis on lifetime activities, such as martial arts, yoga, scuba diving, and other pursuits, which may be engaged in through outings or club activities.

Family Involvement

For young adults who marry and raise families, leisure begins to center around children and the home, in backyard games and picnics, travel to camping areas or family-oriented theme parks, or parental involvement in scouting programs, Little League, or church or synagogue family programs.

There has been growing recognition of the value of family-oriented recreation in promoting healthy family relationships. As a consequence, many public recreation and park departments now sponsor family programs, and such specialized leisure industry components as travel and tourism, ski centers, and even gambling casinos now package special attractions to meet family leisure interests.

Despite the assumption that active recreation declines with increasing age, Rodney Warnick has cited research evidence showing that both twenty-five to thirty-four-year-olds and those in the thirty-five to forty-four age bracket have higher participation rates in a number of outdoor recreation activities than those in younger age groups.[10]

Middle Adult Years

As adults move into the middle adult years, family commitments tend to lessen, and as a result men and women are freer to engage in more varied leisure interests and social activities.

Gaylene Carpenter points out that many of our long-held stereotypes about the middle adult years are questioned today. She comments that the so-called empty-nest syndrome, once commonly experienced by full-time mothers when their young children became more independent, or when their older children left home, is less prevalent today than it once was, since women today are likely to be employed outside the home and pursue personal interests more than they did in the past. She writes:

"In the 1960s, it was easy to understand middle age. Everybody in it was 'over the hill' and could easily be dismissed. . . . Now there is increasing appreciation for the 30-plus years. . . . It is hoped that more and better programs and services will be initiated as recreation professionals become better informed and more creative in their approach to meeting the ongoing leisure needs and diverse expectations of middle-aged adults."[11]

Based on such changes, millions of North Americans in the middle-age adult bracket are able to expand their interest in hobbies, travel, sports, fitness, cultural activities, and other pastimes in public, nonprofit, commercial, and other recreational settings. However, these generalizations do not apply to all individuals in their middle years. Many have divorced and remarried and have new, pressing family responsibilities, while others have lost or changed jobs, with resultant economic insecurity that limits their ability to enjoy leisure freely.

Pre-Retirement Years

As most adults approach retirement, there is increased opportunity to take part in enjoyable recreational activities. Some individuals begin to take longer vacations or have a lightened schedule in the years immediately before retirement. Many employers sponsor pre-retirement workshops that stress health, economic well-being, housing, and other factors, along with leisure values and lifestyles.

Too often, however, older persons work at full schedules until the last moment before retirement. They then are suddenly freed of job responsibilities that have normally filled their days, provided a degree of challenge and personal responsibility, and even offered a supportive social milieu. For such individuals, retirement may pose a serious challenge.

During the period of later maturity, therefore, the intelligent individual should be preparing for retirement. This may include developing new recreational interests, skills, and hobbies; joining appropriate groups; engaging in travel; or taking leisure-related classes that are often sponsored by public recreation and park departments, adult education systems, or community colleges.

Recreation for Elderly Persons

The elderly segment of U.S. and Canadian citizens is immensely diverse. Aging itself is a complex of physiological, social, and psychological changes that vary greatly from person to person. Many individuals begin to age in terms of varied forms of withdrawal or personal decline in their fifties or early sixties, while others maintain high levels of independence and creative activity well into their eighties or even nineties. Social scientists have concluded that there are actually several stages of elderly persons, ranging from those who are extremely vital, healthy, and involved, to those who require intensive personal care and are often in nursing homes.

With growing life expectancy and improving health care, the number of older persons in the United States and Canada is rapidly increasing; it has been predicted that by about the third decade of the twenty-first century, one out of every five Americans will be sixty-five or older, and there will be one retired person for every two of working age, compared with one in slightly less than five at present.

The historical, stereotypical view of aging has been that it is a time when individuals become increasingly ill or disabled, financially dependent, socially isolated, and mentally incapable. However, basic concepts developed by the National Council on Aging stress that aging is a normal part of the development process, with its impact varying greatly from person to person. The former director of the National Institute on Aging, Dr. Robert Butler, writes:

> We used to think that if people lived long enough they would become senile. That's not true. . . . Several studies have demonstrated that decline in intellectual function occurs much less than was reported earlier and is usually caused by a disease—not by the aging process. Quality of life is critical. If you don't keep learning, you don't keep growing; it then becomes less exciting to stay alive.[12]

Recreation's Value for Elderly Persons

In a detailed study of the psychological benefits of recreation for older persons, Tinsley, Teaff, and Colbs identified several important areas of value:

Self-expression, the creative use of one's talents;
Companionship with others;
A *sense of power* in being able to organize one's life effectively;
The *security* of engaging in activities in familiar, safe surroundings;

Compensation for losses in one's life by finding new interests;
Intellectual and *cultural stimulation;* and
Solitude, involving one's ability to spend time alone in a rewarding way.[13]

The overall positive outcomes of leisure activity for elderly persons may be classified under several heading:

1. *Regular physical activity* is invaluable in maintaining cardiovascular fitness; reducing the incidence of strokes; increasing strength, flexibility, and functional capacity to carry out routine daily tasks; and minimizing the adverse consequences of the biological aging process.

Many elderly persons today engage in active sports, such as organized softball, track-and-field activities, or other Senior Olympics activities. However, less physically demanding activities, such as golf, bowling, fishing, gardening, and walking, also contribute to physical well-being, and many leisure-service agencies today offer modified aerobics activities or pool exercise programs to meet the needs of the elderly.

2. Organized recreation programs, such as those found in senior centers or Golden Age Clubs, provide the opportunity for *social contacts, companionship,* and *group involvements* that are critically important for older persons who no longer are employed and may be widowed or otherwise socially isolated. Such programs, as well as others sponsored within retirement communities, churches, or in other leisure-service settings, frequently provide their members with the opportunity to engage in volunteer services, helping the homebound, tutoring children, or playing other roles that contribute to members' sense of self-worth.

3. From a *mental-health perspective,* deeply involving recreational activity helps to relieve stress and tension, provides interest in life, overcomes boredom, and gives elderly persons a sense of accomplishment and mastery over their own lives. Numerous research studies have confirmed that satisfying leisure is a key factor in the satisfaction of elderly persons with their own lives. As they continue to learn and grow, explore new hobbies, or engage in educational programs such as those conducted by Elderhostel, a travel and study program serving hundreds of thousands of older persons, this population group is able to maintain its vitality and enjoyment of life.

Scope of Programming by Public Agencies

A study reported in 1994 by the National Recreation and Park Association and the University of Northern Colorado described the leisure programs for elderly persons sponsored by 4,800 different public agencies. In addition to providing details of membership, scheduling and staffing, the report gave statistics of the specific activities offered:

A number of cultural and educational opportunities are offered by senior centers/programs. Over half offer crafts, dance, music, visual arts, TV/movies, and cultural events. Social recreation activities are provided by a high percentage of respondents with special events as the most popular, followed by parties and social group activities.

The most frequent outdoor recreation activities provided are hiking/biking/walking (50.7%) and nature activities (32.3%). Less than 10% offer camping and backpacking and adventure/risk activities.

Card games, bingo, and board games are provided by more than 75% of senior centers/programs. Pool/billiards, swimming, and bowling are the most popular individual sports; horseshoes is the most popular dual sport, and softball is the most popular team sport offered. Over half of the programs offer the opportunity for their participants to be involved in Senior Games.[14]

In addition to direct sponsorship of recreational activities, many centers offer nutritional programs; varied forms of health assistance or care; counseling on family, legal, or financial matters; transportation aid; and other types of social services for the elderly. In addition, some public recreation and park boards sponsor citywide senior citizens' federations or councils, publish senior newspapers or newsletters, develop discount-card programs, plan trips and outings, and schedule senior recognition days or weeks.

Gender Influences on Recreation and Leisure

In addition to age, a second important influence on recreational values and behaviors has been the *gender* or sex of participants. While the words *gender* and *sex* are often used interchangeably, the term *sex* should technically be used to mean the biological identity of an individual while *gender* refers to all of the societally based roles, traits, and expectations applied to males and females—in recreation, as in other areas of daily life.

Influence of Past Beliefs

Until relatively recently in the western world, girls and women have been regarded and treated as subordinate to males in a variety of respects. They have been considered to be fragile, overly emotional, lacking in technical or business-related skills, and suited chiefly for domestic tasks, such as raising children or maintaining households. Linked to such stereotypical beliefs, women and girls have been widely discriminated against, in terms of legal and political rights, educational and career opportunities, and other important spheres of daily life.

Within the realm of play, these concepts of appropriate gender-related roles were reinforced at every level. Little girls were traditionally encouraged to play with dolls or to engage in such "feminine" pastimes as playing house, make-believe care of babies, cooking, and sewing, or creative and expressive music, dance, or art.

In terms of organized programs, the sexes were frequently separated, both within the activities offered by across-the-board agencies like public recreation and park departments, and in separate organizations designed to serve either boys or girls. In both types of settings, programs for girls and women tended to receive substantially less support than those designed to serve boys and men.

Recent Trends in Gender-Related Programming

Over the past two or three decades, there has been a remarkable shift in gender-related recreation programming, stemming from the impact of the feminist movement. Many of the past beliefs about the differences between the sexes have been discarded, and girls and women today have much fuller opportunities in terms of education, professional careers, political influence, and family-related roles.

Much of the change has come about through a new awareness of what constitutes appropriate roles for men and women. Today, women race horses, fly planes, compete in marathons and triathlons, serve in the military, and work as police officers and fire-fighters. Stewardesses are now known as flight attendants, and may be men or women. In terms of sports, due in part to Title IX, federal legislation requiring the equal treatment of males and females in schools and colleges, there are far greater athletic opportunities for girls and women than in the past.

Beyond this, the arbitrary separation of organized recreation activities in other spheres of play has been largely eliminated. Instead of separate girls' and boys' programs and activities in many areas of public recreation and park programming, most activities are no longer differentiated by the sex of participants.

In terms of recreation-oriented youth-serving organizations, a number of formerly sex-segregated agencies, such as Camp Fire and Boys and Girls Clubs, have merged their programs or now serve both sexes. This is not to say that all gender-related influences on leisure have disappeared. Certainly, boys continue to take part more fully than girls in active team sports, particularly those of a contact nature, such as football, ice hockey, boxing, and wrestling, while girls continue to predominate in recreational activities that are linked to their traditional roles and interests, such as homemaking and domestic arts, and aesthetic pursuits.

At the same time, many youth-serving agencies that serve girls and women predominantly or exclusively, such as the Girl Scouts and the Y.W.C.A., base much of their programming on the changing needs of females in modern society. Clubs, classes, and workshops increasingly deal with issues related to sex and marriage relationships, career development, personal safety, sexual harassment, financial planning and investments, automobile maintenance, and a range of practical skills that are essential to independent living.[15]

Other Sex-Related Issues

A major societal concern today has to do with the growing role of sex as a form of play, or enjoyable leisure pursuit. Numerous research studies make clear that sexual activity is no longer viewed as carried on primarily for the purpose of procreation, as it was formerly regarded by most traditional religious denominations. Instead, it is widely engaged in as a form of pleasure-seeking behavior, and provides a staple of popular entertainment, both legally and in such illicit forms as prostitution or pornography.

This trend is of particular concern to recreation programmers because of the growing involvement of younger and younger teen-agers in sexual activity that results in more infants born to single parents, and the spread of sexually-transmitted diseases. While other societal agencies, such as schools, the church, and the family, bear major responsibility for guiding young people and imparting positive and healthy sexual values, many recreation organizations that are deeply involved with youth also have an important role to play. At every level, and particularly in clubs, discussion groups, camping programs, and other activities serving the full range of teenage boys and girls, it is important to provide sensible and constructive guidance, to teach sound, socially approved values, and to represent positive adult role models.

A related concern has to do with the provision of special programs and services for homosexual youth. In the past, homosexual activity was both illegal and viewed officially as a form of psychological illness. Today, although homosexuality continues to be highly controversial in terms of setting public policy, there is a fuller recognition of the rights of gays and lesbians in U.S. and Canadian society. Many functioning organizations provide leisure opportunities for homosexuals, including athletic, social, entertainment, and travel organizations.

Arnold Grossman points out that public and nonprofit youth-serving organizations have a responsibility to serve homosexual youth in their communities, with appropriate programming, counseling, and the provision of positive role models.[16] While there are few such efforts at present that have been publicized, it seems likely that they will represent a growing priority for leisure-service agencies in the years ahead.

Racial Aspects of Recreation Programming

A third important factor that affects recreation programming involves the racial and ethnic backgrounds of participants. For example, although the United States was regarded as a democracy from the time of its founding, racial and ethnic minorities historically have been kept in subordinated social, economic, and political roles. In the United States, African Americans and in varying degrees members of other racial minorities were barred at one time from most playgrounds, recreation centers, organized sports, and other recreational facilities or programs used by Caucasians. These prohibitions were enforced by law throughout the South and by community custom through much of the North. Similar restrictions applied in many commercial recreation settings, and most nonprofit agencies like the Ys or Scouts either maintained segregated memberships or did not serve racial minority populations at all.

In Canada, while patterns of discrimination have not been as severe, in the eastern part of the nation there has been long-standing friction between the English-speaking majority population and the descendants of French settlers. Native populations such as Eskimo and Canadian Indian tribes have been isolated and subject to much lower standards of living, including educational, employment, and social opportunity.

During the 1950s and 1960s, as the Civil Rights movement in the United States gained momentum through demonstrations, court decisions, and legislation, radical improvement was made in opportunities for racial and ethnic minorities in such areas as housing, politics, education, and the justice system.

Public recreation and park agencies in the United States improved facilities and programs for racial and ethnic minorities. Many voluntary agencies ended their discriminatory practices and made new, intensive efforts to serve minorities. Commercial recreation businesses were pressured, sometimes through lawsuits, to serve non-whites more fully than in the past. African Americans and Latinos have become more prominent in college and professional sports and in the popular entertainment media, and these advances have helped to overcome past negative stereotypes.

Priorities and Program Goals Today

Recognizing the progress that has been made, what are the special leisure-related concerns in this area that affect recreation program planners today? They include the need to:

1. Develop programs that involve racial and ethnic groups more fully, or that meet their specialized program interests and concerns, by giving them a fuller voice in policy-making and program planning;
2. Develop intercultural programs involving varied ethnic populations, to improve social relationships and understanding, and to present a fuller picture of the contributions made by minorities in U.S. and Canadian society;
3. Overcome barriers that still exist as a result of socioeconomic disparities and continuing racial prejudice and patterns of exclusion; and
4. Use organized leisure-service programs as part of the total community effort to improve the lives of racial or ethnic minorities who are part of "under-class" urban populations.

In Canada, such goals were expressed in a brief presented by the Canadian Park and Recreation Association to the nation's Royal Commission on Aboriginal Peoples. This statement stressed the need for partnerships among agencies working with Eskimo and other native populations, recommending action to:

Encourage and support First Nations people to develop their own recreation delivery system;
Promote First Nations people to speak for themselves about recreation to all levels of government, and to participate at all levels of the recreation delivery system;

Recognize and celebrate cultural differences and promote recreation activities specific to First Nations people;
Promote professional and technical training and recreation studies and ensure these opportunities are available within First Nations communities; and
Promote the inclusion of culturally sensitive leadership training materials in existing national training programs, and take a strong stand on racism, a "zero level of intolerance."[17]

In the United States, numerous communities today sponsor festivals, historical celebrations, educational, and museum-centered events, to promote multicultural understanding and improve relationships among different community groups. As an example of such
programs, the Prince George's County, Maryland, Department of Recreation sponsors an
extensive series of cultural events during an annual Black History Week. The series
includes film showings, workshops, theater performances, and musical presentations dealing with both the African roots and the history of African Americans in North America
from the colonial period to the present. In addition to such programs, Prince George's
County also sponsors outstanding annual festivals of music, song, dance, foods, costumes,
and folklore in Hispanic, Asian, Jewish, and other traditions.

Programming for Persons with Disabilities

A fourth major element to be considered in analyzing participant characteristics that affect
recreation program planning involves their degree of ability or disability. As described in
Chapter 3, a key component of the organized leisure-service system today is therapeutic
recreation service, a specialization designed to serve approximately forty-three million
U.S. citizens and two-and-a-half million Canadians with disabilities.

The term *disability* refers to an impairment that hinders an individual in achieving full
physical, mental, or social potential, and that is hampering in one or more areas of life,
such as education, work, or family relationships. In the past, people who were significantly
disabled tended to be barred from most areas of opportunity for normal living; frequently
they were confined to large, custodial institutions, or hidden and over-protected by their
families.

Today, thanks to a more humane and sensible
public understanding of the meaning of disability,
as well as the passage of key legislation in the
United States and Canada, people with disabilities
are guaranteed the right to education within the
"least restrictive" environment, and to protection
against job discrimination because of their physical
or mental impairments.

Increasingly, people who formerly would have
been institutionalized because of developmental
disability, mental illness, or severe physical disability are living in the community independently, or in
group homes or other sheltered environments, and a
growing number are gaining job skills and becoming economically productive.

Significance of Recreation for Persons with Disabilities

Recreation in its varied forms is immensely important for individuals with disabilities.
First, as part of the normal process of human development, recreation promotes healthy
physical, emotional, social, and intellectual growth. Children who are deprived of recreation tend to lack the needed skills or social abilities that will help them function successfully in community life.

From a physical perspective, active forms of play contribute not only to one's strength, endurance, balance, and overall fitness, but also to continuing patterns of healthy living, regardless of one's limitations.

Emotionally, for people of all abilities, recreation provides release from stress, or tension, a sense of personal accomplishment and creative expression, and a means of overcoming boredom or isolation.

Socially, leisure activities offer a means of being part of a group, making friends and overcoming isolation, learning the skills of give-and-take, leadership and fellowship, and meeting other special needs of people with disabilities.

Taken as a whole, positive recreational experiences provide opportunities for families to share positive and enjoyable leisure pursuits with their family members with disabilities, and for individuals with significant impairments to become integrated as fully as possible into overall community life.

Programs and Sponsors

Programs with a primary focus on treatment or rehabilitation under a medically prescribed or other clinical approach are usually offered in hospitals or other special institutions providing residential care for individuals with developmental disability, mental illness, visual or hearing deficiency, stroke or accident trauma, or a similar impairment.

The majority of persons with disabilities, however, do not live in such clinical settings, but are in the community with their families or in other special facilities. They are served by several different kinds of special recreation sponsors:

1. Agencies devoted solely to meeting the recreational and related social and educational needs of people with varied types of disabilities. An outstanding example is San Francisco's RCH, Inc., which provides comprehensive services for individuals of all ages, and is supported by both highly qualified professional leadership and hundreds of volunteers.

2. Camping programs, which may be independently sponsored by their own boards and with their own fund-raising efforts to serve a particular disability, or which may be supported by other organizations, such as Kiwanis, Elks, Moose, or the Easter Seal Society.

3. Organizations that focus on a particular type of activity, such as Special Olympics. Under the leadership of Eunice Kennedy Shriver, Special Olympics pioneered in providing instruction and competition in a wide range of sports for children and youth with developmental disabilities, often in cooperation with schools, civic groups, or other recreation agencies.

4. Nonprofit youth-serving organizations, such as Boy Scouts and Girl Scouts, Boys' and Girls' Clubs, Ys, and church groups, which frequently establish separate units designed to serve those with physical or mental disabilities, or which integrate them, whenever possible, in programming for their membership at large.

5. Public recreation, and park agencies on every level, which build special facilities or equip outdoor and indoor recreation areas for use by people with disabilities, or which sponsor special programs to meet the needs of this population. Many agencies have developed effective policies and services in this area.

Examples of Public Agencies' Policies and Services

Many county and municipality recreation and park departments have established forceful and progressive policies to serve community residents with disabilities (see Figure 6-3).

In fulfilling their mandates to serve individuals of all ages with disabilities, many public recreation and park departments offer extensive programs in sports, hobbies, arts and crafts, outings, aquatics, and social activities. In addition, they may serve in a counseling and referral role, helping families or individuals get in touch with other social agencies or coordinating their own services with other organizations serving those with disabilities. Examples of program elements are shown in Figure 6-4.

It is the policy of the City of North York to include and support persons with a disability in all our recreation services and programs. It is our shared responsibility to live up to this policy by welcoming persons with a disability into our activities.

We will do our best to provide whatever support is necessary. This may mean altering the staff-participant ratio, moving to an accessible location, etc. Support should be natural and unobtrusive, in order to promote real relationships and connections with others. One-on-one support is rarely necessary, and most persons with a disability can be accommodated with very little effort.

We believe that we should start with the assumption that persons with a disability may wish to participate in any one of our programs, not just specialized or segregated ones. We therefore consider it our responsibility to support the needs of all participants in every possible case.

We believe that the community has many resources to help us fulfill our responsibilities in welcoming and supporting persons with a disability. Participants, agencies, advocates, parents, etc. all have valuable insights and experiences which influence the manner in which we provide support. These persons and groups are often included in the process of determining and providing appropriate support.

We believe that our facilities ought to be accessible to all persons. All new facilities are constructed in compliance with building codes on accessibility. As existing facilities are renovated, increased accessibility is an important consideration.

The terms we use when referring to persons with a disability are very significant, as they shape and reinforce attitudes. While bearing in mind that appropriate terminology changes (for example, the word "retarded" was once acceptable but is no longer) and varies from place to place ("spastic" is still used in some countries but not in Canada), here are some basic guidelines for dignified terminology: (1) emphasize personhood rather than disability; (2) use positive or neutral terms, avoiding negative terms, such as "handicapped" or "crippled;" (3) use common sense in judging whether any term or reference would insult your own dignity if you have a disability.

Figure 6-3. "Inclusion and Support"—example of policy statement.

Source: City of North York, Ontario, Canada

Dining Out Program.   Ages 18 and up. Dinner program for developmentally disabled young adults at local restaurants. Participants pay own meal costs. 1st and 3rd Wed. of month.

Indoor Sports and Games for Disabled Adults.   Games and indoor sports activities. 1st Sat. of month.

Square Dance Class.   Ages 15 and up. An 8-week program for developmentally disabled. Mon., 7–9 p.m.

Mommy and Me Aquatics.   A five-week session to introduce youth with disabilities, ages 5–8, to water safety and beginning swimming instruction. One hour, twice weekly program.

Recreation for the Deaf.   Activities for adults, including cards, bingo and games. Tues., 9 a.m.–2 p.m. and Thurs. 10 a.m.–2 p.m.

Sailing for Physically Challenged.   For beginners and intermediates. Rigging modification, cockpit adaptation and techniques for persons with physical limitations. Class free to all qualified disabled persons.

Self-Defense for the Disabled.   Ages 18 and up. Interested in learning self-defense? Then sign up quickly for this limited enrollment class.

Wheelchair Tennis.   Ages 21 and under. Instruction for the game's beginners. 9–11 a.m., day and location to be announced.

Stroke Activity Center.   Center offers social rehabilitation for stroke patients. W/F, 8:30 a.m.–2:30 p.m.

Figure 6-4.   Example of "Adaptive Recreation" programs and services (1992).

Source: Program brochure, Long Beach, California, Department of Parks, Recreation and Marine. Although these listings do not adhere strictly to current terminology guidelines, and although they stress separate rather than integrated program groupings, they represent a broad and diversified range of activities for persons with disabilities.

Summary

This chapter has presented an overview of the influence of four important demographic elements—age, gender, race and ethnicity, and disability—on the needs of leisure-service program participants, and on their ability or desire to participate in recreation programs. In addition, a number of other factors, such as socioeconomic status and place of residence, may also influence participants' needs and interests and should be considered in program planning.

It is not always possible or realistic for a program planner to analyze all of these factors in great detail. Some recreation programming texts, for example, present highly complex, detailed approaches to understanding human growth and development. However, in many cases the information required to analyze participants based on these approaches would be extremely difficult to obtain. Beyond this, with the exception of clinically oriented therapeutic recreation programs that carry out detailed patient or client analyses, it would be difficult to use the knowledge gathered in any practical way in program planning and leadership—particularly in activities serving large numbers of participants.

Therefore, in most cases, leisure-service programmers should rely on a basic understanding of the typical needs, drives, and interests of participants, keyed to the four sets of characteristics described in this chapter. Programmers also must be perceptive to the individual traits and personality patterns of participants, and to the findings of needs-assessment studies that reveal the recreation-related values and behavior patterns of the groups served. Such awareness is critical to the overall task of recreation, park, and leisure-service program planning.

Discussion Questions or Class Projects

1. Based on the chapter's content and on individual students' personal experience and observation, discuss each of the four major age groups with respect to (1) the values and goals of recreational participation for each age group; (2) the special problems or barriers that each group may have in leisure activities; and (3) the most common and successful forms of leisure involvement for each group.

2. To highlight the influence of sex and gender on recreational interests and participation, the class can divide into two groups, male and female. In a separate "buzz session," each group should identify its primary leisure interests and motivations, and then discuss its members' perceptions of the other group's recreational values and involvements. Then, both groups can meet as a whole and share their views with each other. What distinct differences are there between the sexes? What values or interests do they share? What misconceptions do groups have about the opposite sex?

3. To explore issues of racial and ethnic identity, class members can share their own family or group traditions in the area of recreation and leisure. In what constructive ways could leisure be used to promote intergroup understanding and positive relationships?

4. Members of the class having personal contact with disabled individuals describe their disabled acquaintances' leisure interests, outlets, and barriers. What are the positive and negative aspects of segregated and integrated recreation programs that serve people with disabilities?

References

1. Rob Gilhuly, "Leisure Needs Assessment Surveys: The Saskatoon Experience," *Recreation Canada*, Vol. 51, No. 2, 1993, p. 31.

2. See for example Christine Z. Howe and Gaylene M. Carpenter, *Programming Leisure Experiences* (Englewood Cliffs, NJ: Prentice-Hall, Inc., 1985).

3. Erik Erikson, "Eight Stages of Human Life," in *Daedalus, Journal of American Academy of Arts and Sciences,* Spring 1975.

4. Patricia Farrell and Herberta M. Lundegren, *The Process of Recreation Programming: Theory and Techniques* (New York: John Wiley and Sons, 1983).

5. "Tune in to Well-Being," in *Contemporary Issues Series,* Girl Scouts of the U.S.A., 1994.

6. Douglas Kleiber, Reed Larson and Milhaly Csikszentmihalyi, "The Experience of Leisure in Adolescence," *Journal of Leisure Research,* Vol. 18, No. 3, 1986, pp. 169–176.

7. R.J. Cardin, "A Youth Perspective on Outdoor Recreation," *Parks and Recreation,* June 1994, pp. 58–61.

8. Linda L. Caldwell, "Research on Adolescents and Leisure Activities," *Parks and Recreation,* Mar. 1993, p. 19.

9. Christopher R. Edginton, Carole J. Hanson, and Susan R. Edginton, *Leisure Programming: Concepts, Trends and Professional Practice* (Dubuque: IA: Brown and Benchmark, 1992), p. 101.

10. Rodney Warnick, "Recreation and Leisure Participation Patterns Among the Adult Middle-Aged Market from 1975 to 1984," *Journal of Physical Education, Recreation and Dance,* Oct. 1987, p. 49.

11. Gaylene Carpenter, "Serving Those in Middle Age: 30–60," *Parks and Recreation,* June 1984, p. 58.

12. Robert Butler, "Today's Senior Citizens: Pioneers of New Golden Era," *U.S. News and World Report,* July 2, 1984, p. 52.

13. Howard E.A. Tinsley, Joseph D. Teaff and Sandy Colbs, *The Need Satisfying Properties of Leisure Activities for the Elderly.* Project Report, Southern Illinois University and Andrus Foundation, n.d., p. 2–3. For a fuller overview of this subject, see: Francis McGuire, Rosangela Boyd and Raymond Tedrick, *Leisure and Aging* (Champaign, IL: Sagamore Publishing, 1996).

14. "NRPA Concludes Comprehensive Leisure and Aging Study," *National Recreation and Park Dateline,* April 1994, pp. 1, 5.

15. For a fuller discussion of women and recreation, see Karla Henderson, M. Deborah Bialeschki, Susan Shaw and Valerie Freysinger, *A Leisure of One's Own: A Feminist Perspective on Women's Leisure* (State College, PA: Venture Publishing, 1989). From a Canadian perspective, see: Pat Bolla, Don Dawson and Maureen Harrington, "Women and Leisure: A Study of Meanings, Experiences and Constraints," *Recreation Canada,* Vol. 51, No. 3, 1993, pp. 23–26.

16. Arnold Grossman, "Until There Is Acceptance," *Journal of Physical Education, Recreation and Dance—Leisure Today* (April 1995): 47.

17. Ralph Nielsen, "Brief to the Royal Commission on Aboriginal People," *Recreation Canada,* Vol. 51, No. 5, 1993, p. 34.

Chapter 7

Recreation Program Elements: Activities and Services

The [Montgomery County, Maryland] Department of Recreation has provided quality leisure classes through its County-Wide Class Program for over thirty years. Recognized nationally for quality and diversity, County-Wide Classes serve thousands of County residents each day. The program consistently offers the opportunity to pursue a healthier and fuller lifestyle. Whether your goal is to become more physically fit, express yourself creatively, expand your skills or to meet people with similar interests, you can take the first step by registering now for one or more class programs.[1]

The next step in the program planning process is to select appropriate recreation activities or related services from a wide range of possible elements. This chapter examines ten major categories of such activities that may be provided by recreation, park, and leisure-service agencies, ranging from sports, games, and fitness activities, to social-service functions.

Examples of each activity classification are provided, and methods of examining specific program elements are described, in terms of their physical, social, or other requirements. The chapter concludes with a discussion of how activities may be modified to suit special needs, and the varied formats through which they may be presented to fulfill program objectives.

The following learning objectives, established for undergraduate programs in recreation, park resources, and leisure services by the NRPA/AALR Council on Accreditation, are addressed in this chapter:

> Understanding of and ability to utilize programmatically a breadth of diverse activity content areas. (9C.01)

> Ability to conceptualize, develop, and implement recreation programs for various populations, marshaling diverse community and human service resources. (9C.03)

> Understanding of and ability to apply leisure education content and techniques to the therapeutic recreation client. (9D.11)

> Understanding of principles and procedures for planning leisure services, resources, areas, and facilities. (8.22)

Overview of Recreation Program Areas

When the recreation and park movement first got under way, program activities tended to be limited to a comparatively small group of games, sports, creative activities, and nature pastimes suited for playgrounds, day camps, and similar settings. Today, leisure-service program elements cover a much greater diversity of personal and social experiences.

Some recreational pursuits are physically active and demanding, while others are relatively passive and casual in the experiences they provide. Some involve interaction with the natural environment, while others focus on aesthetic and creative personal experiences. Many recreation activities are pursued as ends in themselves, while others represent purposeful means of achieving important personal goals.

Recognizing these differences among recreation program elements, it is helpful to identify ten major categories of commonly provided activities and services, to assist in developing program plans.

1. Sports, Games, and Fitness Activities

Organized sports represent a major interest of people young and old throughout the world. *Sports* may be defined as participant or spectator physical activities requiring both exertion and skill, based on competition, with both formal rules and informal standards of etiquette and fair play. Activities may involve both organized and relatively unstructured play, and may be carried on at varying levels of proficiency, ranging from total beginner to highly skilled player. The term *games* may be applied to sports, as in the case of the Olympic Games, or football or baseball games. However, there are numerous types of games that are not sports as such, like many children's playground games. Similarly, various sports such as archery and boxing are not usually thought of as games. Finally, the term *fitness* may include sports involvement, as well as such non-sports activity as aerobic exercises and casual jogging. It is the element of vigorous physical activity that these three types of leisure involvement have in common.

Active sports are usually classified under two headings: *team sports,* and *individual* or *dual sports.* Examples of team sports are:

baseball	lacrosse
basketball	soccer
football	softball
hockey	volleyball

There are many popular variations of these sports that can be used in recreation programs, such as touch or flag football, floor or street hockey, and slow-pitch softball. Individual or dual sports include:

archery	karate
badminton	racquetball
bowling	shuffleboard
boxing	table tennis
fencing	tennis
golf	track and field

Closely linked to sports are games that use athletic skills and are popular in playground, camp, and school programs. These include such examples as tag, kickball, and lead-up games that are modifications of popular team games.

Fitness activities might conceivably include any active sport or outdoor pursuit, but usually are considered to include the following: jogging or running as a conditioning exercise; varied forms of aerobic exercise, including aerobic dancing or Jazzercise; biking; swimming laps or other pool-based exercise; weight training or use of exercise machines; and varied racquet sports.

Program Values

Sports, active games, and fitness activities have numerous values and administrative advantages as recreation program activities. First, they are extremely popular, as both participating and spectator events. Indeed, so fervent is the interest in college and professional sports that some sociologists describe them as a form of contemporary religion.

Little League World Series is held annually in Williamsport, Pennsylvannia; boys and girls compete in Westchester County, New York, Playground Olympics. Archery tournament is sponsored by Police Athletic League in Ohio, and Washington State Cougars play basketball against Oregon State opponents in Pullman, Washington.

Because of their competitive nature, sports are said to represent important social values and to be a useful means of training children and youth in such areas as self-discipline, good sportsmanship, acceptance of rules, and commitment to group goals. At the same time, many argue that we have overstressed the goal of winning in sports, and have given too much attention to highly skilled players at the expense of ordinary or less-skilled players.

Sports are an excellent type of activity from an administrative point of view in that they can be used with groups of all sizes and can sustain interest over a period of time. They offer exciting spectator appeal for nonplayers, draw colorful publicity, and represent a key link between recreation and park services, since so many sports use outdoor play facilities. In addition, sports are an excellent means of developing positive community involvement. Parents' clubs and volunteer community sports associations often organize leagues, coach and manage teams, raise necessary funds, maintain facilities, and operate many programs with a minimum of paid professional leadership.

Most public recreation and park departments offer a varied range of sports facilities and programs, including instruction and competition for different age groups, as well as participation at different skill or interest levels. In many cases, competition may involve separate programming for males and females, while some leagues may encourage co-recreational team structures. More than most other types of recreation activities, sports can also be used to develop contacts among different groups within a community.

In armed forces recreation, programs have typically included five elements: (1) *instruction* in basic sports skills; (2) *self-directed,* informal play; (3) *intramural* play, among teams or individuals on the same base; (4) *extramural* competition against teams from nearby bases or communities; and (5) *high-level, varsity* play by highly skilled players on a national or even an international level.

Many organizations today provide sports opportunities to people with disabilities. Others have made concerted efforts to provide programs for formerly unserved minority-group members. Little League Baseball, for example, has established numerous leagues in disadvantaged inner-city areas, and the U.S. Rowing Association has sought also to involve racial-minority youth.

Fitness Program Values.　Numerous corporations throughout the United States and Canada cite significant increases in productivity and decreases in employee turnover, as well as millions of dollars saved in health-care costs, linked to employee fitness programs. Companies such as AT&T, Johnson and Johnson, the Adolph Coors Company, and Mesa, one of the largest producers of oil and gas, have instituted extensive sports and fitness programs. For example, Mesa has built a

> . . . *30,000 square foot, $2.5 million on-site fitness center for all employees and dependents (12 years and older). However, the wellness center is much more than a health facility. A wide range of recreation and fitness programs, such as volleyball, aerobics, medical profiles, fitness screening, educational classes, lectures and seminars, stress management, weight control and lower back care are available on a regular basis.*[2]

2. *Outdoor Recreation and Environmental Activities*

A second major category of recreation program activities consists of outdoor recreation and related environmental pursuits. These are defined as leisure pastimes that are carried out outdoors and that are significantly related to the natural environment. To illustrate, fishing and hunting are heavily dependent on the outdoor setting and so are considered forms of outdoor recreation, while basketball is not, although it might be played on playground or schoolyard courts. Examples of outdoor recreation might include any of the following:

backpacking	bird walks
gardening	coasting or tobogganing
hunting	hiking
ice skating	ice boating
mountaineering	kite flying
outdoor cooking	orienteering
snowshoeing	skiing (downhill or cross-country)
surfing	target shooting (rifle or pistol)

Two other types of activities are also related to outdoor recreation:

1. Environmental studies, volunteer cleanup projects, and other activities that are carried on in leisure and that expose participants to the world of nature, such as visits to zoos, botanical gardens, or wildlife sanctuaries; and

2. The broad field of travel and tourism, which frequently involves trips to scenic or exotic environments, or has as its purpose varied forms of outdoor recreation.

Program Values

Like sports, outdoor recreation pursuits are immensely popular. Customarily, they do not involve competition, although some forms, such as fishing contests and cross-country snowmobile races, may be competitive. Instead, outdoor recreation provides exposure to the outdoors, and brings participants in contact with woods, fields, streams, and the great beauty of nature.

Outdoor recreation pursuits also have great appeal because they may be enjoyed by people of all ages, ranging from tiny infants on family camping outings, to elderly participants in quiet nature hobby activities. Today, many people with disabilities take part in outdoor recreation, including such challenging ventures as mountain climbing for people in wheelchairs, and skiing by individuals who are blind.

Ideally, all outdoor pursuits should promote respect for the environment, avoiding pollution and other types of ecological harm. Mechanized outdoor recreation, such as the careless use of off-road vehicles, often represents a threat to wildlife and vegetation. In terms of leisure motivations, conflicts often occur between those who prefer quiet, noninvasive forms of outdoor recreation, and others who crowd rivers or wilderness areas with noisy and polluting forms of play.

National Outdoor Leadership School in Lander, Wyoming, introduces many participants to white-water rafting; U.S. Space Camp, affiliated with NASA, teaches teenagers aviation skills, including survival techniques. Theme camp visitors at Silver Springs, Florida, travel to outpost where injured animals and birds are treated and then returned to the wild. Family groups enjoy skiing at Sugarbush Resort, Warren, Vermont.

Many communities in relatively rural areas offer a variety of close-to-home leisure pursuits based on outdoor themes or folk traditions. The City of Dartmouth, Nova Scotia, for example, sponsors canoe and kayaking instruction, horseback riding, maple syrup-making, coastline and wetlands hiking programs, maritime folklore programs, and similar ventures.

Other Canadian park and recreation departments, as well as those in the northern United States, have developed extensive programs of wintertime outdoor play, including organized ice skating, ice fishing, hockey, and curling. Snowshoeing, tobogganing, downhill skiing, and cross-country skiing are all popular, and numerous resort and state or provincial park authorities have constructed both indoor rinks and arenas, and outdoor trails for skiing and snowshoeing.[3]

Numerous commercial concerns today package varied forms of wilderness play, ranging from whitewater rafting to hunting and fishing expeditions, wilderness exploration, and backpacking trips. Many nonprofit organizations, such as the Sierra Club, Wilderness Education Association, National Outdoor Leadership School, and Woodswomen, Inc., sponsor training courses in varied outdoor pursuits.

Recognizing the sustained and growing interest in outdoor recreation, many communities have built rich networks of facilities for outdoor play. As a single example, Edmonton, Alberta, Canada, with the assistance of provincial funding based on oil and gas revenues, has established a ten-mile long urban parks program in its Capital City Recreation Park. The overall system includes three thousand acres in eleven separate parks along a twelve-mile stretch on both sides of Edmonton's river valley, with numerous sites for picnicking, sports, and summer and winter play. Nearly one hundred different special-interest clubs use the park system, ranging from hot-air balloonists to orienteering groups, canoeists, cross-country skiers, and hang-gliders.

As indicated earlier, a special aspect of outdoor recreation involves travel and tourism to wilderness areas, scenic and historic parks, and other attractions. A developing aspect of tourism today involves travel by people with disabilities. For example, The Guided Tour, an organization in Elkins Park, Pennsylvania, serving men and women with developmental disabilities, has taken thousands of participants to vacations on tropical islands, at world-famous resorts, and to major cities around the globe.

3. *Aquatic Program Activities*

Swimming and numerous other forms of water-based recreation might be classified either as competitive sports activities or as outdoor recreation pursuits, since they meet the essential criteria of both kinds of leisure activity.

They are presented here as a separate category of recreation, because they share a common environment and often are identified as a separate area of management responsibility in public departments. More than most activities, water recreation activities require special facilities, such as indoor and outdoor swimming pools, ponds, lakes or oceanside beaches, or the elaborately engineered structures found in water-play parks, including wave pools, streams for floating, sprays and fountains, twisting slides and chutes, and other innovative facilities.

Examples of aquatic activities include:

boating (canoeing, powerboating, rowing, and sailing)	diving
	life-saving classes
	swimming and bathing
fishing	surfing
skin and scuba diving	water polo
synchronized swimming	water skiing
water aerobics and exercise programs	para-sailing and jet skiing
	competitive swim meets

Program Values

Swimming and related water-based activities are among the most popular leisure pursuits in the United States and Canada. Varied aquatic activities may be organized in many different kinds of formats to serve different population groups. Obviously, they require very careful supervision and safety measures, because of the risk of drowning. However, with adequate supervision, swimming should be a thoroughly safe activity that appeals to all age groups and many special populations as well.

Swimming is enjoyed across the full life span, with many leisure-service agencies offering introductory pool programs for infants—who sometimes learn to swim before they can walk—and for a growing number of middle-aged or elderly swimmers who compete by the tens of thousands in Masters Swimming Championships. Swimming is regarded as an almost perfect form of exercise, improving the strength and flexibility of everything from one's neck to one's toes, without the injuries and strains that often result from other kinds of exercises.

4. Creative Pursuits: Arts, Crafts, and Related Hobbies

Another major area of organized recreation programming involves creative or aesthetic forms of expression. These have grown markedly in popularity in recent years.

Fine arts activities are usually considered to be creative pursuits that are intended to yield not useful products, but decorative objects involving aesthetic expression. They include:

drawing and sketching	oil painting
sculpture (clay, metal, stone or wood)	watercolor painting
graphics (includes various types of print-making, such as lithography, etching, silk-screen or wood-block printing)	

Crafts are generally distinguished from fine arts in that they usually are considered to have a more practical or functional purpose. Historically, crafts were usually thought to have less aesthetic value than fine arts. However, today it is recognized that craft projects may involve a high degree of skill and personal expressiveness. Examples include:

carving (wood, soap, bone, or plastic foam)	ceramics or ceramic sculpture
	jewelry
leather working	macrame
metalcraft	printing and book making
photography	calligraphy
weaving	woodworking

Many craft-like activities may also include varied forms of hobbies that involve construction, such as making model planes, cars, or trains, and various science hobbies that involve making displays or carrying on experiments. Hobbies also include collection of all types, and other pursuits that may require artistic or craftlike presentations.

Program Values

Arts and crafts are extremely useful activities for organized recreation programs, in that they have a wide range of appeal, and may be offered different formats, including instruction, special-interest groups, and exhibitions. Arts and crafts are particularly appropriate for working with individuals with disabilities. Although some crafts may require expensive or elaborate equipment, such as kilns, presses, or weaving looms, others may be carried out with a minimum of special tools or equipment.

Another important advantage of arts and crafts is that they may appeal to beginners at the most basic level of participation, with such simple activities as fingerpainting, drawing with crayons or modeling with clay, or at extremely advanced levels of creative expression. Some recreation and park departments and voluntary agencies maintain entire art centers with ceramics shops or sculpture and painting studios, and they employ well-qualified specialists as instructors.

In terms of their unique values as forms of leisure activity, arts and crafts involve personal creative growth and aesthetic appreciation. They may result in products that can be displayed in shows or exhibits, thus contributing to the participant's sense of pride and accomplishment, and to the community's appreciation of the agency's work. Arts and crafts activities are usually noncompetitive (although prizes are often awarded in arts and crafts shows).

5. Performing Arts: Music, Drama, and Dance

The performing arts are unique in that they represent a form of artistic expression in which no product is created, except for the sound or visual effect of the performance in time and space. Music, drama, and dance are all extremely popular forms of cultural activity in modern society, as they have been for many centuries.

As forms of artistic expression, they can be used to communicate emotions and themes of every sort. The performing arts throughout history have appealed both to the nobility and highly cultured classes, and to the lower socioeconomic classes. Each one takes many forms and may be approached on a social or recreational level as well as creative, performing-arts level.

Listed under each of the following headings are both *art* forms and *social* or *recreational* types of performing arts.

Music

chamber music groups	choruses
drum and bugle corps	folk singing
glee clubs	instrumental instruction
jazz bands	opera or operetta
symphony orchestras	rock-and-role music

Drama

children's theater	charades and dramatic games
experimental theater	creative dramatics
one-act plays	marionettes, puppets, and mask-making
storytelling	theater parties
variety and talent shows	

Dance

ballet	creative dance for children
jazz dance	folk, square, and round dance
rock-and-roll dance	modern dance
disco dance	social or ballroom dance

Program Values

Like arts and crafts, the performing arts may be presented at many levels of proficiency. They often are highly social activities and lend themselves to regular group classes or performing groups that meet regularly, week after week and year after year. They are ideal co-recreational activities, and normally have participants of both sexes and varied ages, particularly in dramatic programs in which play casting requires such diversity.

Performance-oriented groups have additional values, in that they usually require many other participants, beyond those who are actually performing, to carry out such tasks as designing and building scenery for the stage, selling tickets, doing publicity, and making costumes. They are also visible and attractive ways of getting public attention and support.

Many municipal or county recreation and park departments have developed extensive performing arts programs, including repertory theater companies, dance classes at every level of skill, and summer music camps. Performing and fine arts classes of all types are provided in community centers, and some departments work closely with professional music, dance, and theater companies.

6. *Special Events*

Special events represent a unique program feature in many leisure-service agencies, ranging from huge community-wide celebrations to smaller holiday festivals or parties of different types. Generally they provide an important highlight to community life. Some of the special programs sponsored by leisure-service agencies include:

aquatic shows	gospel music or jazz festivals
carnivals for children and families	Mardi Gras, mummers parades, and
founder's day celebrations	similar events
holiday parties	rodeos or western-theme festivals
arts and crafts fairs	
ethnic heritage festivals featuring music,	
food, dance, and folk customs	

Program Values

There are numerous reasons why special events provide an important ingredient in the lives of community residents. They promote a spirit of celebration and festive mingling among different community groups, serving to cement a common bond among residents by encouraging them to work together and to share common interests. Often special events provide a stage on which the leisure interests or hobbies of special-interest groups may be displayed. Large-scale, spectacular events often tend to bring many visitors to a city or region, with a resulting spending of tourist dollars and a boost to the local economy.

One recreation programmer, Ken Cicora, points out that for most park and recreation departments, planning for special events has evolved from simple kite-flying contests, pet shows, or exhibits of children's playground art, to major events with sophisticated planning and promotional strategies and large-scale budgets. He writes:

> *No longer do we produce a community special event [in Fort Lauderdale, Florida] with just our staff and a few prizes donated by local merchants. Now we must consider marketing and promotions, production, maintenance, decorations, security and logistical costs. . . . Today, the Fort Lauderdale Parks and Recreation Department relies heavily upon sponsors for the ten events and festivals it produces annually. . . . Special events can produce a large profit [from admissions, concessions, and souvenir sales] allowing us to offset costs in other department programming areas that do not generate sufficient revenue.[4]*

Therapeutic recreation agencies in particular make frequent use of special events for fund-raising and public-relations purposes. For example, Camp Confidence, a therapeutic recreation camp in Brainerd, Minnesota, sponsors numerous large fund-raising events such as golf tournaments, and the New Lisbon, New Jersey, State School has hosted huge annual picnics for the families of developmentally disabled residents, along with state officials and other members of the public.

7. *Social Recreation and Club Activities*

A related category of recreation program activities consists of informal social recreation pursuits and club programs. Social recreation may be defined as the type of recreation program that stresses the informal mixing of people and the enjoyment of casual, noncompetitive socializing activities that are often traditional or folk-like.

Typical social recreation programs include:

Banquets	Barbecues and picnics
Card parties	Campfires and marshmallow roasts
Fun nights	Carnivals
Play days	Potluck or covered-dish suppers
Scavenger hunts or treasure hunts	Talent shows

Social recreation programs often include participation in such activities as:

Charades, skits, and informal dramatics	Community singing
Folk, square, and social dancing	Icebreakers, stunts, and mixers
Group games, such as guessing games and quizzes	Table games, cards, chess, and checkers

Program Values

Social recreation is especially useful in meeting the leisure needs of specific population groups, such as teenagers, single adults, elderly persons, and people with disabilities.

As compared to passive forms of commercially sponsored entertainment, social recreation provides active participation and interpersonal contacts. Social recreation normally should be inexpensive, noncompetitive, and welcoming rather than exclusive, and it should involve group members in planning and leadership roles whenever possible.

Social recreation is particularly valuable in meeting the needs of elderly persons. For example, senior center programs operated by the Department of Parks, Recreation and Marine of Long Beach, California, include a mix of dances of different types, holiday parties, game programs, and other social recreation activities, along with lectures, seminars, and workshops dealing with travel, religion, health, economic strategies, and other concerns of elderly persons. Retirement communities such as Sun City, Arizona, typically sponsor dozens of special-interest clubs that include varied hobbies, sports, and social recreation activities carried on in different centers throughout the community, as shown in Figure 7-1.

Commercial recreation businesses in the travel, tourism, hospitality, and sociability fields often schedule social recreation activities for their patrons. These tend to be directed by professional staff members and to be based on popular television shows, or other forms of light and humorous entertainment that promote a relaxed social atmosphere. For exam-

Activities	Locations				
	Bell	Fairway	Lakeview	Marinette	Mtn. View
Aerobics	•				
Aerobic Dance	•				•
Agriculture		•			
Art	•	•	•		
Basketball				•	
Bicycle			•		
Billiards	•	•	•		
Boating			•		
Bocce	•		•	•	
Bowling	•		•		
Calligraphy				•	
Cards	•	•	•	•	
Ceramics	•	•	•		
Chess			•		
China Painting		•		•	
Clay-free Form			•	•	
Coin		•			
Coffee Shops	•		•		
Computer				•	
Croquet		•			
Dancing	•	•		•	
Drama					•
Exercise Room	•		•	•	•
Fishing			•		
Handball	•				
Handicapables		•			
Handicrafts	•	•	•	•	
Horseshoes				•	•
Jogging Track				•	
Lapidary	•	•	•		
Languages		•		•	
Lawn Bowls	•	•	•		•

Figure 7-1.   Special-interest clubs and activity groups, Sun City, Arizona.

Note: This is a partial listing of Sun City club programs. Other activities include leathercrafts, model railroading, photo lab, rockhound museums, rollerskating, sewing, stamp collecting, swimming, woodworking, yoga, and numerous others.

ple, on a single week-long cruise conducted by a popular Caribbean cruise line, the following activities and events were scheduled:

> *Passenger talent show—Bridge tours—Singles party—Rum "swizzle" party—Travel and shop talks—Trivia—Video interviews—Piano bar sing-a-long—Trapshooting—Captain's welcome aboard party—Horse racing—Grandmothers and honeymooners party—Newlywed and not-so-newlywed game—Pool games—Midnight deck*

parties—Limbo contest, Sea feud—Country dance class—Ice carving demonstration—Dr. Ruth's sex quiz—Ping pong tournament—Farewell parties—Bingo—Masquerade party—Lottery—Wine and cheese party—Guacamole and salsa party—Midnight cabaret shows—Knobby knee contest—and Debarkation talk.

8. Literary or Mental Forms of Recreation

Another major category of recreation program elements consists of quiet activities of a literary, mental, or other cognitive nature. Such pursuits are often part of social recreation programs, hobby activities, classes, or club programs in leisure-service settings. While such activities are obviously part of daily life, and of the business/professional world, they may also be approached as enjoyable leisure activities, either individually or in group settings. They include:

Book club	Computer club
Current events discussion group or forum	Mathematics tricks
	Mental games
Leisure counseling or other personal discussion groups	Poetry club or workshop
	Radio club or radio station
Paper and pencil games	Writers' workshop
Puzzles	

As an example of how such activities are provided in a program serving youth and adults, the New York City YWCA offers numerous courses in business and creative writing, including these titles: "Writing for Business," "Writing From Personal Experience," "Fiction Writing Workshop for Beginners," "Women and Journal Writing," "Have Fun Writing a Murder Mystery," and "How to Get Your First Article Published."

Program Values

Literary and mental activities may be sponsored in public, corporate, campus, or voluntary agency settings that provide diversified leisure experiences. In some cases, they may simply represent a form of intellectual fun or competition. In others, they involve learning skills that may possibly be linked to career development or learning vocational skills. Hospitals and other treatment centers may have newsletters written and edited by patients and may encourage intellectual pursuits, particularly helpful for individuals who have sustained serious physical trauma or other functional losses, and who need to develop new, compensatory skills and interests.

9. Life-Adjustment and Personal Enrichment Activities

Illustrating the point that many leisure-service agencies sponsor programs that go far beyond simply providing fun, pleasure, or relaxation to participants, many recreation programs include classes, workshops, or other activities designed to contribute to the personal growth, coping skills, or self-actualization of individual participants.

While these activities are often educational in nature, they are not directed toward formal educational goals, but are simply forms of leisure involvement that have somewhat more serious or purposeful motivations than most other leisure pursuits.

Classes and workshops of this type have many emphases. They may be designed to build competence in personal investments, home management skills, health and fitness, interpersonal relationships, personal grooming, vocational development, or other community roles and areas of individual growth. The brochures of an urban YM-YWHA and a suburban YWCA include the following titles:

aerobic exercise and body tone	travel agents training course
childbirth education	women and finance
cooking, gourmet	stress for success: How to make stress
english as a second language	work for you
home repair—survival in a	letting go of clutter
mechanical world	becoming a selfish single
self-defense skills	don't be afraid of your car
weight-reduction	the art of make-up and skin care
dynamics of Jewish history	introduction to computers and word
divorced and separated discussion	processing
group	reversing the aging process
mother-toddler play workshop	

Program Values

Although these are not typical forms of recreation or play activity, such program elements have distinct administrative advantages for recreation and park agencies. They are usually offered in class-like settings, over periods of eight to ten weeks, and with fees that make each course or workshop economically self-supporting. In terms of staffing, self-enrichment activities are usually led by outside specialists who are paid on a per-session or per-course basis, and agree to direct a class based on its having a sufficient pre-enrollment to justify being offered.

10. Social-Service Program Elements

A final important program area of many recreation and park agencies involves services that meet specific nonrecreational needs of participants, addressing life needs or community concerns. Distinguished from the life-adjustment category, which includes many activities of a purely personal nature on a fairly superficial level, these social-service functions relate to significant health, vocational, legal, housing, educational, family, and other areas of social need.

Such program elements are particularly appropriate in recreation agencies that serve various age groups and special populations. Recreation leaders may be able to assist such groups directly through counseling, referral to other agencies, or specially designed programs aimed at meeting specific needs. Such activities and services include:

anti-delinquency projects	career or vocational counseling
discount purchasing plans	drug and alcohol abuse programs
day-care programs for latchkey children	educational counseling, tutoring, or study-hour programs
health clinics, such as glaucoma screening and dental services	legal assistance and referral services
	physical fitness programs
nutritional or meals-on-wheels programs	roving leader services for youth gangs
preretirement workshops	

Many agencies provide an extensive range of such services. The New York City YWCA, for example, sponsors a host of special programs that include a literacy center, alternative high school, and employment services for teen mothers and fathers, pre-school and after-school day-care programs, services for disabled women and girls, services for displaced homemakers, and other programs.

In Phoenix, Arizona, the City Streets/At Risk Youth Division of the Department of Parks, Recreation and Library, has undertaken numerous special programs and services for youth. In the mid-1990s, these included the following:

The innovative Juvenile Curfew Program, in which the department accepted and processed youthful violators of the city's curfew ordinance, providing referral services, counseling with teenagers and their parents, coordinating social services with other agencies, and involving youth in volunteer and community service activities.

An extensive program of job training and development for youth, including varied job internships and the Ranger Cadet Program for work in the parks.

Sponsorship of teen councils, a youth advisory board, conferences, newsletters, youth forums, and new teen centers in high-risk areas of the city.

A collaborative sports program with the city's Housing Department, with funding from the U.S. Housing and Urban Development Department, designed to reduce drugs, gangs, and violence, particularly in public-housing areas.

Program Values

The benefits of such social-service program elements are obvious, both for participants and for the agencies themselves. Those served are assisted in problem areas of their lives in a convenient and effective way, whereas if they had to search out such forms of assistance elsewhere, they might well not do it. In addition, these programs strengthen the overall contribution of the leisure-service agency when they meet such needs, and help support a higher level of respect for recreation and park organizations because they make significant contributions to community life.

Since many recreation, park, and leisure-service agencies already provide extensive services for the youth, the elderly, or people with disabilities, it makes sense for them to provide assistance beyond purely recreational programs.

Realistically, many recreation leaders may not be qualified to conduct a number of such programs that require special training or certification. In such cases, leaders work in cooperation with agencies that specialize in providing such services, or they may hire part-time, specially qualified practitioners.

Volunteer Programs.   A final important social service provided by many recreation agencies consists of the opportunities they offer to individuals to make significant community contributions as volunteers in their leisure time.

For example, in Westchester County, New York, the public Department of Parks, Recreation and Conservation sponsors a large-scale "Volunteers in the Park" program for school and college students who wish to become involved in environmental education, trail maintenance, natural resources inventory tasks, historical research, visitor orientation, or other aspects of park management. The Saskatoon, Canada, Leisure Services Department encourages individuals with disabilities of various types to volunteer in recreation and park settings. And in Long Beach, California, the Parks, Recreation and Marine Department involves thousands of volunteers in tree planting, beach cleanup, and other environmental or recreation leadership projects (see Figure 7-2).

Factors Influencing Selection of Program Elements

Having considered the ten major categories of key recreation activities and related services, how do program planners make intelligent choices from this wide range of possible elements?

Clearly, several factors come into play. The characteristics of participants, described in Chapter 6, must be carefully considered: age, gender, race or ethnic background, and degree of ability or disability. Certainly, their past recreational backgrounds and expressed needs and interests, revealed by the needs-assessment process, must be given appropriate weight, as indications of their probable participation in specific program offerings.

The administrative requirements of different activities or services must also be carefully weighed. What facilities or equipment does a particular sport require? Must program leaders have specialized skills or qualifications to direct a program? What limits must be placed on the number of participants in a workshop, for registrants to receive individual instruction? What cost and revenue factors will make a trip program either feasible or impractical, from a budgetary perspective?

Benefits-Driven Factors

Beyond such questions, it is also essential to examine possible program elements from a benefits-driven point of view. Do they support the sponsoring agency's overall mission and

Annual Coastal Cleanup Day - September 19, 8-11 a.m.

Join in the Long Beach Cleanup Day with the Department of Parks, Recreation and Marine Beach Maintenance Division and hundreds of volunteers across the city in an effort to clean up our beaches.

There'll be free refreshments, certificates and plenty of free parking. So come to the Beach Maintenance Yard, 4320 Olympic Plaza, just left of Belmont Plaza Pool, in Long Beach.

Dedicate-A-Tree Program

Long Beach Parks, Recreation and Marine has developed a new program which offers you a very unique and thoughtful way to celebrate life and love while making an extremely meaningful contribution to your community. The Dedicate-A-Tree program.

This program provides the chance to have a tree planted in a city park to celebrate special occasions such as weddings, birthdays, anniversaries and more. This is a great way for groups to display their pride in our parks.

Long Beach Adopt-A-Beach Program

Due to California's coast drowning under a tide of ugly, unhealthy and dangerous debris, Long Beach Parks, Recreation and Marine has developed a unique program called Adopt-A-Beach.

Your group, business, club or community association can take action by adopting 1/4 mile of shoreline and cleaning up the litter four times a year for one year.

For more information concerning the above programs, contact Jennifer Brooks at 421-9431, ext. 3136.

City of Long Beach Volunteer Team

VOLUNTEER TEAM

If you would also like to play a part in a Parks, Recreation and Marine program, why not join the more than 2000 volunteers who are already involved?

You can meet people, make friends, explore new interests and make a significant contribution to your community! We currently need volunteers to assist with the upcoming Senior Olympics in November. Needed are:

souvenir sales	*timers*	*Special Events assistant*
clerical help	*scorekeepers*	*registration/check-in*
award presentation aides		

Events include track and field, swimming, horseshoes, tennis, table tennis, bowling, billiards, golf, softball, lawn bowling, racquetball, fly and plug casting, and shuffleboard.

Figure 7-2   Volunteerism Brochure: Long Beach, California.

philosophical orientation? Will they help achieve its specific objectives? Are they in harmony with the prevailing social and moral values of the community, or the standards of the organization's membership? Are they designed to enhance and enrich the personalities of participants, or do they have potential negative effects?

Activity Analysis

To determine their suitability for inclusion in the overall program plan, recreation activities may be analyzed from three vantage points: (1) the *kinds of experiences* they provide participants; (2) the *skills or personal capacities* they require of participants, for successful accomplishment; and (3) the *formats or types of structures* within which the activities may be offered.

Nature of Recreation Experiences or Involvements

A number of major behaviors or forms of involvement in leisure pursuits that cut across the ten activity categories listed in this chapter include the following:

1. *Socializing behaviors,* activities such as social dancing, group singing, picnics or parties, in which people relate to each other in informal and unpressured ways.

2. *Shared-interest drives,* pursuits in which people group together because of common leisure interests, such as horseback riding, mountain climbing, contract bridge, coin collecting, or similar hobbies.

3. *Competitive behaviors,* including all sports and games, as well as competition in the performing arts, outdoor recreation activities, or even animal-raising or domestic skills contests, as in state or county fairs.

4. *Risk-taking behaviors,* such as a wide range of outdoor adventure pursuits in which the stakes are often physical injury or even death, and also other thrill-seeking activities, such as gambling and informal drag racing.

5. *Exploratory behaviors,* including travel and tourism, hiking and camping, and other pursuits that introduce participants to new environments.

6. *Vicarious involvement,* such as various forms of spectatorship or passive entertainment, including watching television and movies, and attending sports events, concerts, or theater programs.

7. *Sensory stimulation,* behaviors that involve stimulation of the senses and the search for pleasure as primary motives, such as alcohol consumption, drug use, sexual activity, and visual and auditory experiences such as rock concerts or light shows.

8. *Physical emphasis,* such as running, swimming, or dancing for its own sake, rather than as part of competition against others.

9. *Aesthetic activities,* including personally creative experiences in the fine, performing, or literary arts that extend beyond spectatorship into active involvement.

10. *Cognitive and intellectual behaviors,* experiences in the realm of ideas, including reading, writing, or discussion groups.

11. *Volunteer service,* in which individuals provide services to others or to the community without pay, as personally rewarding leisure experiences.

12. *Spiritual involvement,* which may come from a formal religious involvement, or from such forms of leisure activity as yoga or other types of eastern exercise or meditation practices, or from retreats, exposure to the outdoors, or similar experiences.[5]

Obviously, a number of these kinds of involvements overlap with each other, in the sense that a given activity may provide several different kinds of personal outcomes. However, they represent twelve distinctly different kinds of *primary emphases* to be found in leisure pursuits, and so offer a useful framework for selecting recreation program elements.

Skills or Capacities Required for Successful Involvement

A second approach to examining activities systematically consists of identifying and measuring the skills and capacities required of participants, under four main headings: (1) *physical* or *psychomotor;* (2) *emotional* or *affective;* (3) *cognitive* or *intellectual;* and (4) *social* or *interpersonal.*

Physical/Psychomotor Activity Requirements

From a casual perspective, one might simply identify the basic physical skills that are necessary to engage in an activity with a reasonable degree of success.

For example, to play racquetball or table tennis, it is necessary to be able to grasp a paddle, have enough shoulder, arm, and wrist control to hit the ball, possess a reasonable degree of hand-eye coordination, and have enough mobility to be able to move quickly within a limited area. Other sports or outdoor pursuits may require more substantial degrees of strength, endurance, or agility. However, even these modest levels of skill may not always be required. People in wheelchairs frequently play tennis, and many individuals who are legally deaf are able to dance simply by feeling the rhythmic pulse of the music with their feet.

While this sort of simple appraisal may be sufficient in most recreational settings, therapeutic recreation specialists are often called upon to carry out a much more detailed analysis of activities in order to develop clinical treatment plans for patients or clients. For example, Peterson and Gunn outline a suggested rating form that deals with such elements as primary body position required, strength, speed, endurance, energy, muscle coordination, hand-eye coordination, flexibility, and coordination. Three sections of this rating form are shown in Figure 7-3.

Emotional/Affective Activity Requirements

Analyzing activities in terms of their emotional or affective aspects is concerned primarily with the positive or negative impact that they are likely to have on participants.

For example, the children's play activities in which one youngster is chosen as "it" and must compete against the overall group in a tag, chasing, or ball game, may result in the "it" child's being frustrated, ridiculed, or scapegoated by the others because of the very nature of the game. Obviously, such a game may be destructive and inappropriate, particularly for children who have weak self-concepts, or are timid, insecure, or emotionally unstable.

From a broader perspective, several different kinds of basic human emotions may readily be identified among participants' responses to recreation activities. These include joy, happiness, guilt, fear, or anger. Recreation activities may be analyzed in terms of their potential for promoting these emotions. Program planners might ask, do activities offer the

What types of movement does the activity require?

bending	————————————	catching	————————————
stretching	————————————	throwing	————————————
standing	————————————	hitting	————————————
walking	————————————	skipping	————————————
reaching	————————————	hopping	————————————
grasping	————————————	running	————————————
punching	————————————		

What are the primary senses required for the activity?
Rate: 0 = not at all; 1 = rarely; 2 = occasionally; 3 = often

touch   ————————————
taste   ————————————
sight   ————————————
sound   ————————————
smell   ————————————

How much of the body is involved?

_____ top half	_____ arms	_____ hands	_____ ears
_____ bottom half	_____ legs	_____ feet	_____ neck
	_____ torso	_____ eyes	
	_____ head	_____ mouth	

Figure 7-3.   Selected psychomotor rating elements (Peterson/Gunn).[6]

opportunity for participants to gain positive satisfaction from accomplishment, and feel in control of their environments? Or do activities tend to result in frustration or hostile, aggressive, or destructive behavior?

Again, in therapeutic recreation settings, the emotional/affective aspects of program activities are of much greater concern than they normally would be in typical community leisure settings. To illustrate, Peterson and Gunn suggest a rating system for the in-depth analysis of activities from an emotional perspective (see Figure 7-4). Recognizing the need for systematic analysis of program tools in therapeutic recreation, one might nevertheless ask whether instruments of this type are not overly detailed, and whether they are not likely to rely heavily on subjective judgment or even guesswork.

Cognitive/Intellectual Activity Requirements
This aspect of activity analysis consists of determining the extent to which given program elements demand mental abilities of participants that are reasonably congruent with their overall cognitive and intellectual development.

Rate the opportunities for the expression of the following emotions during this activity.

	Often				Never
Joy	1	2	3	4	5
Guilt	1	2	3	4	5
Pain	1	2	3	4	5
Anger	1	2	3	4	5
Fear	1	2	3	4	5
Frustration	1	2	3	4	5

Rate the likely responses.

Success	1	2	3	4	5	Failure
Satisfaction	1	2	3	4	5	Dissatisfaction
Intrinsic						Extrinsic
reward	1	2	3	4	5	reward
Acceptance	1	2	3	4	5	Rejection
Confidence	1	2	3	4	5	Inferiority
Excitement	1	2	3	4	5	Apathy
Cooperation	1	2	3	4	5	Defiance
Patience	1	2	3	4	5	Impatience
Manipulation	1	2	3	4	5	Nonmanipulation
Awareness						Awareness
of others	1	2	3	4	5	of self

Figure 7-4.   Selected emotional rating elements (Peterson/Gunn).[7]

For example, numerous games or other communication-based activities may require a range of vocabulary and verbal skills. Others typically demand the ability to concentrate, or require memory retention. Strategic elements are important parts of most sports, as well as an awareness of rules and appropriate behavior in different competitive situations.

Other activities may require the ability to learn to use special equipment or tools, manipulate objects, or carry out mathematical calculations. At the same time that leaders should be cautious about involving participants in activities that are far beyond their cognitive abilities and may result in failure and frustration, they must also realize that such experiences provide the opportunity for learning important concepts and skills, if carefully presented.

Social and Interpersonal Aspects of Activities

A fourth important aspect of program activities concerns their social or group-dynamics requirements. For example, varied activities may require interactional skills having to do with cooperation, acceptance of others, and the ability to follow rules, demonstrate ideals of fair play, and take responsibility.

Activity Interaction Model

To understand the potential of different activities for developing positive social values and interactional skills, it is helpful to analyze the group processes they involve. Elliott Avedon developed a model that identifies eight different kinds of participant relationships:

1. *Intraindividual:* action carried on by an individual, involving no outside person or objects. *Examples:* yoga, daydreaming.
2. *Extraindividual:* action involving an outside object but no other person or object. *Examples:* gardening, ceramics.
3. *Aggregate:* action directed by a group of persons toward an object or other environmental element, without interaction among each other. *Examples:* several individuals jogging in proximity to each other, a group playing Bingo.
4. *Interindividual:* two persons in one-to-one competition with each other. *Examples:* chess, singles tennis.
5. *Unilateral:* competitive action among three or more persons, with one person selected as "it." *Examples:* tag and chase games, hide-and-seek.
6. *Multilateral:* competition among three or more persons, with each person competing against all the others. *Examples:* Scrabble, spelling bee.
7. *Intragroup:* cooperation between two or more persons with a common purpose or goal. *Examples:* choral group, environmental project.
8. *Intergroup:* competition between two or more intragroups. *Examples:* Any team game or contest, such as baseball or football game, or one-act play competition among little theater groups.[8]

Ideally, participants should have the opportunity to experience different kinds of group structures and interpersonal experiences, and leaders should deliberately select activities to achieve positive social outcomes or promote desired behavioral change.

Modification of Program Activities

It may be necessary for leaders to modify program activities to make them more accessible or enjoyable for participants. This is often done by therapeutic recreation specialists, to ensure successful participation or to help patients or clients progress from simple to more complex and challenging pursuits.

Equipment.   Varied forms of special equipment have been developed to permit people with visual, orthopedic, or other disabilities to take part in sports such as bowling, archery, swimming, and even baseball. In bowling, some wheelchair users utilize special ramps to release the ball, and lighter, more maneuverable chairs have been developed for use in sports such as tennis and basketball.

Other helpful equipment modifications are holding racks for cards, electric card shufflers, and Braille playing cards designed for blind persons, as well as board games with raised squares. Increasingly, computers are being used to help participants with limited communicative or manipulative abilities to engage in varied pursuits.

Game Rules and Skills. Activity rules or playing procedures may be adapted to accommodate successful play. Players with orthopedic, neurological, or developmental disabilities may swing at a ball on a tee, in an adaptation of baseball, or to take an indefinite number of swings until they hit the ball. In some cases, actions may be carried out on a stop-and-go basis. For example, in volleyball, instead of hitting the ball with continuous action, players may catch the ball and then throw it, or hit it on the bounce.

Facility Adaptation. This may take two forms: (1) modifying the facility by providing ramps, properly designed rest rooms, water fountains, doors, and other elements; and (2) laying out the playing space so that it can be used by individuals with mobility limitations. In a game such as softball, this might mean putting more players into a smaller area, to allow for better coverage, or it might mean using a larger, lighter ball.

Formats for Participation

A final important aspect of recreation activities and services is the structures through which they may be presented to groups. Essentially, these different formats provide a diversified range of experiences or group situations to meet varied leisure needs. They include the following:

1. *Free Play or Open Facility.* This format includes unorganized play, such as children using playground equipment, or teenagers playing unsupervised pickup games of basketball. It may also include the use of picnic grounds, hiking trails, drop-in centers, and similar forms of unstructured leisure involvement.
2. *Classes and Instructional Programs.* Many programs include a wide variety of classes in such subjects as arts and crafts, music, drama and dance, sports, hobbies, languages, and a host of other areas of personal growth or leisure interests.
3. *Organized Competition.* This format applies chiefly to sports, where teams and leagues in varied individual and group sports may appeal to all ages. However, competition may be used in outdoor recreation, as in fishing contests, in games such as chess and checkers, or in agricultural or homemaking projects. It may even be used in dance, music, or theater competition.
4. *Performances, Demonstrations, and Exhibits.* Special events that display the achievements of leisure programs, such as art shows, hobby or craft exhibits, dance or music performances, martial arts demonstrations, and similar events, serve both to educate the public about different leisure activities, and to motivate program participants by giving them an exciting goal or culminating event to work toward.
5. *Other Special Events.* Many leisure-service agencies sponsor such special events as holiday parties, historical celebrations or parades, picnics and barbecues, award banquets, carnivals, and festivals.
6. *Trips and Outings.* These may range from simple bus trips to a nearby beach or state park, to educational visits to museums, packaged ski trips, or charter flights to vacation resorts, both domestic and foreign.
7. *Special-Interest and Social Clubs.* Organized groups with continuing membership are often sponsored by retirement communities, corporate recreation depart-

ments, colleges or universities, armed forces recreation, and other agencies. Their purposes may be to engage in a particular hobby, outdoor recreation pastime, or other leisure interest, or simply to provide social outlets for their members.

8. *Leadership Training.* Many leisure-service agencies conduct leadership training in such areas as coaching, umpiring, or other sports-related functions; first aid and cardiopulmonary resuscitation; swimming or lifesaving resuscitation; boating skills; and other recreation skills. Agencies also may provide workshops, clinics, and classes for other community groups.

In addition to these eight formats, program activities within the categories of self-enrichment or human-service functions may also use such approaches as support groups, one-to-one counseling, or other specialized therapeutic techniques that do not fit within the more traditional formats.

The needs and interests of different population groups, and the variety of leisure-service activities and services that may be provided in organized recreation programs, are essential elements in the service-delivery process. Chapter 8 discusses two other key elements: facilities and leadership.

Summary

This chapter describes ten major categories of recreation program activities and services that are provided within organized leisure-service agencies today. It shows how program elements may range from extremely basic or simple experiences in terms of children's games, arts and craft activities, or sports and nature projects, to more advanced pursuits in terms of the skills or degree of personal commitment that are needed for success.

In each major program category, the personal values or outcomes of participation are identified, along with the administrative advantages of the activity for the sponsoring organization. Several categories include activities that would not typically be thought of as recreation in a narrow, pleasure-seeking sense, such as classes, workshops, or clinics dealing with life-adjustment skills or with remedial or social services. However, these programs are offered by many types of leisure-service agencies today, as shown by examples throughout the chapter, and are best considered within a benefits-driven approach to programming.

The chapter explores methods of analyzing and modifying activities, in terms of the demands they make on participants' physical, emotional, cognitive, or social capabilities. Finally, the chapter identifies eight different kinds of formats or structures for involvement, which help to diversify program content and to satisfy different needs of participants.

Suggested Class Assignments or Projects

1. As a class assignment, students may put together a file, scrapbook, or other organized collection of activities within a specific program category such as sports or social recreation. This should include descriptions of specific activities, suggested age levels, guidelines for leadership, and other appropriate information.

2. As a field assignment, small groups of students may visit a large municipal, county, nonprofit, or other leisure-service agency, to observe its pro-

gram activities, gather program materials, and interview staff members. Based on this, students may develop an overall plan of the agency's activities and services, assigning them to the categories presented in the chapter, and indicating the formats used to serve different groups of participants.

3. Individual students may present a specific activity to the class, suited to the classroom setting or an available outdoor setting, if the class schedule and location permit this. After they have participated in the activity, class members may analyze the presentation and the activity itself, based on the physical, emotional, cognitive, and social criteria suggested in the chapter.

References

1. *Annual Program Brochure,* Montgomery County, Maryland, Department of Recreation, 1994.
2. "The Importance of Good Physical Fitness: Flash or Fact?" *Parks and Recreation,* Oct. 1994, p. 58.
3. Randy B. Swedburg and Lisa Ostiguy, "Welcome to the Ice Age," *Parks and Recreation,* Jan. 1994, pp. 56–61.
4. Ken Cicora, "Sponsoring Special Events," *Parks and Recreation,* Dec. 1991, p. 27.
5. Adapted from James F. Murphy, et al., *Leisure Service Delivery System: A Modern Perspective* (Philadelphia: Lea and Febiger, 1973), pp. 73–76.
6. Carol Ann Peterson and Scout Lee Gunn, *Therapeutic Recreation Program Design: Principles and Procedures* (Englewood Cliffs, NJ: Prentice-Hall 1984), pp. 174–175.)
7. *Ibid.,* pp. 178–179.
8. See Elliott M. Avedon, *Therapeutic Recreation Service: An Applied Behavioral Perspective* (Englewood Cliffs, NJ: Prentice-Hall, Inc., 1973), pp. 162–170.

Chapter 8

Recreation Leadership and Facilities Planning

Within the [City of Mississauga] Community Services, Recreation and Parks Division, we talked a lot about the importance of . . . customer service. . . . In some areas, we were doing an excellent job in delivering quality service; in others we were failing miserably. Our young, part-time work force provided most of our services during prime-time customer use—evenings and weekends. We questioned how well we were training and developing our staff to deal with the demands of a well-educated consumer. With over 1,200 part-time staff, we needed to provide more than just lip service . . . we needed to provide new tools and problem-solving skills . . . .[1]

Combining an existing indoor community center swimming pool with the new facilities of an outdoor family aquatic center has provided the city of Kettering, Ohio, with an exciting, popular, and financially successful leisure attraction. Families, adults, and children are participating in record numbers as aquatic attendance and revenues reach new heights. The fact that revenues from the newly combined indoor and outdoor aquatic facility consistently exceeded operating expenses has become a goal successfully met by the City's new Family Aquatic Center.[2]

Two additional important elements in the recreation, park, and leisure-service programming process consist of leadership and facilities. While some may regard these as separate management functions or as operational strategies related to programming, they both influence the choice of possible program activities and services, and their success in achieving desired program outcomes.

This chapter describes concepts of group leadership, categories of leaders in leisure-service agencies, staff development practices, and leadership methods in varied program areas. It also deals with the planning and operation of recreation and park areas and facilities, with emphasis on recent trends that affect programming.

The following learning objectives, established for undergraduate programs in recreation, park resources, and leisure services by the NRPA/AALR Council on Accreditation, are addressed in this chapter:

> Understanding of and the ability to use various leadership techniques and strategies to enhance the individual's leisure experiences for all populations, including those with special needs. (8.18)

> Understanding of and the ability to apply personnel management techniques, including job analysis, recruitment, selection, training, motivation, career development, and evaluation of staff and volunteers. (8.30)

> Ability to organize and lead/conduct in one or more programmatic areas. (9C.02)

> Knowledge of the interrelationship between leisure behavior and the natural environment. (8.05)

> Understanding of the concept and use of leisure resources to facilitate participant involvement. (8.19)

The Role of Recreation Leadership

Recreation leadership consists of the human element that plays an important role in all leisure-service programming. It includes promoting, guiding, and evaluating participation on every level. Leadership has been defined as any of the following:

> A *phenomenon in group life,* involving the direct, face-to-face contact between leaders and follower, and the dynamic process that emerges in their interaction.

> An *ability or trait* possessed by certain individuals, which enables them to motivate others and to help them identify and achieve important personal and group-related goals.

> A *process of working with others,* involving specific skills and techniques that result in effective problem-solving and a high level of participant motivation and performance.

Theories of Effective Leadership

Various theories of effective leadership have been developed that apply to the role and degree of effectiveness of leaders within such group settings. These include: (1) the *trait* theory, which suggests that leaders have certain important personal qualities, or traits, such as intelligence, energy, aggressiveness, willingness to take responsibility, sound judgment, and interpersonal skills; (2) the *situational* theory, which argues that different situations demand different kinds of competence from leaders, in terms of technical knowledge or interpersonal skills, so that leadership effectiveness or the group's choice of a leader depends heavily on its situational needs; (3) the *functional* theory, which suggests that leadership is a widely shared function of the group, in dealing with such specific tasks as defining goals and objectives, decision-making or problem-solving, and maintaining group cohesiveness or external relationships; and (4) the *contingency* theory, which holds that the group's choice of a leader and the leader's effectiveness both depend on the interplay of such elements as the group's make-up and its value system, the demands of the situation, and the leader's personal characteristics.[3]

Leadership in Leisure-Service Agencies

In a broad sense, leadership in recreation, park, and leisure-service agencies is a function of many different individuals. Administrators, supervisors, division heads, program specialists, and others are all responsible for providing leadership, in terms of establishing goals, solving problems, or similar functions.

More narrowly, leadership is often considered to be a specific job level, title, or position. The term *leader* has usually been applied to staff members assuming a direct, face-to-face, action level of responsibility, in terms of guiding group activities, teaching program skills, or similar functions. Typically, in the past, most civil service job codes or position classifications identified one or more such levels of leadership, such as leader I, II, or III or leader, senior leader, or leader aide.

In working with groups of recreational participants, the leader's task is often defined as teaching sports, crafts, outdoor skills, or other activities. However, even in such assignments, there are often problems involving interpersonal relationships, group planning of special events or programs, irregular attendance, disciplinary control, or poor morale. Thus, even in activity-centered groups, the social interaction of participants represents an important concern.

Position Classifications and Job Descriptions

Within every type of modern organization, it is customary to develop classification systems that identify the different divisions of service, staffing levels, and specific areas of job responsibility, all linked to hiring qualifications and requirements, levels of pay, personnel benefits, and similar elements.

In most recreation, park, and leisure-service agencies, particularly those under public, voluntary nonprofit, military, or therapeutic sponsorship, jobs typically are classified with respect to their title, civil service grade (if the agency is a branch of government), hiring eligibility requirements, job responsibilities and/or areas of required competence, and other forms of relevant information.

Job descriptions are usually developed that systematically define the tasks that must be performed, appropriate work behaviors, needed knowledge and leadership skills, orientation and training needs, and other details of the work situation, as shown in the following examples.

Job Functions of Playground or Recreation Center Leaders

Leadership manuals of several public recreation and park departments indicate that the major job functions of leaders in playground or recreation center programs include the following responsibilities:

1. *Plan, Organize, and Conduct Programs.* The leader is responsible, under the general direction of his or her district supervisor or department head, for planning, organizing, and carrying out a full range of attractive and enjoyable activities designed to achieve the key goals of the sponsoring agency, and to promote both the learning of useful leisure skills and the development of the constructive social values of sportsmanship and good citizenship.

2. *Lead and Direct Activities.* In addition to his or her overall program responsibilities, the leader is normally expected to teach, lead, direct, coach, or officiate in a variety of program activity areas, including arts and crafts, storytelling, dance, drama, sports, trips, and nature activities.

3. *Guide and Direct Participants.* The leader must work with individuals or groups of participants to promote positive and socially constructive forms of behavior. This includes guiding them in cooperative group relationships, effective group planning and decision-making, and respect for public property and community social values.

4. *Maintain Control and Discipline.* The leader must maintain order and discipline on the playground or in the center, preventing vandalism, fighting, or other antisocial behavior. In addition, he or she is usually expected to enforce departmental regulations devoted to smoking, gambling, drinking, the use of undesirable language, or other prohibited acts, and to apply disciplinary measures when required.

5. *Provide a Desirable Model.* Leaders are expected to provide desirable adult models for children and youth in their own behavior and personal habits, and to represent the department positively in all contacts with the public or other municipal employees. This involves strict adherence to departmental regulations and seizing every opportunity to present a favorable image of the department and recreation itself as an important form of community service.

6. *Accident Prevention and First Aid.* An essential leadership function is to maintain an effective safety and accident prevention program. This includes vigilant attention to all possible safety hazards, such as defective equipment, and immediate follow-up on having them repaired, as well as constant teaching and enforcement of desirable safety attitudes and practices in *all* areas of playground or center activity.

7. *Facilities, Equipment, and Supplies.* As indicated, the leader is responsible for regular inspection and supervision of facilities, and for reporting problems of cleanliness or maintenance, as well as safety hazards. He or she is also responsible for maintaining an up-to-date inventory of equipment and supplies, for supervising their use, and for requisitioning new materials when necessary. Leaders may also be in charge of scheduling recreation facilities (such as ball fields) for use by other community groups.

8. *Supervise Volunteers.* An important function of recreation leaders or center directors is to recruit or enlist volunteers from the community to train and assign them, and generally to supervise them in program service.

Job Description in Voluntary Agency: YMCA

Many nonprofit community organizations have detailed position descriptions for staff members on various levels. The Young Men's Christian Association has developed descriptions for titles as general director, youth director, physical education or fitness director, membership director, and business director. An example follows:

Responsibilities of YMCA youth director

1. Assists boys and girls through organized groups and informal education to develop attitudes and social habits consistent with Christian principles.
2. Integrates programs and activities with efforts of parents, school, church, and community leaders.
3. Guides the Youth Program Committee of the Board of Directors in formulating policies for youth programs.
4. Identifies youth needs and organizes group programs to meet these.
5. Enlists, trains, and supervises volunteer group leaders.
6. Interprets YMCA to youth members, parents, and public.
7. Manages business aspects of youth department.
8. Is generally responsible for day camp and sometimes for resident camp program direction.
9. Maintains adequate records and makes reports.

Job Description in Armed Force Recreation: Sports Director

Within each branch of the armed forces, the functions of recreation employees are defined at varying levels of responsibility or authority, and within specific program specializations. In the U.S. Air Force, an individual in the post of intramural sports director must work closely with a sports council consisting of squadron sports directors, members of base standing committees, team managers, and others, to fulfill the following tasks:

1. Plan, direct, and supervise the general conduct of all intramural activities.
2. Assist group and squadron sports directors and team managers in an advisory capacity.
3. Develop intramural policies in collaboration with the base sports director, the sports council, the sports staff, and the participants.
4. Systematically publicize and promote the program.

5. Draw up schedules, organize leagues, meets, and tournaments, and plan special events.

6. Select, train, assign, and supervise intramural officials.

7. Interpret the intramural program to base personnel.

8. Provide for the safety and well-being of all participants.

9. Evaluate the program.

10. Compile and publish game results and individual and team records.

11. Develop and publish rules relating to program administration.

12. Develop and supply to squadron sports directors and organization managers the necessary forms for reporting game results, signing out equipment, reserving practice areas, making a protest, and so forth.

13. Control equipment furnished for contests.

14. Prepare budget estimates.

Volunteer Roles in Therapeutic Recreation: RCH, Inc.

Many organizations develop job descriptions for volunteer leaders. For example, San Francisco's RCH, Inc., has prepared the following form:

POSITION AVAILABLE: VOLUNTEER

DEPARTMENT: CHILDREN/TEENS, LEISURE/OUTREACH, COMMUNITY LEISURE TRAINING, ADULT DEVELOPMENT, VOCATIONAL INTEGRATION PROGRAM, AQUATICS/P.E. AND ADMINISTRATION.

DESCRIPTION:

Under the general supervision of the Volunteer Specialist a Volunteer will work with people of various ages and disabilities.

Volunteers will work directly with clients in a variety of activities such as, arts and crafts, adaptive swimming and P.E., dance, drama, community outings and self-help skills. Volunteers will be given the opportunity to assist with planning and implementation of specific projects or activities for the group or groups they are working with.

Volunteers may also have the opportunity to participate with staff in a variety of special projects such as dances, ski trips, camping, and other outdoor environmental activities.

There are a number of non-program related activities in which people can offer their volunteer services. We need volunteers to help us perform administrative functions, assist with Bingo, mailings, phones, and filing.

JOB STANDARDS:

1. Ability and desire to work with a variety of different people.
2. Interest in working with all types of disabilities.
3. Must be at least 16 years old.

HOURS: Flexible hours: Monday - Friday, evening hours available.

Needed Competencies in Other Settings

The program skills required by leaders in a number of other leisure-service settings have been identified by researchers. For example, recreational sports directors in colleges and universities should be competent in such areas as officiating, scheduling, special events programming, staff training and supervision, facility operations, safety and first aid, promotion and publicity, evaluation methods, and computer utilization.

In employee recreation and services associations in companies or other institutions, staff members may be expected to plan social events, sports leagues or classes, supervise fitness facilities, and provide individualized activity guidance, organize travel tours, or operate employee stores or discount buying services.

In commercial settings such as health spas and fitness centers, staff members may have specialized roles, ranging from lifeguards, aerobic dance teachers, or weight-training experts, to serving as sales representatives, giving prospective members tours of the facility, promoting memberships, supervising individual fitness programs, and counseling.

Trends in Leadership Assignments and Titles

Based on such examples, two important trends in recreation, park, and leisure-service agencies may be identified.

First, the actual job title of "leader" tends to be used less, as more and more different types of agencies have taken on leisure-service responsibilities. Instead, other job titles that are more applicable to the service setting tend to be used. For example, such titles as "youth director," "recreation therapist," "sports manager" or "intramurals director," "personnel services specialist," "student activities manager," or "creative arts specialist" have replaced the general title of "leader."

Linked to this change, as greater numbers of part-time specialists, seasonal employees, and volunteers are used to direct program activities, full-time, year-round professionals are given broader responsibilities. Instead of being concerned chiefly with teaching skills and coordinating program activities, they often have middle-management functions related to budget making and financial management, program scheduling, public and community relations, evaluation, and similar supervisory functions.

Personnel Process in Leisure-Service Agencies

The overall leadership development and personnel process in leisure-service agencies includes several important steps, including recruitment and hiring, supervision, and evaluation of personnel.

Recruitment, Selection, and Hiring

Recruitment may be more or less complex, depending on the size of an agency and its number of full-time professional, part-time, and seasonal employees. Often, new full-time staff members are recruited from those who have previously worked for a department on a part-time, seasonal, or internship basis.

In voluntary agencies and armed forces recreation, national newsletters may publicize position openings and their requirements. Depending on the organization itself, fliers, announcements at professional conferences, or advertisements may be used to attract applicants. This method may begin at an early point in the personnel process, with an agency recruiting staff members for summer aquatic programs (see Figure 8-1), and may continue to the point of advertising openings for executive positions for commissioners or general managers.

The selection process may include any or all of the following procedures: (1) having the candidate fill out a detailed job application form; (2) detailed consideration of the candidate's background, past performance, and references; (3) a personal interview with the candidate; (4) a written examination, usually part of a state, county, or municipal civil service series; (5) a physical examination; (6) a character investigation; and (7) in some cases a performance test in specific skill areas.

Preparatory work should be done before an interview is scheduled. The candidate's references should be carefully checked by either mail or telephone, with the confidentiality of responses assured. The individual's background should be thoroughly examined to determine the appropriateness of his or her experience or education, and to identify possible unexplained gaps in employment, frequent job changes, or other indications of personal or professional instability or difficulty.

The goals of the actual interview are several: (1) to gather fuller information about the relevance of the applicant's experience and education to the position; (2) to assess the applicant's personality and character, including apparent levels of motivation, achievement drive, leadership quality, and personal style; and (3) to evaluate the applicant's overall intelligence, adaptability, and problem-solving or analytical ability.

Appointment and probation.   After being hired, candidates normally undergo a three-to-six month probationary period. New employees should be carefully observed and evaluated during this period. If their performance is satisfactory, they are then eligible for permanent employment and may not be discharged except for cause, according to the personnel procedures or union contracts that normally govern such actions.

Orientation and In-Service Education

At the conclusion of the recruitment and hiring process, the beginning employee joins the leisure-service agency. Customarily, he or she is given an orientation designed to familiarize new employees with the job setting and their responsibilities, and to provide other needed forms of preparation.

Many recreation and park departments sponsor varied in-service training programs dealing with leadership skills. For example, Figure 8-2 illustrates a required lifeguard training course. Other training programs may have to do with supervisory skills, resolving conflicts, customer relations, safety and health practices, registration procedures, bookkeeping and computer skills, substance abuse, and various technical aspects of recreation and park maintenance.

Figure 8-1. Summer job recruitment brochure: Oakland, California.

City of Oakland   Office of Parks and Recreation

SPORTS & AQUATICS UNIT
Presents:

Basic LIFEGUARD TRAINING COURSES
(CERTIFICATION COURSES FOR ENTRY-LEVEL POOL LIFEGUARDS)

DATES:

- **SESSION #1-**   **February 1st-22nd, 1994**
                              Tues. & Thurs., 6:30-10:00 pm

- **SESSION #2-**   **March 1st-23rd, 1994**
                              Mon. & Wed., 6:30-10:00 pm

- **SESSION #3-**   **April 5th-10th, 1994 -** *SPRING BREAK*
                              Tues.-Sunday, 8:30-4:30 pm

- **SESSION #4-**   **April 19th-May 10th, 1994**
                              Tues. & Thurs., 6:30-10:00 pm

LOCATION: TEMESCAL POOL (beside Oakland Technical High School)
                      371 - 45th Street, Oakland, CA   (510) 238-2202

COST: $60 - Includes book and certification fee

COURSE PREREQUISITES: Participants must be 15 years or older. Participants must be certified in Community Safety Course within 30 days of course completion of Basic Lifeguard Training. Specific skills required for course acceptance: 500-yd swim, recovery of a diving brick in 9-ft of water, 15-yds underwater swimming. Course is geared towards strong swimmers. Be sure to be in good physical condition before enrolling in course.

FOR MORE INFORMATION - Call the OPR Aquatics Unit at (510) 238-3494.

REGISTRATION: Complete form below and MAIL to: **OPR Aquatics Unit**
                          (Make all checks payable to same)   **1520 Lakeside Drive**
                                                                   Oakland, CA 94612

Course space is limited--register early--first come, first serve on paid
registration-confirmations will be mailed upon receipt of registration.

BASIC LIFEGUARDING COURSE REGISTRATION FORM - 1994

Name: _____ Age:_____ DOB:_____

Address: _____ City: _____ Zip: _____

Session desired: #1   #2   #3   #4   Phone #: _____ Emergency #: _____

- I would like OPR Aquatics employment information: Yes _____ No _____
- I am under 18 years of age and need parent permission supplement: Yes _____ No _____

TITLE VI COMPLIANCE AGAINST DISCRIMINATION 43 CFR 17.6(b): Federal and City of Oakland regulations strictly prohibit unlawful discrimination on the basis of race, color, gender, national origin, age, disability, sexual orientation or AIDS & ARC. Auxiliary aids and services may be provided upon request. Contact the Office of Parks and Recreation at 1520 Lakeside Drive, Oakland, CA 94612 or call (510) 238-3092.

Figure 8-2.   Example of in-service training: Oakland, California.

Improving Leadership Skills

In addition to sponsoring in-service workshops or courses, many leisure-service agencies prepare printed handbooks or manuals that present recommended program activities and leadership methods, within the most popular areas of recreational participation.

Beyond describing such activities, both in-service training sessions and program manuals provide more general kinds of leadership guidelines. Recreation leaders must be able to conduct groups effectively in the broader sense of knowing how and when to introduce new skills, set group goals to motivate participants, schedule special events, and similar group management tasks. Examples of such guidelines within three program areas follow.

Arts and Crafts Leadership

Arts and crafts are approached on many different levels. They may be the partial responsibility of a leader or director who does not have special skill or background in this area, but who can direct a number of fairly simple projects. On playgrounds, arts and crafts are usually provided at regular times each week, as part of the recreation schedule, for all who wish to take part. In community centers, arts and crafts instruction is usually approached in more formal ways, with actual classes being set up on the basis of age levels, degree of skill, or type of activity being presented.

Although each of these situations may impose its own requirements or approaches, certain guidelines apply to the management of all arts and crafts activities in recreation settings.

1. Schedule arts and crafts activities on a regular basis, making sure the schedule is known to all participants through posters, fliers, and announcements.
2. Keep a display of finished arts and crafts projects as a means of praising those who have done good work in the activity and interesting others to take part.
3. Know in advance what projects will be presented, and have a sample of the product to show participants at the preceding session to encourage attendance.
4. Be sure to have all the materials and equipment needed for the project.
5. Demonstrate each step of the craft activity clearly and precisely as it progresses. Encourage children to ask questions, making sure they are fully answered. As the group works, it should be closely supervised at all times and given help as needed.
6. Allow enough time to complete the activity. If it cannot be done in a single session, make sure that all work in progress can be stored safely until the next time.
7. Maintain good discipline and order in the crafts session to avoid accidents and to permit all participants to work seriously on their projects in a quiet, controlled atmosphere.
8. Allow enough time for cleanup, and expect all participants to join in as a matter of group responsibility. Keep a clean, well-organized area, and make sure that damaged equipment is repaired or replaced. Since it usually takes time for arts and crafts materials to be ordered and sent, all needed materials should be requisitioned well in advance.
9. If possible, plan for an arts and crafts exhibit, and invite parents and other community members. Although the goal is not to overemphasize competition, it is a

good idea to give awards (ribbons, scrolls, and so on) to the best artists or craftspersons in a number of categories.

Games Leadership

Many different types of games may be used in community recreation settings such as playgrounds, day camps, or after-school sessions in community centers. These include active group games, social games and mixers, dramatic games, mental games and puzzles, and a host of others. The following guidelines outline the process of leading active playground games for children in the elementary-school range.

After selecting several games that are appropriate to the age level and number of participants, the leader should review the games thoroughly and make sure that any needed equipment is available and that boundary lines, if required, are marked. In terms of actual instruction, while different methods may be used, the following guidelines are based on leadership manuals published by several public recreation departments:

1. After you have gotten the group into the proper teams or formation, make sure you have their attention. If you have a whistle, blow it as a signal for quiet. Do not overuse it. Make sure that you have everyone's attention; do not talk over crowd noise.
2. When presenting the game, stand where the maximum number of players can see you and hear you, and where you will be facing them, rather than with your back to them.
3. Create an air of expectancy by your own enthusiasm. Quickly announce the game with a brief introduction, and then begin to teach it.
4. Make your explanations clear, brief, and correct. If necessary, use one or more players to demonstrate the activity. If it is at all complicated, repeat this.
5. Ask for questions if any of the players seem confused. Then start the game without further delay.
6. Minor errors or faults in play may be corrected by blowing the whistle, stopping the game briefly, showing the correct action, and continuing play.
7. Make sure that rules are obeyed. If necessary, stop the game to enforce them, and then continue.
8. Keep interest high, and encourage the players enthusiastically.
9. If the game involves keeping score, let the players know the team scores from time to time.
10. End the game while interest is still relatively high rather than let it drag on and become boring.

Conducting Nature Activities

A third broad area of direct program leadership for children and youth involves nature-based activities. The list of possible nature-based program elements is almost endless. However, here are three categories of useful hobbies, crafts, and projects suited for different age levels. A few require special leadership expertise, but most are quite simple.

1. *Nature Hobbies and Crafts.* These may encompass any of the following:
   a. Preparing labels for tree or plant identification.
   b. Doing spatter-printing with leaves.
   c. Making Christmas tree ornaments out of seed pods, pine cones, or other natural objects.
   d. Sketching, painting, or photographing nature subjects.
   e. Doing creative writing on nature themes for camp, center, or playground newspapers.
2. *Nature Science Experiments.* These involve more formal projects, and necessitate careful observation and recording of results over a period of time. Examples are as follows:
   a. Observing how long it takes beans or other types of seeds to germinate under different conditions (type of soil, light, warmth, and so forth).
   b. Building simple weather stations and recording temperature, humidity, wind changes, and similar information.
   c. Making careful observations of plant flowering, tree leafing, bird migration, correct times for planting, and so on.
3. *Nature Games.* Many games are specially suited for the natural environment, and promote observation and awareness of the outdoors.
   a. Nature-retrieving or treasure-hunt games involving races or relays in collecting natural objects.
   b. Nature sounds and smells—observing the environment and recording sights, sounds, smells, or other observable phenomena as a form of contest.
   c. Nature word games or memory contests, based on knowledge of the outdoors.

In all such activities, extreme care must be taken to ensure that damage is not done to the natural environment, and that participants are exposed to sound ecological values.

While this text does not include detailed descriptions of arts and crafts, games, nature projects, or other music, dance, or sports leadership guidelines, most college libraries and many public libraries do contain books showing those guidelines. Often, leaders who work in face-to-face group situations put together their own collections or scrapbooks of activities as they have learned them from other leaders or have taken them from useful sources.

Principles of Effective Teaching

In many program situations, recreation leaders are called upon to teach specific activity skills. Beyond the guidelines that have just been presented for effective leadership of arts and crafts, games, nature activities, and social events, it is important to understand several principles that underlie successful instruction in a wide range of program activities.

1. *Awareness of individual differences.* Each learner (or program participant) is an individual and tends to learn in his or her own way. Leaders should be aware of such dif-

ferences, and should adapt their teaching approaches to the needs of each learner, in terms of methods of presenting materials, and expectations about participants' progress.

2. *Learning by doing.* In general, people learn best by doing—that is, by taking part in the activity directly—rather than by reading about it, hearing a lecture, or seeing a film.

3. *Analyzing the learning task.* The leaders should understand clearly the nature of the learning task before presenting it to participants. What exactly are the key elements that must be learned? What actions are not important?

4. *"Whole" versus "part" instruction.* There has been a long-standing controversy about the best way to present any activity or learning task: as a *whole,* so that individuals may learn it all at once, or in *parts,* through step-by-step instruction. Both methods have merit; the method selected should depend largely on the complexity of the activity. However, even when it is a fairly complex skill that is being taught, such as swimming or doing a lengthy dance, the sooner the separate parts or skills can be combined into a whole presentation, the better it will be for the learner.

5. *Motivation and learning readiness.* These are key factors in successful teaching. Efforts must be made to arouse participant interest or eagerness for involvement. Learning readiness is based in part on the developmental stage of the participant and in part on past recreational experience; both must be considered.

6. *Transfer of learning.* Once a basic skill or understanding has been achieved, learning related tasks becomes easier. The leader should therefore be consciously aware of teaching a progression of skills, and encouraging the participant to rely on past learning to master new challenges.

Other learning principles involve the following: appropriate *practice of skills,* which goes beyond mere drills and includes new learnings or insights; setting *reasonable goals* for learning, goals that are high enough to be challenging, but not too high to be realistic; and using *ability groupings* when feasible, so that teaching methods may be adapted to subgroups of participants with similar learning levels and needs.

Role of Program Supervisors

In most recreation settings, program leaders or activity specialists function under the direction of supervisors who assign them to tasks, guide or counsel them in their job performance, and evaluate their effectiveness. While there have been numerous theories of supervision, it is generally agreed today that the behaviors of productive supervisors should include the following:

1. Establish high but achievable expectations for staff leaders and assign them tasks in which their individual abilities are most likely to be utilized fully.

2. Clearly define the responsibilities and accountabilities of staff members, and show confidence in their ability to carry out these tasks.

3. Assist staff members through effective coaching, counseling, and technical assistance to perform at their maximum levels of competence.

4. Encourage staff members to share in policy-planning, decision-making, program development and marketing functions, and maintain a positive work place atmosphere.

5. Systematically observe the performance of staff members under their direction, and use evaluation findings to improve work.[4]

The Role of Facilities in Recreation Programming

Another key element that influences recreation and leisure-service programming involves areas and facilities. Obviously, the places where people play are critical in terms of providing opportunities for creative and enjoyable leisure experiences. A barren schoolyard or refuse-filled park offers little to encourage positive forms of recreational participation.

During the early decades of the twentieth century, U.S. and Canadian public recreation and park departments offered a limited range of playgrounds, parks, sports facilities, and community centers. In time, new and varied kinds of places for play began to be developed in order to meet more diversified leisure interests.

Traditional Types of Recreation Facilities

Several major categories of recreation and park facilities are briefly described below, with the kinds of program elements they house. Chiefly, these represent facilities operated by public recreation and park departments, although in many cases nonprofit, commercial, or other types of leisure-service agencies may also manage such areas and facilities.

Playgrounds. Designed primarily for children and youth, these range in size from tiny "tot-lots" to larger play areas that are often attached to schools or indoor recreation centers. Their equipment may be limited to such familiar items as slides, swings, sandboxes, and jungle gyms, or they may also include statuary or structures based on themes of children's play, or areas and materials used for creative play or exploration, as in so-called "adventure" playgrounds.

Parks. These may include small neighborhood parks, as well as much larger areas or nature reserves, sometimes amounting to hundreds of acres. Larger parks typically offer sports facilities, band shells, riding trails, skating rinks, and other specialized facilities for play.

Recreation Centers. Traditionally these have been buildings with both indoor and outdoor facilities for a variety of sports, social, creative, and other group activities. In addition to providing areas for these types of activities, these centers may include facilities or areas for youth centers, senior centers, or human-service programs, sometimes shared with other community agencies.

Sports Facilities. These include fields, courts, or other outdoor areas for popular team and dual or individual sports, such as baseball, softball, soccer, tennis, and golf. Often the facilities are attached to recreation centers, or in some cases they may be free-standing in parks, as sports complexes serving several seasonal activities. Indoor centers often contain spaces for basketball, volleyball, floor hockey, wrestling, or martial arts.

Art Centers.   In addition to spaces in general recreation centers for arts and crafts, a growing number of cities have art centers that house studios for classes in various creative activities, as well as exhibition galleries and, in some cases, meeting rooms for lectures, or auditoriums that house music, theater, and dance groups.

Civic Arenas and Auditoriums.   Many cities today sponsor civic auditoriums or exposition halls, with rooms of various sizes that are useful for music, dance, or theatrical performances, or for community meetings. In some cases, these facilities are built through a combination of public and private funding and management, and house entertainment events, hobby shows, trade shows, conferences, and garden and home shows.

Facilities Serving People with Disabilities.   Many communities today operate facilities serving individuals with physical or mental disabilities. In some cases, these facilities constitute special sections of other facilities used by nondisabled persons, to facilitate integrated participation in selected program activities. Today, all new recreation facilities or structures being renovated must be designed in accordance with architectural standards ensuring access to persons with disabilities.

Other Facilities.   Other recreation areas today may include marinas or boat-launching ramps, stadiums, zoos and botanical gardens, various types of museums, historic mansions, skating rinks and ski centers, environmental education centers, riding stables, and other, more specialized facilities. In addition, many public agencies own and operate camping sites of various types, ranging from close-by locations for day-camp operations to wilderness camps at a distance.

New Trends in Leisure Facilities

During the period from the 1970s through the 1990s, the gradual acceptance of an entrepreneurial and marketing-based emphasis in many public and voluntary leisure-service agencies created a new pressure to develop facilities and programs that lent themselves to fiscal self-sufficiency. At the same time, commercial recreation businesses expanded dramatically, and began to provide technologically complex facilities with cleverly designed, innovative forms of appeal to the public.

Fitness Centers

Increasingly, public recreation and park departments, commercial fitness centers, Ys, and in some cases private-membership organizations, company-employee sponsors, and universities are building multifaceted, state-of-the-art indoor recreation facilities that include fully equipped weight and exercise rooms, full-size gyms, leisure pools, and in many cases meeting rooms, food courts, and other specialized areas. Schmid summarizes a 1993 survey by *Athletic Business,* which found that numerous cities in the Midwest and Near-West regions of the United States, particularly in Colorado, Ohio, Michigan, Illinois, and Minnesota, were building such facilities or making huge additions to existing buildings.[5]

Table 8-1 shows the variety of recreation facilities in or connected to indoor recreation centers that were examined in the *Athletic Business* survey.

The diversity of activity areas in such centers shows how programs seek to satisfy a wide variety of family or community leisure needs. The Atlantic Club, a private fitness center in Allenwood, New Jersey, houses two aerobic dance studios, a child-care center, conferences and multipurpose rooms, a cafe and a juice bar, a pro shop, and a physical therapy center, in addition to its pool, gymnasium, and weight- and circuit-training rooms.

Aquatic Facilities and Water-Play Parks

In addition to pools that are part of fitness or recreation centers in general, many communities have developed elaborate water-play parks that include wave pools, water slides, and chutes, leisure pools that are usually shallow and designed with a beach-like ambience (as compared to traditional instructional or competitive pools), children's pools and play areas, and in some cases "lazy-floating streams" for tubing. An example of this type of park is a $5 million-plus wave pool in the District of Surrey, British Columbia. This publicly owned Canadian facility is part of a complex of recreational attractions that include a library, an ice arena, and a community center.

Family-Play Facilities

A major thrust in the United States and Canada during the post-World War II decades has been the development of hundreds of theme parks, which have become an important element in travel, tourism, and popular entertainment. Cleverly designed and promoted to attract family audiences to clean, wholesome, and imaginative environments that included technologically advanced rides, shows, and other exotic or amusing settings, these new amusement centers have a variety of themes as the basis for their appeal. Some deal with storybook or fairyland themes, and others with cartoons, jungle, or Wild West settings, or with trips into the future.

On a less expensive scale, many locally based commercial sponsors today offer varied types of family-oriented recreation facilities that are designed to appeal to the entire age range. Such facilities may include video-game galleries, miniature golf, playground equipment for children, pizza and other food services, and varied forms of entertainment, along with modified sports areas.

Often, these facilities include party-planning services as a package offering for families, or they may offer large-group discount rates for organized visits arranged by local public recreation and park departments. For example, Sportsworld Amusement Park, located in Paramus, New Jersey, offers game arcades, rides, batting cages, miniature golf, and food services, all within a safe, controlled environment.

The expansion of the types of revenue-based, innovative play facilities just described has significant implications for recreation program planners. First, these facilities obviously are designed to serve families or individuals who are able to pay membership charges or admission fees. As such, whether sponsored by public, private, or commercial agencies, they tend to be found only in relatively affluent areas and to exclude those who cannot afford their costs.

Table 8-1.   Facilities at indoor recreation centers under construction or planned.

Facility	Percent
Men's Locker/Shower	100%
Women's Locker/Shower	100%
Multipurpose Room(s)	92%
Gymnasium(s)	88%
Child-Care Facilities	79%
Aerobics/Dance Room	75%
Family Locker Rooms	71%
Free-Weight Equipment Area	71%
Cardiovascular/Selectorized Equipment Area	71%
Indoor Lap/Competitive Pool	63%
Indoor Leisure Pool	54%
Concession Stand	50%
Racquetball/Handball Courts	46%
Indoor Track	46%
Whirlpool(s)	42%
Sauna	38%
Pro Shop	21%
Climbing Wall	17%
Outdoor Tennis Courts (at indoor facility)	17%
Steam Room	17%
Indoor Ice Rink	13%
Outdoor Lap/Competitive Pool (at indoor facility)	13%
Squash Courts	8%

Beyond this, they represent a shift away from the kinds of organized, directed programs that were typical of most public and nonprofit leisure-service agencies in the past. With the exception of exercise programs that require instruction or leadership, such as aerobic-dance classes or children's gymnastics and martial arts, they usually consist of casual free play or some form of entertainment or involvement with machinery, in the form of video games, rides, or other mechanized equipment. While safe and controlled, they lack the social, cognitive, or other growth aspects of other forms of directed play. The leader's role, or lack of it, is illustrated by an observation made by the director of the Sportsworld Amusement Park, that while children enjoy playing "Street Fighter," the latest craze in video games, their counselors are free to play billiards, a favorite among the "older" crowd.

Mobile Recreation

Many public recreation and park agencies today operate mobile recreation programs, which make it possible to bring varied recreation attractions to neighborhoods or communities over a broad geographical area.

For example, the Oakland County, Michigan, Parks and Recreation Department sponsors a variety of mobile recreation programs that include trailers stocked with game equipment, tents, mobile stages, bleachers, and buses that are used for community fairs or festivals, company picnics, family events, reunions, and more. As a service to local groups and communities, Oakland County offers a traveling music show, puppet mobile, sports mobile, show mobile, mime troupe, skate mobile, nature discovery, and star-lab planetarium (see Figure 8-3).

When such programs were introduced to the public recreation and park movement, their primary role was to bring portable swimming pools, skating programs, or other forms of recreation and entertainment to economically deprived urban neighborhoods. This occurred during the 1960s, as part of the war on poverty and in response to inner-city rioting. When federal funding to support such programs was terminated in the early 1980s, the Oakland County Parks and Recreation Commission provided special funding to continue the mobile recreation program. Approximately $20,000 has been granted each year to fund between 140 and 160 visits to communities and neighborhoods in Oakland County, based on their socioeconomic needs.

Many other large recreation and park agencies continue to serve disadvantaged neighborhoods with varied play programs and facilities. For example, the City of Oakland, California's Office of Parks and Recreation provides diversified activities through its six city pools, ranging from junior lifeguard, CPR, and standard first aid courses, to public swimming, lap swimming, classes for all ages, a youth rowing program, and evening alcohol- and drug-free parties for teens. Figure 8-4 shows how twenty-one different aquatic and social programs are offered, seasonally or year-round, at Oakland's pools.

Example of Diversified Park Programming

To illustrate the broad range of outdoor recreation facilities offered by many county agencies today, the Westchester County, New York, Department of Parks, Recreation and Conservation operates numerous parks, reservations, lakes, swimming pools, golf

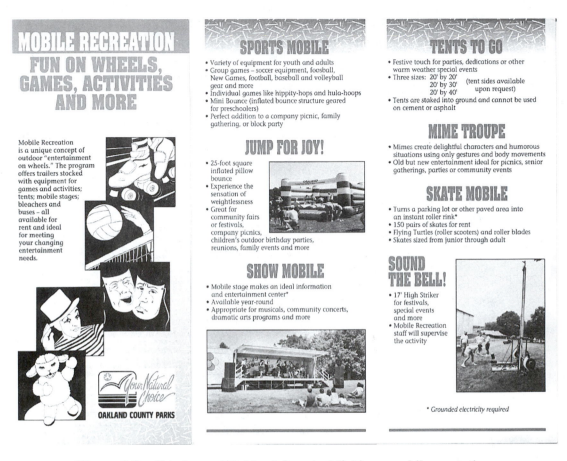

Figure 8-3.   Brochure of Oakland County, Michigan, mobile recreation program.

courses, ice rinks, boating facilities, a special music camp, environmental centers, and historical sites.

Different facilities host specially designed program elements. For example, the calendar of events at Washington's Headquarters Museum, an authentic historical site, includes Revolutionary-period crafts of quilting, yarn spinning, chair reeding, basketry, and colonial herb gardening, as well as celebration of holidays or events related to the Revolutionary War era.

The examples that have just been cited show how different facilities lend themselves to providing a huge range of program activities. In some agencies, the leadership that is required involves careful planning of events, teaching of skills, or supervision of participation. In others, the involvement of participants is relatively unstructured and free, and the leadership role is less critical. Taken all together, such leisure experiences and services must be fitted into a carefully designed overall program plan, as Chapter 9 will show.

• Aquatics/Pools •

The OPR Aquatics program offers a full variety of activities through its six City pools. These programs vary from public swim, group lessons and specialize swim teams (see grid). The Summer Aquatics season will open its Learn to Swim Program on June 29, 1993 at each pool and public swimming begins June 28 . Safety is a primary concern, therefore strict rules and regulations are enforced for everyone's protection. For specific questions on rules and regulations, brochure and registration information call Aquatics Unit at (510) 238-3494.

City Pools

deFremery Pool . . . .1269 18th St. 238-2205
Fremont Pool . . . . . .4550 Foothill Blvd. 238-2203
Lions Pool . . . . 3860 Handy Rd. 238-3494
Live Oak Pool . . . . . 1055 MacArthur Blvd. . . .238-2292
McClymonds Pool . . 2607 Myrtle 834-8395
Temescal Pool . . . . 371 45th St. 238-2202
Aquatics Unit . . . . . . Main Office 238-3494
1520 Lakeside Dr.

Aquatics Advisory Council meets bi-monthly on Mon. evenings at 1520 Lakeside Drive . For more information, call 238-3494.

- Seasonal
- Year Round

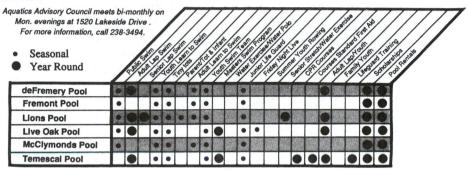

Figure 8-4.   Oakland, California, aquatics program.

Summary

Leadership and facilities represent two critical elements in recreation, park, and leisure-service program development.

This chapter summarizes varied theories of group leadership and identifies current trends in the professional functioning of leisure-service leaders and program specialists. It offers several examples of job descriptions in public, voluntary, therapeutic, and commercial agencies, and outlines key phases of the personnel management process in recreation and parks. The improvement of leadership skills in such program areas as arts and crafts, games, and nature pursuits is reviewed, with an overview of the basic principles of effective teaching.

The importance of facilities in recreation programming is examined, with a description of the range of places for play that have traditionally been operated by public recreation and park departments. Several examples of newer types of more complex, revenue-oriented facilities are then presented, such as fitness centers, water-play parks, and family-play centers, along with their implications for programming and leadership.

Finally, while showing how such trends in facilities development favor more affluent community residents, the chapter concludes by describing diversified recreation and park systems that continue to serve a broad range of people with varied leisure opportunities.

Class Assignments and Activities

1. As a practical exercise in leadership, several students may present to the class activities such as social or group games, craft projects, informal dramatics, or demonstrations of activities adapted for people with disabilities. Following each presentation, class members should critique it, stressing its positive aspects but also suggesting ways of improving leadership techniques.

2. Guest practitioners from different types of leisure-service agencies may visit the class, to describe their agencies' programs as well as their own leadership responsibilities and trends in their field. Preferably, these should be individuals who are qualified professionals, who may discuss their past specialized training as well as the role of continuing education and membership in professional societies, in terms of their own career development and on-the-job performance.

3. If the class schedule makes it possible, the class should visit and tour a major leisure-service agency's facility, so that students may get an overview of the agency's program operation. If this kind of visit is not possible, class members may be assigned to gather and review program materials (schedules, brochures, reports, etc.) from various agencies, to gain a fuller picture of current recreation program practices.

References

1. Diane La Pointe, "Tools for Customer Service Training in the 1990s," *Recreation Canada,* Vol. 51, No. 2, 1993, p. 36.

2. Carl F. Fuerst, "The Family Aquatic Center," *Parks and Recreation,* July 1993, p. 34.

3. For a fuller discussion of leadership theories, see Christopher R. Edginton and Phyllis M. Ford, *Leadership in Recreation and Leisure Service Organizations* (New York: John Wiley and Sons, 1985), pp. 22–47.

4. See E. William Niepoth, *Leisure Leadership: Working with People in Recreation and Park Settings* (Englewood Cliffs, NJ: Prentice-Hall, Inc., 1983), pp. 291–298.

5. Sue Schmid, "Cities on the Move," *Athletic Business,* Oct. 1993, p. 30.

Chapter **9**

Developing the Program Plan

The written program plan is analogous to the architect's blueprint or the project manager's network diagram. . . . [It] outlines all of the activities to be accomplished and the development of a timeline for their completion. . . . The management plan should identify all activities necessary for implementing the program, and it should identify the person responsible for implementing each activity.[1]

. . . the following factors are common to all program development situations. With the specific customer group(s) in mind, the leisure-service professional will focus on the program area, program format, program content, time factors, facilities, setting, equipment and supplies, staffing, cost, promotion, activity analysis, and risk management.[2]

The program plan represents a comprehensive, orderly model of the total range of activities and services that the recreation, park, and leisure-service agency intends to offer, along with details of specific program elements, such as scheduling, staff assignments, and the fiscal practices necessary for implementing the program.

The program plan serves as a plan of action, outlining the broad sweep of agency operations for the time period ahead. In addition to the overall agency plan, there also may be separate plans for different program elements, facilities, or groups of participants. Each of the important tasks involved in developing the program plan is discussed in this chapter, in order to satisfy the following undergraduate curriculum standards established by the NRPA/AALR Council on Accreditation:

Ability to formulate, plan for implementation, and evaluate extent to which goals and objectives for the leisure service and for groups and individuals within the service have been met. (8.27)

Ability to apply activity and task analysis to various populations and settings. (9D.12)

Understanding of and ability to utilize programmatically a breadth of diverse activity content areas. (9C.01)

Ability to conceptualize, develop, and implement recreation programs for various populations, marshaling diverse community and human service resources. (9C.03)

Role of the Program Plan

The program plan is based on all the factors that were described in the preceding chapters of this text—an agency's philosophy, goals, and objectives; its physical, personnel, and fiscal resources; and the needs and interests of participants and community groups to be served. It should be benefits-driven in the sense that it seeks to accomplish a clearly defined set of positive, measurable outcomes in both personal and social terms.

The plan systematically outlines the intentions of the agency with respect to program offerings during the year ahead or other defined time period, identifying all activities and services; their locations, schedules, and staffing assignments; projected costs and anticipated revenues; and other details of program operations. As a behind-the-scenes working document, the program plan has a factual and statistical format. It does not discuss the priorities that were considered in making programmatic decisions. It does not include colorful descriptions, human-interest appeals, photographs or other illustrations, such as those that might be found in promotional program brochures.

Organization of the Plan

The program plan is usually developed over a period of several months, with input from staff members on various levels, and with ultimate decision-making by agency administrators.

Structurally, the plan may have sections dealing with:

1. *Major program categories,* such as sports and fitness activities, performing and creative arts, or aquatic activities;

2. *Population groups served,* usually designated as different age groups, but also with a special category for people with disabilities;

3. *Program locations,* such as a breakdown of offerings by geographical districts or other political units (within a county recreation and park system, for example), or within different recreation centers or other special facilities;

4. *Time sequences,* showing the duration or sequencing of activities and events through different seasons of the year; and

5. The *responsibilities of administrative units* of the agency, such as personnel, maintenance, financial management, and public relations.

Each of these separate ways of organizing the plan must be coordinated with the others so that all elements interlock smoothly. Each program element or facility must be scheduled efficiently, to ensure a balanced offering in terms of populations and locations served, staffing assignments, and needed support services.

In a physical sense, the program plan may take any of several formats. At the simplest level—for example, within a small therapeutic recreation unit within a larger department of physical rehabilitation service—the plan may simply be typed and duplicated, item by item, giving the relevant information that describes each program element and its operational details.

Use of Computer Spreadsheets

In larger or more complex leisure-service agencies, programs are likely to be entered into a computer, using software that organizes all data regarding participants, scheduling, staffing, location, financial details, and similar information, as shown in Figure 9-1.

In terms of continuing operation, this computer-based planning system receives and processes additional data, such as registration, income, and attendance statistics during the course of the program's implementation. It lends itself to an instant appraisal of the status of any program element, with feedback that may be used to make needed changes in the overall plan.

To assure ready access to the plan and to have a convenient reminder of needed details, separate sheets or layouts may be prepared that display staffing assignments within a given center, the progress of specific programs such as tournaments or festivals, or the hour-by-hour and day-by-day scheduled activities in a facility.

Visual Formats

Some leisure-service agencies have developed convenient ways of visually presenting program plans, to facilitate efficient staff operations.

Program Diagraph.   One such method involves a "diagraph," a combined diagram and graph that outlines all events or continuing activities in an easily understood form. The dia-

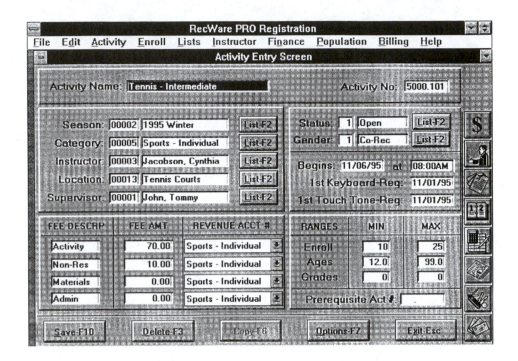

Figure 9-1.   Example of programming software: RecWare PRO System.

Source: Sierra Digital Co., Sacramento, California.

graph consists of a quarter-inch-thick rectangular board, usually four feet by six feet, formed by two skins of white gloss paper separated by Styrofoam. It is used in staff program planning sessions and throughout ongoing operations.[3]

Twelve vertical columns represent the months of the year and are labeled as such. Activities of three types are represented horizontally on the board in the form of half-inch Scotch tape that is color coded for identification, marking the exact time period each type of activity will fill during the year. These activities are *scheduled sequences,* which take place over a given period of time, such as a course in square dance instruction, or a day camp program; *sustained sequences,* which continue through all or most of the year, such as golf course play, or jogging trails; and *special events,* which normally involve only a day or two during the year.

In addition to indicating the active period of each program activity, tape markers may be used to indicate planning deadlines, final report due-dates, maintenance, or setup schedules, and similar information.

Program Maps.   Another type of visual presentation makes use of community-wide maps, in which various major facilities and programs are shown on a large geographical layout, using color-coded pins. This approach is useful in identifying the under- or over-provision of different types of activities and services throughout the community, and also in determining their appropriateness in terms of the demographic factors outlined in Chapter 6.

Customarily, maps of this type are prepared on a large scale and hung in a department's office, where they are readily visible to both staff members and members of the public visiting the agency. As a variant of this, many public recreation and park departments make use of brochures that include a map of facilities of all types within a large geographical area, with each facility marked by a coded number. Accompanying the map is a listing of all activity categories, or programs offered within different age-group categories. Check marks or small symbolic markers are used to indicate which of the overall group of activities are offered at each of the facilities, as shown in Figure 9-2 and Figure 9-3.

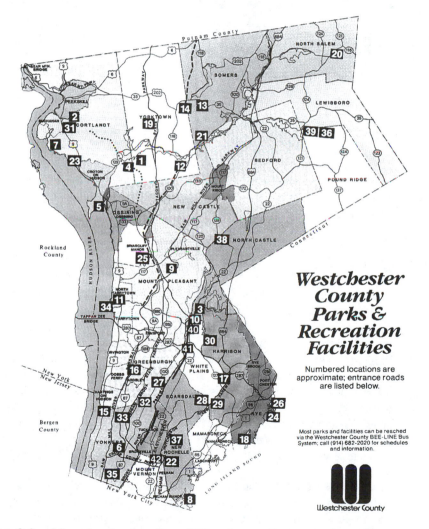

Figure 9-2. **Map showing location of Westchester County Park Facilities.**

Key indicates general accessibility of parking & restrooms; it does not imply that every area of the Park is accessible. If accessibility is a concern, call prior to your visit.

1 Bald Mountain
Blinn Road, Yorktown — 593-2600

2 Blue Mountain Reservation
Welcher Avenue, Peekskill — 737-2194

3 Cranberry Lake Preserve
Off Route 22, Old Orchard Street, N. White Plains — 428-1005

4 Croton Gorge
Via Route 9 to Route 129, Cortlandt — 271-3293

5 Croton Point Park
Croton Point Avenue, Off Route 9, Croton-on-Hudson — 271-3293

6 Dunwoodie Golf Course
Wasylenko Lane, Off Yonkers Avenue, Yonkers — 476-5151

7 George's Island Park
Dutch Street, Off Route 9A, Montrose — 737-7530

16 Macy, V. Everit, Park (Park Pass Required)
Saw Mill River Road, Ardsley — 946-8133

17 Maple Moor Golf Course
North Street, White Plains — 949-6752

18 Marshlands Conservancy
Route 1, Rye — 835-4466

19 Mohansic Golf Course
Baldwin Road, Off Taconic, Yorktown Heights — 962-4065

20 Mountain Lakes
Hawley Road, North Salem — 669-5793

21 Muscoot Farm
Route 100, Somers — 232-7118

22 Nature Study Woods
Webster Avenue, New Rochelle — 593-2600

31 Sportsman Center
Watch Hill Road, Cortlandt — 737-7450

32 Sprain Lake Golf Course
Grassy Sprain Road, Yonkers — 779-5180

33 Sprain Ridge Park (Park Pass Required)
Jackson Avenue, Yonkers — 478-2300

34 Tarrytown Lighthouse, Kingsland Point Park
Palmer Avenue, Off Route 9, North Tarrytown — 593-2634

35 Tibbetts Brook Park (Park Pass Required)
Midland Avenue, Yonkers — 965-1901

36 Trailside Nature Museum, Ward Pound Ridge Reservation
Routes 35 and 121, Cross River — 763-3993

37 Twin Lakes
California Road, Eastchester — 593-2600

Figure 9-3.   Section of listing showing activities available at each facility.

Content of the Program Plan

We now examine the five important elements that constitute the overall program plan: (1) the *selection of activities or services to be offered;* (2) the *scheduling of activities and services;* (3) the *locations of program offerings;* (4) *staffing arrangements;* and (5) *fiscal analysis.*

Selection of Activities

The selection of activities and services to be fitted into the agency's program plan begins with a *review of past offerings.*

Review of Past Offerings

Program planners should examine the agency's offerings over the past year or two, to determine which programs should be continued, expanded, reduced, modified, or eliminated. One obvious way to do this is to analyze the patterns of enrollment, registration, or participation. If these have gone up steadily over time, the increase suggests that a given activity is popular, meets a public need, and should be continued. If they have declined sharply, these questions must be asked: Is the activity one in which the public no longer is interested? Were there other specific reasons that the activity did poorly?

Program Life Cycle.   The concept of the program life cycle, as shown in Figure 9-4, has been adapted from business marketing theory. It suggests that many products or services go through a typical sequence of being introduced, growing in public interest or acceptance, reaching a healthy peak or plateau of participation, and then beginning to decline.

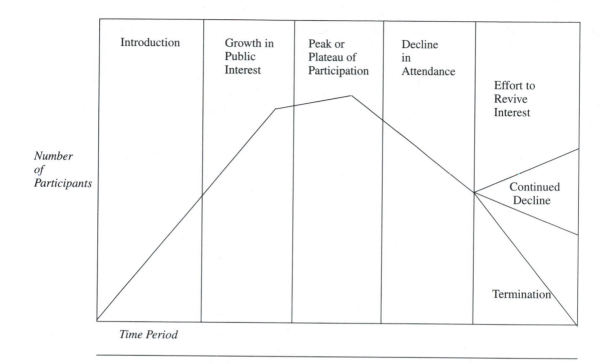

Figure 9-4. *Program life cycle.* **Adapted from John L. Crompton, "Programs Have Life Cycles, Too,"** *Parks and Recreation,* **October 1979, p. 53.**

In terms of recreation and park programming, some popular activities will continue to draw impressive numbers of participants year after year, while others may show sharp, sudden rises in public interest and equally rapid declines in participation, suggesting that their appeal is of a fad nature, rather than being based on an enduring set of personal motivations or leisure interests.

Review of enrollment or participation statistics should be combined with analysis of program evaluation reports. For instance, if there has been a sharp decline of public interest and involvement in a program activity, was it because of a stretch of bad weather? Was it because of new, competing programs or events? Were there accidents or other unfavorable happenings that affected the public's perception of the activity?

Based on a careful analysis of the factors involved with an activity whose participation level has dropped, program planners may decide to promote the activity more fully, and to add new, more attractive elements to increase its appeal and return it to a high level of involvement. Or, planners might decide to continue it at a lessened rate of involvement, because it does continue to have value, although for a smaller number of participants. Or, if they decide that its interest was of a temporary, superficial nature, and that the effort to revive interest in the activity is not justified, the decision may be made to cut back the activity sharply or to terminate it entirely.

Findings of Needs-and-Interests Surveys

As shown in Chapter 5, surveys of the needs, interests, and satisfaction levels of past or present patrons of recreation, park, and leisure-service agencies may be used to identify public attitudes regarding the full range of potential program offerings.

Leisure needs-and-interests surveys may indicate other important information, such as the preferred locations for certain program activities, the kinds of fees that people would be willing to pay, and the best times for participation, in terms of the day of the week or the hour of the day. Surveys also may be used to identify barriers that have prevented people from taking part in a given activity. This information would be useful for programmers in making key decisions about schedule, location, and cost. Such information can be combined with the opinions or suggestions provided by advisory councils, participant evaluation forms, or focus groups.

Response to Trends in the Field

A final important influence affecting program planning stems from the agency staff's awareness of current trends and innovations in the field. Based on correspondence with fellow professionals; attendance at conferences, symposiums, or workshops; and reading the professional literature, program planners should be knowledgeable about new and exciting program activities being provided elsewhere, and about opportunities for support of innovative program services.

As a related factor, in organizations such as the Police Athletic League, Boys and Girls Clubs, the YMCA and YWCA, the Catholic Youth Organization, and Jewish community centers, program recommendations frequently are made by planning groups at national headquarters that conduct studies in order to identify key priorities or new program directions.

Analysis of Potential Activities

Before making a final determination of which program elements to include in the overall plan, it is helpful for planners to analyze each potential offering in terms of the experience it provides for participants and its administrative requirements. This analysis should include asking the following questions:

1. *Social interaction patterns.* Is the activity carried on by individual participants, in small groups or large groups, or in other types of social settings? Does it involve competition or cooperation as a primary mode of behavior?
2. *Individual experience.* Is the activity primarily psychomotor, cognitive, or affective in nature? Does it contribute to the participant's physical, intellectual, emotional, or social development?
3. *Leadership, equipment, and facilities.* Does the activity require skilled leadership? If so, what is the needed ratio of leader to participants? Can the activity be carried on independently, without paid leaders, or with volunteer supervision? What are its requirements in terms of equipment and facilities?

4. *Participants.* Does this activity require a set number of participants, or can it be undertaken with flexible numbers? Can it be used with different age groups, or is it most appropriate for a single age group?

5. *Time and duration.* Is there an ideal time for offering this activity, or can it be given at different times? What is the typical duration of a session or period of involvement?

Particularly in working with special groups, such as individuals with physical, mental, or social disabilities, it is essential to examine the nature of the leisure experience, both in terms of the positive outcomes it can offer, and in terms of the demands it may make on participants.

Based on all of these factors and on planners' determination of the key needs and interests of their own clientele, in terms of age, gender, ethnic or racial factors, socioeconomic and educational background, and other demographic variables, a ranked listing of high-, medium-, and low-priority activities and services should be developed.

Final Decision Making

In the last stage of decision making with respect to the activities and services that are to be offered in the overall program plan, many leisure-service agencies have developed rating systems or formulas to ensure that all important factors are given appropriate weight.

U.S. Navy "Smart Compass"

U.S. Navy planners within the Morale, Welfare and Recreation system make use of a marketing analysis known as "Smart Compass," which conducts systematic needs assessments and utilizes patron feedback information, linked to usage statistics and other data, to provide a basis for future planning. Figure 9-5 illustrates the summary form used to collate the information gathered, as a basis for marketing-oriented decision making.

On the summary form, each program, such as golf, club operations, or use of the fitness center, is analyzed on a single page. The number of resources, or facilities, provided for this program element are recorded, with information about those sponsored by Navy and non-Navy agencies, their condition, numbers of hours used, and fee levels. Past and future participation by different groups of patrons are recorded or projected, along with evaluations of quality and satisfaction made by three levels of users—high, medium, and low. Program costs and revenues and other data are summarized, leading to conclusions and recommendations.

Sunnyvale Activity Rating System.   The information gathered may be analyzed using a mathematical formula that scores the various factors to be considered in determining whether to offer a given program element. For example, the Sunnyvale, California, Leisure Service Department has developed an activity rating form in which each program element—in this case, instructional classes—is rated in terms of such factors as market competition, profitability, current demand, staff time required, and potential partnership arrangements (i.e., cosponsorship with other agencies) (see Figure 9-6). With the more important factors given a

Resource Assessment: PROGRAM:_____

	Number	Condition				# Days	# Hours	Fee	Comments:
	Units	M	A	SS	I				
Navy									
Non-Navy									

Needs Assessment - Participation Patterns:

Group:	Past %	Future %	Comments:
Active Duty			
Spouses			
Retired			

High Participation:	Low Participation:

Needs Assessment - Facility Evaluation:

High Users:	Medium Users:	Low Users:

Overall Satisfaction:	Range:

Lowest Rated Item:

Major Problems:	

Other Comments:	

COST ASSESSMENT:		PROGRAM ASSESSMENT:
Net Program Costs:	$	Applicable Ratings (if any):
NAF Revenue % of NAF Costs:	%	
NAF Revenue of Total Costs:	%	
Annual Number of Users:	#	
Total Cost Per User:	$	
Subsidized Cost Per User:	$	

Figure 9-5. U.S. Navy Smart Compass Program/facility summary form.

CLASS BEING RATED _____ **TOTAL SCORE** _____

* RATING FOR POTENTIAL PARTNERSHIP _____

** Rating Scale 1 - 10
   (1) Indicates Lowest Demand/Recommendation for the Class,
   (10) Indicates Highest Demand/Recommendation for the Class.

	Rate	WT	Score
Competition: Similar activities already being offered by private business other nearby agencies. High competition = low score Low competition = high score	8	x 1.0 =	8

Profitability
  Revenue _____
  Expenses _____
	7	x 1.0 =	7

Expense/Participant ratio	6	x 1.0 =	6
Availability and Capacity of Facility	9	x 1.0 =	9
Trends in Market Interest growing/declining	10	x 1.0 =	10
Current Demand Interest in this type of activity	5	x 2.0 =	10
Staff Time Acceptable amount of staff time required	2	x 1.0 =	2

Political or Special Factors
  Special population needs or any other factor that would
  supercede the other scores.
	10	x 2.0 =	20

TOTAL SCORE			**72**

A score 80 or above, or (10) under Political or Special Factor, suggests an activity should be offered.
**Scores to be based on responses to Activity Market Surveys conducted. (attached).

*If, based on Market Survey, there is a potential for Partnership for this activity, complete the Activity Rating Form again, factoring the partnership concept into your responses.

Comments:_____
_____
_____

Figure 9-6.   Sunnyvale, California, activity rating form.

double weight, each class is rated and then given a total score that helps to determine whether or not it should be scheduled.

Choice of Formats

Before moving to the next step of the programming process, scheduling of activities, it is necessary for planners to determine the format or formats through which selected activities will be presented to participants. As described in Chapter 7, these range from free play or open-facility settings to leadership training. While not all activities can be presented in all types of formats, ingenious planning can assure considerable variety in program offerings, as shown in Figure 9-7.

The Scheduling Process

Having determined which activities and services should be offered during the coming year, the planner must fit them into a time scheme that will coordinate the agency's facilities and staff members with the free-time patterns and priorities of potential program participants.

Scheduling Single Facilities

The task of scheduling single facilities serving a narrow range of interests is relatively simple. The emphasis is on maximizing the use of the facility by serving the largest number of patrons during prime hours, while arranging special times to serve other groups.

Ice rink managers, for example, must schedule the use of their rinks for mass skating sessions, practice by individual or group figure skaters, ice-hockey practices, or competition and other uses. The activity with the greatest number of participants is likely to be given prime-time hours, while activities with relatively fewer participants are assigned less convenient hours. Typically, many figure skaters or youthful ice hockey players practice in the early morning or pre-dawn hours.

Tennis complexes provide another example of how a single facility may be used for varied program formats. The director of a commercially operated tennis center must be inventive in scheduling court hours for instruction, singles or doubles play, special day camps or clinics, tournaments, and other program elements. While the bulk of the tennis center's revenue is derived from general court play, each of these other program features is used to promote player interest, bring along a new crop of players, provide highlights to regular play, and build revenues.

Annual and Seasonal Scheduling

Recreation scheduling during the course of the year consists of determining when a given activity should be offered, over how long a period of time, and how frequently.

Climatic and Seasonal Factors.   While some activities may be carried on throughout the year, particularly in regions with moderate climates that permit outdoor play through the year, weather considerations often dictate the scheduling of activities. In some areas, the late

Activity Category	Free Play	Instruction	Competition	Performance/ Exhibition	Special Event	Trip or Outing	Special Interest Group	Leadership Training
Sports, Games, Fitness	Basketball in school yard	Tennis class	Senior softball tournament	Gymnastics demonstration	Police Athletic League awards event	Trip to Baseball Hall of Fame	Sports card collectors club	Workshop in playground games
Outdoor Recreation	Informal hike or picnic	Riflery class	Cross country snowmobile race	Flycasting demonstration	Environmental cleanup project	Visit to historic park	Company ski club	Mountain climbing leader training
Aquatics	Swimming at beach	Pre-school water survival class	Diving meet	Synchronized swim show	Community pool party	Trip to water play park	Kayaking club	Lifesaving and CPR clinic
Arts and Crafts	Informal sketching in park	Ceramics class	Art show competition	Glass-blowing demonstration	Banquet honoring local artist	Trip to art museum	Photography hobby group	Girl Scout leaders' crafts workshop
Performing Arts	Teen-age dancing in lounge	Violin class in recreation center	Ballet company competition	Choral concert	Children's theater weekend	Folk dance group tour	Senior's music appreciation club	Young conductors class
Literary Activities	Story-telling at campfire	Speed reading class	Spelling bee	Poetry reading	High school political debate	Trip to city library	Famous books discussion group	Training for volunteer tutors

Figure 9-7. Examples of program formats in major activity categories.

189

spring, summer, and early fall represent the times for outdoor play, although in warmer climates the summer months may be oppressive for active sports.

Fall, winter, and spring are generally the most appropriate times for organized classes with set enrollments and time schedules involving six-, eight-, or ten-week courses. Summer programs tend to rely less on fixed programs with formal registration, since many families take vacations at this time, although sports leagues and day camps may continue through July and part of August.

Typically, winter programs place heavier emphasis on classes, social clubs, or other group activities in recreation centers. Many departments feature winter activities that are based on climate factors. The Detroit Recreation Department, for example, has featured winter programming including ice skating at natural and artificial rinks, sledding and tobogganing under supervision, sleigh rides, cross-country skiing on approved trails, and winter picnics.

Within each season, many activities go through a sequence of programming that includes planning, training or practice, competition on progressive levels, and culminating tournaments or exhibitions. In terms of sports, for example, the Chicago Park District has traditionally scheduled competitive play in varied sports and games over a period of several months, moving from participation in local parks, to area or district-wide competition, and ultimately to city-wide activities.

Seasonal programming may also include scheduling of special events based on historical traditions, religious holidays, or civic commemorations. An example of the scheduling of special events is shown in Figure 9-8, which presents varied tournaments, swap meets, shows, and performances held at the Westchester County, New York, County Center during a recent winter season.

Weekly and Daily Programming

Within each season, program activities that meet regularly must be fitted into weekly and daily schedules in a coordinated way, based on time blocks that fit into a regular or repeated schedule.

To illustrate, a recreation center's swimming pool might involve such time allocations as these: open swim for adults, family swim periods, instructional classes at different skill or age levels, exercise or water aerobics sessions, scuba diving, swimming for disabled people, swim team practice, and numerous other special uses. In some cases, a large pool may have different groups using different lanes or sections at the same time, provided that their program uses do not conflict with each other.

Typically, such time blocks are assigned based on public demand and interest and on the priority of certain activities, in terms of the agency's goals. Often, an activity is scheduled for a period ranging from one to three hours, depending on the activity's time requirements. For example, evening adult classes in languages, hobbies, or arts and crafts are likely to be scheduled for at least ninety minutes or two hours, while a vigorous fitness program would probably be scheduled for no more than one hour.

Another example of weekly programming, a suggested five-day schedule of an outdoor school, is shown in Figure 9-9. Unlike the swimming pool schedule, where the more popular activities, such as open-swim periods, tend to be scheduled each day, featured activities vary each day of the week.

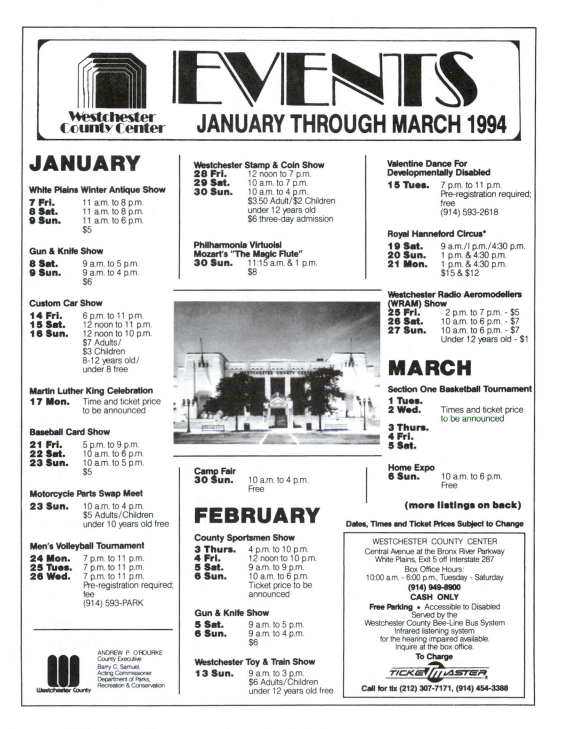

Figure 9-8. Seasonal special events scheduling: Westchester County, New York.

7:15	Reveille—If you get up earlier—6:30 earliest, please be quiet so you don't disturb the rest of the campers			
7:40	K.P. and Flag Raising Bell: (Four campers raise the American and Maryland flags)			
8:00	Breakfast—followed by lively songs. Individuals or class groups lead these. Weather Report.			
8:45	Clean-up—Cabin and Wash Room, Staff Meeting			

Monday	Tuesday	Wednesday	Thursday	Friday

Cabin Assignment
 	
9:00 Flag Raising
 	
Camp Tour of
  Nature Cabin,
  Weather Station,
  Dining Hall,
  Rec Hall,
  Nature Craft,
  Nurses Cabin
	All Day Field Trip
	
	Temp. Changes
	  Changes in plant
	  growth
	Water's effect
	  on rocks
		Compass-Water-
		  Shed Quest
		How to spot a fire
		Use of compass
		Maps: sketch &
		  topographic
		Discussion of a
		  a watershed
			Mountain View
			  Rock Formation
			Study rocks: color,
			  texture, hardness
			Terms: Piedmont
			  plateau, fault,
			  inland seas
			Mountain formation:
			  age, volcanic
				Nature Craft,
				  Sketching Tools
				Use of axes,
				  crosscuts, sledges
				Sketch with
				  charcoal
				Whittle:
				  totem-pole,
				  pencil-holder

12:15	Lunch: Weather Report, Songs, K.P.'s report at 12:00 to set the tables. One K.P. per table. (Each class group has 4 or 5 meals).			
	Lazy Time: Whittle, crafts, nature cabin, rest in cabins.			

1:30 Field Note
  Hike
Hike in forest
Take field notes
Use five senses
 	
3:30 Teams of 4 or
  5 children
	Cook-Out
	Each cooks his/her
	  own in mess kit
	Care of forest
	Compass Hike
	Use of compass in
	  woods
	Observation of
	  plant and animal
	  life
		Trout Hatchery
		See 18" trout
		Slides of trout
		View trout ponds, or
		  Pond study,
		  fishing
		Life in pond
		Temp changes
		  in water
		Dissect frog, fish
			Forestry-Tree
			  Planting
			Types of trees
			Age of trees
			  Interesting growth
			Plant succession
			Plant pine tree
			Animal life
			What is a forest
				Busses Leave
				Catoctin Furnace
				You may wish to
				  visit this historic
				  area enroute
				  home

4:30	Shower and Free Time: Nature cabin, Run on Greentop, Nature crafts, Whittle, Rest
5:15	Supper: Skits, stunts, or jokes from boys and girls. Weather report.
6:30	Class Meetings, classroom teacher in charge.
7:30	Evening Activities: Games, stunts, campfires, stories and songs.
9:00	Taps

Figure 9-9.   Sample outdoor school schedule: Frederick County, Maryland.

An example of daily programming on a playground appears in Figure 9-10, showing the basic schedule used by the Phoenix, Arizona Department of Parks, Recreation and Library.

In addition to planning daily schedules, playground programmers might also include a special theme for each week, to be used in planning arts and crafts, music, dance, drama, or other activities. Different sports clinics, tournaments, and evening programs to involve family groups might also be scheduled from week to week.

In all such weekly and daily schedules, it is essential that time be allowed for transition between program activities, for groups to move from place to place, for leaders to set out needed equipment, or for other housekeeping functions to be carried out.

Determining Location of Program Offerings

A third key element in the program plan involves the assignment of activities and services to areas and facilities where they will be readily available to groups of participants.

As Chapter 8 points out, large public recreation and park departments customarily have the widest variety of facilities, ranging from parks, playgrounds, sports, and centers to such specialized facilities as marinas, stadiums, or other major structures or areas to meet program needs. In addition, many public departments may also use facilities owned by other organizations, on a contractual exchange basis. Other types of agencies, such as Ys, Boys and Girls Clubs, and other youth-serving organizations, typically own their own buildings, although they may also use publicly owned areas for camping or sports activities.

In the past, nationally published standards established recommended levels of facility availability designed to meet the minimum recreation program needs in communities. Typically, such standards recommended that there should be a neighborhood playground within a quarter-mile of each elementary school child's home, and that there should be a neighborhood recreation center within a half-mile of each high-school-age youth's home. In addition, authorities recommended that certain key facilities be provided to meet program needs based on population numbers to be served (see page 249).

Today, recognizing the extreme differences among most communities, there is little effort to enforce such recommended standards, particularly in large, older cities with severe fiscal restraints. At the same time, a number of guidelines may be used to ensure that facilities are used to their maximum capability in recreation program planning and operations.

Facility-Usage Guidelines

1. Program elements should be assigned to facilities or locations both to assure a fair balance of leisure opportunities throughout a community, and to reflect special needs with respect to age, socioeconomic status, or other demographic characteristics.

2. To the degree possible, publicly owned facilities should be made available for use by private groups, as in the case of recreation and park agencies' ball fields that are frequently scheduled by youth sports leagues that operate the bulk of actual programming.

3. In all program activities that make use of natural settings, sound ecological principles must be enforced to prevent environmental damage, pollution, or other harmful

A.M. Time Block	Activity	Person Responsible (Name)
	Open area, inspection tour for condition of area, safety of equipment	Leader
	Get equipment out and set up (tetherball, bases, table game, etc.)	Leader, Aide or Volunteer
	Start self-directed activities for early arrivals or those not involved in sports, (Table games, 4-square, tetherball, various ladder tournaments)	Aide or Volunteer
	Active team sports or tournaments (while it's cool).	Leader or Aide
	Start or check self-directed activities for those not participating in activities below	Aide, Volunteer or Leader not involved in next activity
	One or more special interest group activities involving direct leadership (arts & crafts, music, dance, nature-science, games "emphasis of the week")	Leader and/or Aide or Volunteer
Pre-Lunch Lunch Hour	Self-directed activities, conversation general supervision, meetings, lunch	All
P.M. Time Block Afternoon	Indoor activities (hot part of day)	Person Responsible
	Start self-directed activities (table tennis, teen canteen, table games)	Leader, Aide or Volunteer
2 or more time blocks	Special interest group activities involving direct leadership (arts & crafts, music, dance, nature-science, clubs, etc.)	Leader, Aide or Volunteer
Pre-Dinner Dinner Hour	Self-directed activities, meetings, preparation of reports, general supervision, dinner	All
P.M. Time Block Evening	Indoor-outdoor activities	Person Responsible
	Start or check self-directed activities	Aide, Volunteer or Leader
Early Evening	Program slanted toward self-directed activities. Some equipment may be reserved for groups at this time—table tennis, game courts, etc. Co-recreational activities Teen Clubs Sports—Leader circulating as much as possible on area with one Leader Check on supplies, inspect area, lock up	Leader or Aide Leader Leader, Aide

Figure 9-10.   Example of basic daily playground schedule.

effects. Agency policies about the use of alcohol must be enforced, including their application to outside groups using facilities.

4. Similarly, efficiently planned and applied maintenance programs must be used to prevent vandalism, graffiti, or other forms of physical abuse that degrade facilities and make them unsightly or unattractive for public use.

5. The role of well designed and maintained areas and facilities in preventing accidents must be emphasized in all program operations, to ensure public safety and minimize costly liability lawsuits.

Customarily, the assignment of specific activities to different agency facilities appears in two ways within the operational program plan: (1) within the section of the plan that presents activity offerings under broad divisional headings, such as sports, creative arts, or aquatics, all facilities offering specific activities are listed; and (2) each major facility, such as a recreation center or sports complex, lists under its name the varied activities it offers. This cross-referencing approach is also frequently used in program brochures and other publicity media, to facilitate public awareness of specific activities and their locations.

Staffing Elements in the Program Plan

A fourth important element of the operational program plan involves the assignment of staff members. Obviously, recreation, park, and leisure-service leaders should be involved in program development from the initial planning stage to the final steps of evaluation and writing reports. Leaders should be responsible for the following tasks:

Planning and design. Leaders should be involved in assessing the needs and interests of participants and developing recommendations for their programs, including appropriate levels, formats, and other details of activities to be offered.

Organizing and implementing. Leaders should assist in determining the locations where activities are presented, promote and publicize them on a local basis, and make sure that all needed equipment or supplies are available.

Monitoring and evaluating. Once program activities have been set in motion, leaders must monitor them to identify problems or weaknesses while they can be corrected. Both throughout the process and at its conclusion, they are responsible for conducting systematic self-evaluations and submitting program reports as required.

Facility Supervision.   Leaders may also be assigned to facilities that require little direct activity leadership. For example, at outdoor recreation sites such as tennis courts, golf courses, picnic grounds, nature preserves, or similar facilities, leaders may be expected to:

1. Check use permits or assign individuals or teams to areas for organized play.

2. Oversee the maintenance of areas and facilities, the distribution of materials, the repair of equipment, or similar tasks to ensure successful program operation.

3. Register and assign individuals or groups to picnic sites, camp sites, or other locations; collect fees; and carry out other administrative tasks.

4. Supervise participants to ensure that agency policies and rules are being observed, and enforce approved procedures when they are violated.

In facilities such as environmental education centers, historical parks, or similar locations, staff members may be assigned to instructional or interpretive functions. However, often their role is simply one of overseeing the area or facility, making arrangements with participating groups, supervising admissions and maintenance operations, and similar tasks.

In the past, it was usually expected that an individual would be assigned to a specific location or job responsibility throughout the year. Today, the work of full-time professional leaders may vary greatly from season to season. An individual such as an arts and crafts specialist may have various different assignments, such as teaching activities on a local level, conducting leadership clinics on a district level, and planning arts festivals on a county- or city-wide level.

Use of Part-Time and Seasonal Staff Members

Many leisure-service agencies today make use of part-time leaders to teach or lead classes or special-interest groups. Such individuals must be carefully selected in terms of their backgrounds, teaching skills, and certification credentials, where applicable.

The program plan must also include provision for employment of an expanded number of playground leaders, aquatic specialists, and other staff members during the summer season, in the case of public recreation and park agencies. Similarly, many nonprofit youth-serving agencies that operate large-scale camping programs also must develop plans for recruiting, training, and supervising substantial numbers of seasonal counselors and program specialists, usually during the winter and early spring months.

The recruitment, orientation, and in-service training, and ongoing supervision of program volunteers represents another critical concern, particularly in voluntary, nonprofit agencies that rely heavily on the use of unpaid leaders and staff assistants.

Revenue Sources and Pricing Policies

The fifth important element in developing recreation program plans today involves the use of revenue sources. As indicated in earlier chapters, many leisure-service agencies are relying increasingly on fees and charges to support their existing programs and to justify new ventures.

As a vivid example, Bill Mullins describes a period of fiscal transition in the U.S. Navy's Morale, Welfare and Recreation operation, when tax-funded appropriations for recreational programs declined by about one-third. Using new self-sufficiency formulas for support, the Navy was able to increase its revenue substantially, yielding profits from some programs that were then used to help subsidize other program areas. In the early 1990s, Mullins wrote:

While not new, traditional revenue generators, such as bowling and golf operations, have done their part to help military recreation fund leisure programs. Bowling programs in the military continue to be extremely popular and generate substantial profits. However, to increase their revenue-production potential and simultaneously provide services sought by the community, the military services expanded their bowling operations to include attractive and well-maintained game rooms, quality fast-food operations, and an appealing resale area. As a result, services have improved and so have the profits. In fact, in fiscal year 1990, Navy bowling center profits increased 35.7 percent over the previous year.[4]

Similar strategies enabled the Navy MWR program to increase its profits from golf course operations by fifty percent over the same period. Clearly, the opportunity to gain substantial revenues from intelligently marketed programs and services represents a key element in overall program planning.

Pricing Policies

Within the overall revenue management effort, pricing represents a critical function. While its most obvious application involves setting appropriate fees for public participation in activities such as classes, league competition, or admission to recreation attractions, it also has several other components. These include such elements as:

1. Determining appropriate rental charges for the use of publicly owned facilities by other community organizations.

2. Conversely, establishing appropriate rental fees that the public department can pay for the facilities of other organizations that it uses for program activities.

3. Setting fees for organizations, such as companies or private-membership associations, that register groups of participants in public programs, or that obtain other special recreation services.

4. Determining appropriate rates of return from concessionaires operating in public recreation and park areas, or who are subcontracting the operation of public facilities.

Of these various concerns, the most critical involves the pricing of activities and services offered to the public at large. There are two reasons for this. First, the public recreation and park department has a responsibility to provide a floor of basic leisure opportunity for all community residents, and to ensure that unreasonable or excessive pricing policies do not exclude substantial groups of residents from adequate recreational outlets.

Unlike the situation with for-profit organizations, where it would be normal to charge the maximum amount that a given product could command, taking into account the prices charged by competitors and the willingness of customers to pay at given rates, public and voluntary agencies must bear in mind their social marketing role and their commitment to serving the public.

Analysis of Programs Costs and Revenues

Fees charged for any recreation activity or service are usually based on two kinds of factors:

1. The actual costs of a given program, including personnel, materials, equipment, facility usage, transportation, and similar elements, balanced against anticipated revenues; and

2. Non-cost-related factors, such as the fee levels prevailing for similar activities or attractions provided by other agencies, as well as the extent or intensity of consumer demand, along with the social value or benefit associated with a given activity.

In the first case, a recreation and park agency may elect to base a program fee simply on the need to cover the instructional cost of a leader, teacher, or other staff member responsible for the activity. For example, in a folk dancing class for adults, there might be ten scheduled sessions, with a leader who is paid $40.00 per session, a total cost of $400.00. The department might set a per-person fee of $35.00 for the series, with a minimum enrollment number of twelve participants. That would generate revenue of $420.00, enough to pay for the expense of running the class.

However, in setting the fee for an activity, many agencies are likely to include both direct and indirect costs of conducting an activity, along with anticipated revenues (see Figure 9-11). Here, in the same folk dancing class, the direct costs of the instructor and the use of the hall and record-player are combined with a percentage of the department's promotional and other overhead expenses, to determine the revenue that the class must return. Based on this analysis, a higher fee must be set or a higher number of registrants must be required, to justify the class.

Fixed and Variable Costs.   Another factor that influences pricing decisions for recreation program activities involves fixed and variable costs.

Direct Costs of Folk Dancing Class (10 Sessions)

Leader's fee: $40.00 per session	$400.00
Rental of hall, or portion of untilities or custodial charge: $25.00 per session	$250.00
Rental of record-player or other sound equipment: $10.00 per session	$100.00

Indirect Costs

Four percent of department's promotional costs for seasonal brochure and advertising	$100.00
Two percent of other administrative costs, telephone, registration, supervisory costs	$250.00
Total Anticipated Costs	$1,100.00

Alternative Class Fees and Enrollments

25 registrants at $35.00 class fee (requires department subsidy)	$875.00
30 registrants at $35.00 class fee (course pays for itself, approximately)	$1,050.00
40 registrants at $35.00 class fee (course returns surplus revenue to agency)	$1, 200.00

Figure 9-11.   Illustration of cost and revenue analysis of program activity.

Fixed costs are those that are the same for a given activity, no matter how many participants are involved in the activity. For example, in the folk dance class illustration, the costs of conducting the class will be the same whether there are fifteen or thirty-five students, apart from a negligible additional cost for registering them, or the possible need for a larger meeting room.

If a department were to sponsor a ski trip, the costs of publicizing the trip and chartering a bus would be the same (fixed), whether twenty or forty people went on the trip, assuming that the bus's capacity could handle the larger number. However, the added number would involve variable costs, such as additional lift tickets, accommodations, food, and possible staffing costs.

Making Pricing Decisions

The elements of direct and indirect costs, along with an analysis of fixed and variable costs, must be combined with the factors of competing programs, demand for the activity, and its value in terms of the agency's mission, as indicated earlier. As a result, different kinds of leisure-service organizations may have sharply contrasting fee structures, as shown in Figure 9-12, which presents typical daily guest charges and membership fees for five different kinds of fitness centers and clubs in the late 1980s.

Fees charged for essentially the same service may also vary within an agency, to suit potential patrons at different levels of economic capability or willingness to pay for leisure opportunities. Ron McCarville argues that it is highly desirable to provide price alternatives and the option of program discounts. He writes:

You may establish different fee levels depending on use patterns. You can set rates higher during busy or "prime-time" periods. This strategy . . . offers a meaningful choice to your clients. They may pay a premium or may take advantage of a

Type of Establishment	Daily Guest Use Fee	Basic Membership Plan	Full Membership Plan
	Mean Fee*	Mean Monthly Fee	Mean Monthly Fee
Corporate recreation/fitness center	$4.20	$16.60	$17.80
Health/Fitness club	$5.50	$45.80	$54.80
Racquet/tennis club	$4.80	$44.80	$72.90
Private golf/country club	$18.30	$136.20	$127.10
YMCA/YWCA	$4.50	$31.90	$66.00

*Mean is the arithmetic average.

Figure 9-12. Fee structures at different sport and fitness agencies.[5]

discount.... Such differential pricing distributes demand so that fewer consumers fall victim to crowded and closed programs [and] permits more extended use of the facility and more revenue.[6]

Discounts may be made available to patrons who are willing to register for longer periods, accept fewer services, volunteer their services, or assist an agency in other ways, or to patrons who can demonstrate special financial need. Cato and Crofts refer to such differential pricing strategies as a means of erecting "fences" that

.... allow users to logically and rationally segment themselves into an appropriate rate category based on their needs, behaviors and willingness to pay ... price-sensitive users [receive] lower rates in exchange for decreased flexibility.[7]

As an example of market segmentation that lends itself to variable pricing arrangements, Cato and Crofts suggest a possible set of fees that take into account the nature of participation and the user group involved (see Figure 9-13).

Frequently, public recreation and park departments vary their fee structures based not only on the age group or family category of participants, but also on participants' resident or non-resident status, as shown in Figure 9-14, the fee schedule for the Chinn Aquatics and Fitness Center in Prince William County, Virginia, during a recent year.

An example of how commercial recreation businesses may vary their offerings within an extremely wide pricing range is found in the hunting and fishing field. Figure 9-15 shows three bear hunting options offered by a Canadian hunting service in Ungava Bay, which vary in the length of each hunt, the services provided, and the guaranteed results.

Pricing and Social Priorities

As an illustration of the effort to develop flexible pricing policies that take into account social needs, some large-scale agencies in metropolitan or diversified county areas may utilize any of the following methods to permit economically disadvantaged children in particular to enter facilities or programs: (1) setting aside particular days or times when no fees are charged; (2) developing no-fee arrangements for families that are on welfare or

Price	Advance Requirements	Day of Week	Time of Day	Likely Users
50 cents	14-day advanced reservation	Off peak	Off peak	Groups
$1.25	None	Off peak	Off peak	Retirees Under-employed Children
$2.50	None	Peak times	Peak times	Price-insensitive Individuals

Figure 9-13.   Suggested rate "fence" for municipal swimming complex.

DON'T MISS THIS OPPORTUNITY!
RENEW YOUR PASS PLAN NOW!

Pass Plan prices will increase on May 1, 1992

Regular Six-Month Pass

Type	Through April 30, 1992		May 1, 1992	
	Resident	Nonresident	Resident	Nonresident
Adult	$175	$220	$195	$245
Youth (under 18)	$130	$165	$150	$190
Couple	$265	$330	$295	$370
Dependent (3−22)*	$ 50	$ 75	$ 75	$100
Senior	$ 90	$110	$ 90	$110
Senior Couple	$175	$220	$175	$220

Regular One-Year Pass

Type	Through April 30, 1992		May 1, 1992	
	Resident	Nonresident	Resident	Nonresident
Adult	$315	$390	$350	$440
Youth (under 18)	$235	$295	$265	$330
Couple	$475	$585	$525	$655
Dependent (3−22)*	$100	$150	$150	$190
Senior	$160	$195	$160	$195
Senior Couple	$315	$390	$315	$390

* Dependent passes are available with the purchase of an Adult, Couple, Senior, or Senior Couple Pass. If 18−22 years old, the dependent must be a current full-time college student.

No Increase in the Special Pass

Although pass plan renewals will be taken during all hours of operation, the following schedule outlines the times during which additional staff will be available to provide speedy processing.

April 2–23

Tuesdays and Thursdays	6:00−9:00 pm
Sundays	12:00−3:00 pm

April 25–30

Saturday	11:00 am−2:00 pm
Sunday	12:00−3:00 pm
Monday through Thursday	6:00−9:00 pm

For more information call 791-2338, extension 102

Figure 9-14. Fee scale for Chinn Aquatics and Fitness Center.

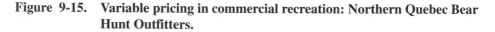

Figure 9-15.   Variable pricing in commercial recreation: Northern Quebec Bear Hunt Outfitters.

otherwise classified as being in a poverty population (preferably utilizing confidentiality procedures to protect the privacy of those receiving such assistance); (3) having a variable fee policy, which requires permits or pass plans in some areas or neighborhoods, and not in others; or (4) providing the possibility of scholarships, sometimes in exchange for a work commitment, for some individuals.

Revenue Factors and Pricing Models

As this chapter has shown, budgetary issues involving program costs and anticipated revenues are critically important in all program planning processes today. In some cases, public and other departments may do sophisticated computer-based projections extending a number of years into the future, for various program elements.

For example, the Sunnyvale, California, Department of Leisure Services develops pricing models for dozens of different classes, events, leagues, and other recreation activities that include projections of future enrollments, costs, and revenues. Figure 9-16 shows such an analysis, excerpted from a more extensive spreadsheet that includes estimates of salaries,

		93/94	96/97	99/100	102/103
4	REVENUE # ____				
5		93/94	96/97	99/100	102/103
6	# Trips/Yr	13	13	13	13
7	Available Space on 2 Busses	94	94	94	94
8	Total Participants for all Trips	657	657	657	657
9	Average occupancy per trip	51	51	51	51
10	Occupancy Rate/Trip	54%	54%	54%	54%
11	Average Fee Per Trip	$37	$39	$42	$44
12	Resident Discount Fee/Trip	$35	$37	$39	$42
13	Lab Fee	$0	$0	$0	$0
14	Trip Conduct Rate	99%	99%	99%	99%
15	Refund factor	90%	90%	90%	90%
16	% Residents	85%	85%	85%	85%
17	% Non Residents	15%	15%	15%	15%
18	Inflation Growth Rate	102%	102%	102%	102%
19	Average House/Trip (Trip Time)	8	8	8	8
20					
21	EXPENDITURES				
22	Coordinator Hours	17	17	17	17
23	Coordinator Cost	$595	$631	$670	$711
24	Asst. Coordinator Hours	10	10	10	10
25	Asst. Coordinator Cost	$255	$271	$287	$305
26	Support Hours for all trips	149	149	149	149
27	Support Cost	$1,788	$1,897	$2,014	$2,137
28	Volunteer Hours (includes registration)	500	500	500	500
29	Cost of Meal/Person	$12	$13	$14	$14
30	Cost of Meals all Trips	$7,096	$7,530	$7,991	$8,480
31	Transportation Cost all Trips	$5,466	$5,801	$6,156	$6,532
32	Staff Hours all Trips (Includes Trip Time)	176	176	176	176
33					
34	COSTS				
35	Cost for all Trips/Yr	$15,200	$16,130	$17,117	$18,165
36	Average Cost/Trip	$1,169	$1,241	$1,317	$1,397
37	Cost per Staff Hour	$86	$92	$97	$103
38	Cost per Participant	$26	$27	$29	$31
39					
40	PARTICIPANT INFO				
41	Total Participants/Yr	657	657	657	657
42	Total Hours/Yr	176	176	176	176
43	Total Participant Hours/Yr	115,632	115,632	115,632	115,632
44	Average Part. Hrs/Trip	8,895	8,895	8,895	8,895

Figure 9-16. Trip pricing model, Sunnyvale, California (1993).

revenues, and market-comparison prices of other public recreation and park departments for similar program activities.

The Program Plan: Process and Product

Clearly, the overall program plan represents a key element in the successful operation of recreation, park, and leisure-service agencies. While it may take many different forms—including seasonal or facility-centered plans—it should be regarded as both process and a product.

The process consists of the sequential stages of developing goals and objectives, conducting needs-assessment and internal and external environmental scans, seeking possible cosponsorship agreements as described in Chapter 5, and implementing the final decision-making steps that have just been presented.

As a product, the program plan provides a comprehensive, invaluable framework for the entire operation of leisure-service delivery during the year. Clearly, the program plan must not be viewed as a rigid, fixed structure that cannot be altered once it has been set on paper or into the computer. Instead, as the following two chapters will show, the plan must be responsive to changing needs and circumstances and to problem situations that may arise during the course of the year.

Summary

The program plan represents a carefully thought-out, comprehensive set of decisions with respect to conducting varied recreational activities and related services during a given time period.

This chapter describes a number of approaches to organizing and presenting program plans, including computer-based analyses, the use of visual or mapped formats, and other methods. It then examines five different aspects of the program plan, including: (1) the selection of activities, based on agency goals and objectives, needs-assessment surveys, and the review of past programs; (2) the scheduling process, including annual, seasonal, weekly, and daily schedules; (3) assigning program elements to appropriate locations; (4) staffing considerations, including the use of part-time personnel; and (5) the use of revenue sources and varied pricing policies as part of program planning.

All of these elements are combined in the decision-making process that results in the program plan, so that ultimately a blueprint is developed that represents the intention of the agency at a given stage, allowing for the option of making needed modifications, based on changes that may occur in the designated period. For leisure-service agencies that have adopted a benefits-driven approach, each stage of the process should emphasize the need to identify and work toward achieving substantial positive personal, social, economic, and environmental benefits for those being served.

Class Assignments and Projects

1. As a class programming exercise, small groups of students can design a set of program activities for one of the following specialized settings: a senior center, a summer day camp for children of elementary-school age, a military base with service men and women and their families, or an environmental center serving school and community needs. As part of this assignment, students should determine the agency's goals and objectives, the formats in which activities will be presented, their scheduling, and program fees and projected revenues, if relevant.

2. As a similar exercise, select a facility, such as a tennis center, pool and aquatic center, bowling center, or center serving youth and adults with disabilities. Identify several target audiences and show how the programmers for this facility may design activities appealing to each of these separate groups.

3. Develop a plan for an overall special event, such as an historic celebration, folk festival, or other large-scale community occasion. Begin by determining the event's theme and overall purposes, and then outline a number of program features, including participatory and spectator elements, that will attract and entertain those attending. Develop a physical layout of the facility where the event will be held, and a schedule of different activities or presentations that will be featured.
Note: Since these assignments represent comprehensive and difficult tasks, if the assignments were to be carried out fully, it should be understood that each project is to be conducted in a preliminary way, with the sketching out of only initial ideas, strategies, and approaches to the task.

References

1. J. Robert Rossman, *Recreation Programming: Designing Leisure Experiences* (Champaign, IL: Sagamore Publishing, 1989), p. 197.

2. Christopher R. Edginton, Carole J. Hanson and Susan R. Edginton, *Leisure Programming: Concepts, Trends, and Professional Practice* (Dubuque, IA: Brown and Benchmark, 1992), p. 158.

3. See Richard G. Kraus and Joseph E. Curtis, *Creative Management in Recreation, Parks and Leisure Services* (St. Louis: Times Mirror/Mosby, 1986), pp. 228–229.

4. Bill Mullins, "Managing Fiscal Transition," *Parks and Recreation,* Oct. 1991, pp. 38–42.

5. Adapted from *Recreation, Sports and Leisure,* July/August 1988, p. 21.

6. Ron McCarville, "Successful Pricing in the Eye of the Beholder," *Parks and Recreation,* Dec. 1992, p. 40.

7. Bertha Cato and John Crofts, "Experimenting with Discount Pricing," *Parks and Recreation,* Dec. 1992, p. 31.

Chapter *10*

The Program in Action: Operational Guidelines

Even after all these preparations have been made and the park and its staff are ready for opening day, there is much more to be done. The Denver metropolitan area has many top-notch recreational facilities competing for the consumer dollar. The Colorado Rockies, the National League's newest baseball team, has been hugely successful in breaking every major league attendance record with crowds averaging well over 50,000 per game.

A number of other major amusement parks, family entertainment centers, movie theaters and countless other attractions are all after limited recreational dollars. In order to remain competitive, Hyland Hills [a publicly owned facility] must advertise and promote Water World as aggressively in the media as any comparable privately owned recreational facility.[1]

This chapter describes the action phase of the recreation, park, and leisure-service program process. It presents guidelines and examples of program implementation that cover the following operational functions:

1. Program publicity designed to promote participation, and the broader concern of year-round public relations.

2. Program registration methods, including procedures for class enrollment and fee payment, and for facilities memberships.

3. Supervision of ongoing activities, including staff performance, the role of agency policies and procedures, and facilities operations.

4. Legal concerns in recreation programming, with emphasis on risk management and safety concerns.

5. Problem-solving and crisis-management strategies.

6. Current emphasis on achieving total program quality and maximum customer/participant satisfaction.

The following learning objectives, established for undergraduate programs in recreation, park resources, and leisure services by the NRPA/AALR Council on Accreditation, are addressed in this chapter:

Understanding of and ability to implement public relations and promotion strategies. (8.33)

Ability to utilize effectively the tools of communication, including technical writing, speech, and audio-visual techniques. (8.34)

Understanding of the principles of risk management planning, and the ability to participate in the development and implementation of a risk management plan. (8.38)

Understanding and ability to utilize diverse interaction and facilitation techniques, including leadership, instructional strategies, counseling techniques, and crisis confrontation and intervention. (7C.01)

Understanding of and ability to apply operational legal concepts related to negligence, specifically the conduct and supervision of activity. (9C.07)

Getting Under Way: Implementing the Program

We are now ready to embark on the key stage of the program development process—actually carrying it out! At this point in program development, all the details of program offerings have been outlined clearly. The schedules of open facilities, classes, workshops, leagues, tournaments, and clubs, and other recreation activities and events, are in the computer or are outlined in flow charts, staff assignment memoranda, or other agency documents.

The challenge now is to make it work, in terms of achieving maximum enrollment, participation, and satisfaction and—at the same time—accomplishing the agency's broader goals and objectives. For this to happen, each phase of the program implementation process must be carried out with a high level of staff commitment and energy, with imagination and creativity, and with a keen sensitivity to the needs of current and potential program participants.

Public Relations and Publicity

The first step is to implement an effective public relations and publicity campaign. Obviously, no leisure-service agency is likely to begin at ground zero, in terms of public awareness and interest. Unless an agency has just been established and is starting with a clean slate, it will have a history of past performance. If the organization has been reasonably successful, it will have a loyal core of past participants who will continue to be actively involved.

However, based on the reality that there is a constant ebb-and-flow in the public's interest—as well as an inevitable turnover in the participants themselves, due to such factors as people moving into and out of communities, changing family situations, or illness and death—it is essential that all new and continuing recreation programs be vigorously and colorfully introduced to the public. This promotion must occur at the onset of a new year or season and at key points throughout the program's week-by-week operation.

The overall term that is applied to this process is *public relations,* which encompasses both the direct forms of publicity that are used to promote immediate interest and involvement, and the long-term, broader concern of maintaining positive community attitudes, customer relations, and effective two-way communications.

Purposes of Public Relations
The primary purpose of an agency's public-relations effort is to reach the public at large with a continuing, comprehensive flow of information designed to promote favorable attitudes toward the agency and involvement in its offerings. A secondary function of public relations is to encourage volunteer leadership, participation in advisory councils or other forms of assistance to the agency, or generally strengthen the public's understanding of the value of recreation and leisure in individual, family, or community life.

Public Relations Channels

The channels through which public relations are carried on include the following: (1) *informational media,* such as newspapers, magazines, television, and radio; and (2) *interpersonal links,* such as advisory groups or recreational councils, appearances before civic groups or departments, task forces, public meetings, or events designed to capture public attention.

Brochures and Newsletters
These represent the most comprehensive and detailed means of disseminating program information to the public. A program brochure usually includes a listing of activities grouped by type, location, or patron group to be served, in an attractive and colorful format that also provides varied information about the agency's facilities, goals, and fees. To illustrate the content of typical brochures, Figures 10-1 and 10-2 show the table-of-contents pages of two such brochures.

Contents

Figure 10-1.   Contents page of New York City YWCA program brochure.

In addition, a more narrowly focused program brochure may present up-to-date information about a single important program or facility, or services designed for a particular group of participants, such as those with disabilities. Customarily activities and services are grouped within brochures, by type, by those being served, or by location. Usually each program offering is accompanied by a brief description, an indication of the age group(s) served, and fees or charges, if any. Individual listings may also include details of location, times and dates activities are being offered, or other needed information.

A brochure designed to publicize a single facility or activity is generally quite brief. However, brochures may be profusely illustrated and attractively designed, as shown in Figure 10-3, the brochure for the Catholic Youth Organization's Camp Christopher, in Akron, Ohio, or Figure 10-4, the brochure for the Chinn Aquatics and Fitness Center in Prince William County, Virginia.

Newsletters may be used to present similar messages to the public—in a slightly different form usually featuring announcements or brief articles in a newspaper-like format that is published and distributed to members or community residents on a monthly or quarterly basis. Newsletters usually are intended to achieve general public relations goals, rather than to promote attendance at a specific program offering.

Brochures and newsletters may be distributed in several ways: (1) direct mail to all individuals or families currently involved in agency programs, or to a mailing list that may include those registered over a period of recent years; (2) a general mailing to all residents

CITY OF KAMLOOPS
PARKS & RECREATION SERVICE

What's Inside...

Parks and Recreation Services Information	3
Registration Information	4
Registration Forms	5
Pre-School Programs	6 - 13
Children's Programs	15 - 18
Teen Programs	19 - 22
Adult Education	23 - 30
Sports	33 - 37
Fitness	38 - 42
Seniors	44 - 47
Aquatics	48 - 60
Art Gallery	61
Museum	62 - 63
Parks Information	64 - 67
Grant Programs	69
Facilities - Arenas and Pools	70 - 71
Special Needs	72
Community Groups & Organizations	73 - 85
Back Page	88

REGISTRATION FORMS	86 & 87
REGISTRATION PROCEDURES	4

Figure 10-2. Contents page of Kamloops, British Columbia, Canada, Parks and Recreation Brochure.

in the community, or to those in specific target neighborhoods; (3) handouts in all park and recreation facilities, in municipal or town halls, or through community organizations such as Parent-Teacher Associations, churches, or other civic groups; or (4) seasonal magazine-like supplements inserted in a community's newspaper.

CYO and Community Services / Diocese of Cleveland
404 Elbon Ave.
Akron, Ohio 44306-1500

No matter where you are located in the Cleveland Diocese . . .
you are minutes from CYO Camp Christopher. Camp
Christopher is situated in the heart of the Cleveland Diocese.
It is located in the scenic rolling countryside of Bath, Ohio at
the corner of Ira and N. Hametown Roads, one and one-half
miles west of Cleveland-Massillon Road, with easy access from
all points.

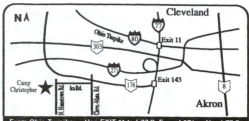

From Ohio Turpike — Use EXIT 11 to I-77 S; From I-271 — Use I-77 S
to Akron; From Cleveland — Use I-77 S to Akron. Get Off at EXIT NO.
143 - US 176 - RICHFIELD. Turn Right at Stop sign. Go to 1st Light -
BRECKSVILLE/CLEVE.-MASS. RD. and turn Left. Take to 2nd Light -
IRA Rd. - turn Right. Follow approximately 3 miles to N. HAMETOWN
RD. Camp Christopher is at the intersection of IRA and N.
HAMETOWN Rds.

From I-71 S take RT. 18 to Akron. Get on I-77 N to Cleveland. From
I-77 N — First exit past US 18 is Ghent Rd. exit. Turn Left. Proceed
to 2nd Light - IRA Rd. - turn Left and see the above

Figure 10-3.   Cover of brochure for C.Y.O. Camp Christopher, Akron, Ohio.

Figure 10-4. **Brochure of Chinn Aquatics and Fitness Center, Prince William County, Virginia, Park Authority.**

News Releases and Articles

Newspaper stories or magazine articles generally are used to promote specific programs shortly before the point of initiation, or registration. They may also be used to provide information about an overall program, or to highlight innovative recreation, park, and leisure-service activities and their positive outcomes. Because of their immediacy, newspaper stories are useful for achieving quick results, while magazine articles have a longer period of production and must be planned for well in advance.

Guidelines for News Releases

Usually, news releases are brief summaries of newsworthy events or programs, human interest stories, or other agency-connected news, and they may be the impetus for calling press conferences or encouraging newspaper editors to send reporters to gather fuller information. A good news release has the following characteristics:

1. It should be kept simple and factual, and should be written in a lively, straightforward style, without editorializing. The lead, or first paragraph, should contain a summary of the story's main points, including the who, what, when, where, and how of the program.
2. The release should be limited to one page, if possible, with less important information in the later paragraphs, since these tend to be cut if space is limited.
3. Material should be neatly typed, with adequate margins and headings. The release should include the department's name and telephone number at the top, and should be submitted with sufficient lead time to permit follow-up and editing.

Magazine articles should be written for local or regional publications and for special-interest magazines that would find recreation programs and events to be of interest, such as those dealing with hobbies, tourism, cultural activities, or sports. Generally, magazine articles should describe particularly interesting or innovative program elements or outcomes, and should be longer and written with greater flair than newspaper stories.

A magazine article should be prepared in conjunction with direct contact with the editor, preferably in advance of writing or sending the article, and it is helpful to prepare high-quality photographs to illustrate it, since picture stories are usually more attractive to editors than solid text.

Use of Mass Media: Television and Radio

Television and radio also provide useful means of reaching the public directly via announcements of interesting programs and events, or via coverage of programs that may have a strong public relations impact.

Other forms of visual publicity media include the use of specially prepared motion pictures or videotapes that may be sent out free of charge for showing at community groups; slide-show talks to be presented by members of the agency's staff; and exhibits and displays, or action demonstrations, to be featured in schools, libraries, civic plazas, or public squares, or other popular locations. Tours, open houses, and similar events open to the public may also accompany the opening of new facilities or the introduction of innovative or newsworthy programs.

Within the marketing framework, effective public relations and publicity campaigns cannot be dismissed as part-time or casual functions to be handled in an amateurish way. Since public relations contributes to the key purposes of leisure-service agencies—involving public support and program participation, it requires careful planning and thorough, professional execution.

Innovative Promotion: San Jose Sharks

Frequently, commercial recreation enterprises, including professional sports teams, demonstrate great ingenuity in developing unusual promotional campaigns. For example, when the San Jose Sharks joined the National Hockey League in 1991, predictions were that it would be difficult to arouse public interest in a traditionally non-hockey northern California community. However, with the help of an attractive logo and a generous community development program known as "Sharks and Parks," in which the hockey club assisted hundreds of local recreation and park agencies throughout the region in establishing street hockey leagues for youth, the Sharks have become immensely successful.[2]

Incentive Programming: Ashland Oil

Within organizations that sponsor recreation and fitness programs for their own members or employees, varied types of incentive awards may be used to promote high levels of participation. Ashland, Inc., is a diversified energy supplier with more than 33,000 employees worldwide, almost 20,000 of them in three Kentucky locations. The company initiated a diversified program of 38 different recreational, fitness, and sporting activities, awarding points for participation at 100-, 250-, and 500-point levels, with such rewards as T-shirts, sweatshirts, jackets, and athletic bags. This approach evolved into monthly programs focusing on fitness standards relating to frequency, intensity, and duration. David Dale writes:

> *A typical incentive program would be our "Mount Everest Challenge" where employees would walk, run, stair climb or cross-country ski to the top of Mount Everest. . . . Other incentive programs: "The Ultimate Triathlon" using running, walking, cycling and stair climbing. A "Road to Indy" promotes our Valvoline Group as it traces the mileage from our fitness centers to the Indianapolis 500 site in Indianapolis. Our upcoming new program called "Calorie Countdown" gives all fitness activities a calorie equivalency and people must burn 5,000 calories in a month to make the incentive.[3]*

The Ashland fitness centers have been integrated into the mainstream of the company, cooperating closely with medical and safety departments, and aimed at the development of healthy and positive lifestyle changes. The operation of the fitness centers clearly is benefits-driven, in that the program is purposefully designed to lower employees' compensation claims, lost time, injuries, absenteeism, and use of health-care systems—and to create a higher level of morale and enthusiasm among all participants.

Overall Thrust of Public Relations

Beyond the sharply focused emphasis of publicity on directly promoting recreation programs, the overall leisure-service profession has become increasingly aware of its need to communicate more effectively with the public, in a variety of ways. Alan Bright points out that more effective communication

> *. . . can help managers identify the recreation preferences of diverse groups, obtain support for plans and programs, enhance visitor enjoyment through interpretation, add to the educational experience of students in our school systems, reduce resource impact and visitor conflicts in recreation settings, inform the public about recreation program offerings, and manage vandalism and depreciative behavior in recreation settings.*[4]

Increasingly, professional recreation and park societies have sought to enrich the public's understanding of the importance of recreation, or to increase its support for specific leisure-related programs. For example, the Parks and Recreation Federation of Ontario, Canada, has established a Speakers' Bureau designed to equip local agencies and professionals with the tools needed to reach varied audiences and community groups with a positive leisure-related message.

Similarly, many municipal recreation and park agencies have sponsored community programs to celebrate "July is Recreation and Parks Month," in cooperation with the National Recreation and Park Association (see Figure 10-5). Such campaigns serve to enhance the public's awareness of recreation and leisure, and to promote the agency's own programs.

The Program Registration Process

The program registration process is a second key element in the efficient operation of recreation, park, and leisure-service programs. Registration is normally a required procedure when any recreation program or facility is formally scheduled or designated for use by a specific number of individuals or groups, or requires payment of a fee.

Registration covers a wide range of program applications, including such examples as signing a child up for a summer day camp, registering a team in a softball or bowling league, renting a campsite in a state park, reserving a slot for a scheduled trip or outing, and dozens of other recreation situations. It is obviously needed when the number of openings, spaces, or pieces of equipment to be used is limited. It is also essential when it is necessary to confirm the number of program participants in advance, in order to determine whether there is sufficient registration to justify holding a class, workshop, or other event. Registration is also a means of assigning individuals to program involvement at the appropriate levels of skill or experience.

Because registration may represent the first contact of the participant with the leisure-service agency, and because enrollment may suffer if it is not carried on efficiently, a primary consideration should be the participant's convenience and satisfaction with the procedure.

JULY IS RECREATION AND PARKS MONTH

INSERT YOUR LOGO HERE

WHEREAS,   physical recreation and meaningful leisure experiences contribute to physical and mental well-being as well as the overall quality of life; and

WHEREAS,   community recreation and leisure opportunities create socially beneficial connections between and among individuals, groups, and communities; and

WHEREAS,   parks and recreation services provide preventative health benefits, support more productive workforces, enhance the desirability of locations for business and families, and stimulate tourism revenues to increase a total community economic development model; and

WHEREAS,   the provision and preservation of parks and open spaces are both an investment and insurance plan for our collective quality of life;

NOW, THEREFORE, BE IT RESOLVED THAT JULY HAS BEEN DESIGNATED AS RECREATION AND PARKS MONTH by the National Recreation and Park Association; and

BE IT FURTHER RESOLVED THAT all citizens of this great city join in this nationwide celebration bringing recognition to all the benefits derived from quality public and private recreation and park resources at the local level.

Signed this first day of July, 1994.

_____

Figure 10-5. Sample proclamation of "July is Recreation and Parks Month," used by community recreation and park agencies.

Mail-In Registration

This procedure is convenient for the participant, if he or she fills out the forms correctly, and if there are no complications, such as a class being filled, the need to provide more information about the activity, or the possibility of applications being lost. Figure 10-6 is an example of a registration form that may be mailed or submitted in person. It includes information about early registration procedures, class cancellation, refunding, and waiting-list arrangements.

In-Person Central Registration

In this procedure, those wishing to enroll must apply in person at a single central location, such as the department's main office, or another recreation center or major facility. Staff members conducting registration should be familiar with all elements of the various programs and should be able to provide immediate information regarding the availability of classes or activities.

24   Registration Information

1. Early Registration Day (March 26 from 9 - 11 am) for Oakland Residents Only. Open registration continues during regular office hours 9:00 - 5:00 pm on March 28.

2. Classes without sufficient advance registration may be cancelled. Patrons will be notified by phone and may transfer classes or get a full refund.

3. Refunds will be given up to one working day before a class or event is scheduled to begin with a 15% service charge being withheld. NO REFUNDS WILL BE MADE AFTER THIS TIME. Please allow 3 - 4 weeks for refunds to be processed.

4. A $5.00 fee will be charged for all returned checks.

5. A $2.00 per class fee will be charged for non-resident of Oakland.

6. Waiting lists are kept for full classes. You will be notified if openings occur and a spot will be held for only 48 hours. If you can not be reached, the next person will be notified.

7. Payment should be made by check & payable to MONTCLAIR RECREATION CENTER ADVISORY COUNCIL. To register by mail return a registration form and a check to Montclair Recreation Center, 6300 Moraga Ave., Oakland, 94611. Mailed in registration will be process after 11:00 am on March 26, in order received.

8. If you register by mail, you will NOT be notified if your registration is accepted; just come to the first class.

FOR YOUR RECORDS

Class	Day	Time

Registration Forms   25

Name:_____

Child's Name:_____ Age:_____

Address:_____ City:_____ Zip:_____

Home #:_____ Work #:_____

Emergency #:_____

The above named child has my permission to participate in the Montclair Recreation Center programs. I understand the City of Oakland does not assume liability in case of injury to my child.

Parent/Guardian's Signature:_____ Date:_____

Alpha	Age	Class(1st choice)	Class(2nd choice)	Fee

Non-Oakland Residents Fee - $2.00 per class $_____

TOTAL AMOUNT $_____

Name:_____

Child's Name:_____ Age:_____

Address:_____ City:_____ Zip:_____

Home #:_____ Work #:_____

Emergency #:_____

The above named child has my permission to participate in the Montclair Recreation Center programs. I understand the City of Oakland does not assume liability in case of injury to my child.

Parent/Guardian's Signature:_____ Date:_____

Alpha	Age	Class(1st choice)	Class(2nd choice)	Fee

Non-Oakland Residents Fee - $2.00 per class $_____

TOTAL AMOUNT $_____

Figure 10-6.   Registration form used by Montclair Recreation Center, Oakland, California.

This approach is efficient from the perspective of being carried on in a single, well-known location, and having a central fee collection procedure. Its weakness is that participants are not able to meet directly with the program's supervisor or leader to ask questions, and are not able to see the facilities involved. This approach may also result in excessively long lines, if registration for numerous different programs is being held at the same time. For this reason, it may be advisable to spread the process over a period of several days.

Telephone Registration

Telephone registration is a convenient approach from a mechanical standpoint, in that there is no need to handle money directly; payment may be made by credit card, or at the first meeting of the program involved. Telephone registration has the disadvantage of not providing a face-to-face encounter between the participant and staff members that might provide fuller information about the activity. However, for routine forms of registration, it can be extremely useful, since it does not require registrants going to a special location or waiting in line.

For example, the Department of Parks, Recreation and Conservation of Westchester County, New York, uses a automated telephone registration system for making "tee-time" reservations at its five golf courses (see Figure 10-7). A person who calls normally has a county park pass and a personal identification number (PIN), used to respond to a series of automated verbal prompts through which the preferred day of the week, number of golfers, time of day, and course of the participant's choice may be entered, and the arrangement confirmed.

In-Person Registration at Program Site

In this procedure, individuals register for a given activity at the location where the program or event will take place, such as a performing arts center, sports complex, or senior center. While this method has the advantage of bringing participants face-to-face with the staff members who will direct the activity, and enabling them to become familiar with the facility, it may make registering more difficult for individuals who are planning to attend more than one program. Many departments use several different registration methods, as shown in Figure 10-8.

Use of Computers

Whatever registration method is used, growing numbers of leisure-service agencies are employing computer technology to improve organizational efficiency. Through terminals located at different centers and registration points, staff members are able to gain instant access to up-to-date registration totals for all classes or activities in the data base. Needed decisions on admission to activities, confirmation of events or courses, refunds, and similar matters can be made promptly and efficiently, and data for periodic and final reports can be assembled easily.

Within specific categories of recreational activity, computers have simplified the tasks of scheduling programs and registering participants. For example, the travel and tourism industry has become almost totally automated, with computer-based reservations providing an instant means of confirming airline or hotel reservations, car rentals, or other ele-

AUTOMATED TEE TIME RESERVATION SYSTEM

WESTCHESTER COUNTY DEPARTMENT OF PARKS, RECREATION AND CONSERVATION

Dunwoodie Golf Course
Mohansic Golf Course
Saxon Woods Golf Course
Sprain Lake Golf Course
Maple Moor Golf Course

(914) 285-GOLF

ANDREW P. O'ROURKE, County Executive
Barry C. Samuel, Acting Commissioner
Department of Parks,
Recreation & Conservation
Westchester County

QUICK GUIDE TO

TEE TIME RESERVATION SYSTEM

TO MAKE THE CALL:

- In order to access the system, you must use a touch-tone phone.

- Dial (914)285-GOLF (285-4653) to reserve a tee time.

- Tee times are available by phone reservation
  Weekends - 8 a.m. to 5:45 p.m.
  Weekdays - 9 a.m. to 5:45 p.m.

- For Westchester County Park Pass holders, reservations can be made up to 7 days in advance. (Example: reservations for Saturday, May 8, will start being accepted after 7 p.m. on Saturday, May 1.)

- For non-Park Pass holders, reservations can be made up to 5 days in advance.

- If you need assistance making a reservation, call (914)593-2609, Monday through Friday, 9 a.m. to 4 p.m.

WHEN THE MESSAGE BEGINS:

Listen closely to all instructions and make the appropriate choices when requested to do so. At the end of the call, you will be allowed to confirm your reservation (by pressing 1), or change it (by pressing 2).

TO RESERVE A TEE TIME:

Press 1 in response to opening prompt. Then, in response to the subsequent prompts and instructions, use the push buttons on your telephone to:

1. Enter the 9-digit personal identification number (PIN) located on the front of your Pass, beneath the bar code. Persons without a Westchester County Park Pass will be asked to enter their Social Security number.

ANDREW P. O'ROURKE
County Executive
Barry C. Samuel, Acting Commissioner
Department of Parks,
Recreation & Conservation
Westchester County

Figure 10-7.   Westchester County golf reservation system.

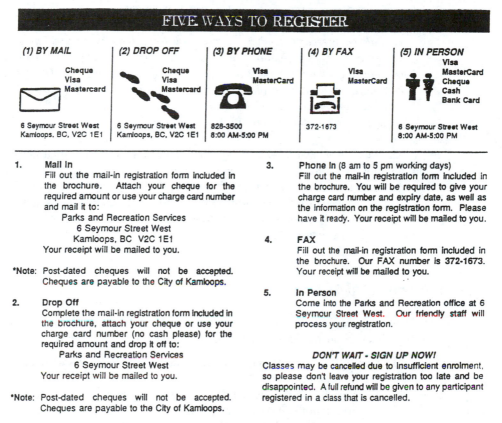

Figure 10-8. **Kamloops, British Columbia, Canada, program registration form.**

ments in a travel package. Similarly, in large-scale intramural sports programs, computers are used to organize and schedule hundreds of teams, determine student eligibility, record scores, identify officials, and maintain total statistics for each team and for league play or tournaments through the year.

Beyond this, computer technology is often used to provide information to potential participants at the point of entry. Travelers to major federal or state parks, or to major tourist regions within a state, may be helped to select hiking trails suited to their personal capabilities and preferences, or to select other destinations through a sequence of questions, with the computer providing appropriate choices as the traveler uses a touch-screen mechanism or simple keyboard operations.

Membership and Access Applications
Extending beyond the registration period, computers are used to record membership information that includes personal details, type of membership, and issue or expiration date.

Photo identification cards may be used to control access, as in the case of a fitness club or other private-membership facility. Edward Szillat writes that more advanced systems designed for member recognition and access management

> . . . . *also may record member characteristics—such as eye or hand images or fingerprints—for identification purposes. . . . Daily member access management includes identifying members as they enter and recording visits. The system may be programmed to flag expired memberships, fraudulent card use, or other problems. It may record each visit by manual computer entry, bar code or magnetic strip reading, or other electronic access devices.*[5]

The ideal membership system, Szillat continues, requires minimal labor to maintain and monitor, but keeps accurate records regarding all membership and participation functions. Pointing out that today's recreation and park agencies often have multiple membership categories with different program features, he concludes that the system of choice is a computer-based registration and identification method that meets the agency's various control needs in a cost-effective way.

Ongoing Program Operations

Following the registration process, as recreation programs get under way, it is essential to ensure that they are carried out with full commitment to the following practices:

1. Careful adherence to stated agency policies and procedures within all areas of program operations.
2. Staff members carrying out their assigned functions with a high degree of enthusiasm and professional commitment.
3. Consistent emphasis on participant and staff safety, particularly in such areas as aquatics, active sports and games, outdoor recreation, and playground use, through a comprehensive risk-management program.
4. Effective supervisory practices with respect to program activities, fiscal management, facility maintenance, and prompt response to problem situations, through conflict-resolution or crisis-management procedures.

Adherence to Agency Policies and Procedures

As a framework for maintaining staff efficiency and program quality, most recreation, park, and leisure-service agencies develop a comprehensive set of approved policies and required procedures that govern program operations. As described on page 24, policies refer to general guidelines based on the agency's philosophical beliefs and overall mission.

Procedural guidelines are much more specific than policies and present detailed rules for the conduct of programs. They may be drawn from varied sources but generally are assembled in leaders' manuals or operational booklets that are used in orientation or in-service training sessions for leaders.

Examples of Policies and Procedures

An example of how an organization's fundamental beliefs may be expressed in its program-planning guidelines may be found in the manuals prepared by the Mormon Church for church youth and adult groups in various areas of sports, creative, and social activities. For example, in a detailed manual on theater programming, the church's values are illustrated by a description of what the church considers to be good theater, and by a specific list of themes or forms of behavior or relationships that should be avoided in church-sponsored drama programs.

As another illustration, the National Board of Directors of the Girl Scouts of the U.S.A. has developed a list of twenty-two policies that each local or regional council must agree to enforce in its application for a Girl Scout charter. These policies are intended to uphold the values of the Girl Scout movement and to protect the organization against misuse or exploitation. They deal with such subjects as membership admission qualifications, the place of religion in girl scouting, health and safety, political or legislative activity, fund-raising methods, and permission for commercial endorsements involving the organization.

In many cases, program guidelines outline strict procedures in areas that might result in lawsuits or other legal problems, if they are not dealt with properly. For example, Little League Baseball publishes a 135-page operating manual that deals with all aspects of programming, from national administration to coaching procedures and the use of equipment. One major area involves principles of conduct, in which policies about sexual harassment are presented, beginning with a statement of Little League Policy:

> *It is the policy of Little League Baseball Incorporated that all of the parties involved in the operation of chartered Little Leagues will provide a League and District Administrator operational environment which is free of all forms of discrimination, including incidents of sexual harassment. No individual shall be subjected to verbal or physical sexual behavior. Sexual harassment will be treated as misconduct, and may result in the application of appropriate corrective action up to and including dismissal.[6]*

Following this policy statement, the manual presents a detailed definition of forms of sexual harassment, report procedures, and the responsibilities of Little League officials in dealing with the problem, if it should appear.

Day Camp Guidelines

Another example of policies and procedures is found in the Summer Day Camp Operations Manual of the Fort Worth, Texas, Park and Recreation Department. The manual provides extensive guidelines dealing with the following:

> *the background and objectives of the day-camp program; suggested schedules and general duties of recreation leaders; procedures for field trips; discipline guidelines; a listing of all Fort Worth Park and Recreation Department centers and pools, with emergency numbers; plus a number of forms for parent/guardian sign-in and -out records, daily lesson plans, class enrollment and attendance records, volunteer applications, and similar forms.*

To illustrate its procedural guidelines, the Summer Day Camp Operations Manual outlines the following rules for field trips to such settings as swimming pools, roller-skating rinks, bowling alleys, zoos and nature centers, and other special attractions:

Procedures for Field Trips

Buses or vans *must* be identified with the *site name* (beginning and ending point).

Participants *must* wear name tags.

Staff and volunteers *must* wear name tags.

Site supervisor should accompany participants.

Parental permission slip *must* be on file for each participant.

Lists of names, addresses, emergency phone numbers, trip location, departure and return times, and names of staff must be left *at the park, taken on the trip,* and *routed to the Assistant Director of Programs' office* prior to the trip.

Head counts *must* be taken *both at the beginning and at the end of the trip.*

Restroom and water trips must be done in groups, and *must be accompanied by staff persons; never send children on their own.*

If the group is split, staff persons *must* accompany each group.

These guidelines illustrate a critical need to protect the safety and well-being of program participants. Typically, because of growing concern about the physical or sexual abuse of children, which has led to highly publicized court cases involving abuse by adult religious leaders, directors of private nurseries or day camps, scout leaders, and others, many leisure-service agencies have formulated very strict rules about adult leaders not touching children, being alone with them in cars, or similar actions.

Legal Concerns and Risk Management

Because of the growing threat of negligence lawsuits stemming from accidents occurring in recreation, park, and leisure-service programs, as well as a genuine concern about the safety of participants, all leisure-service agencies today normally have policies and procedures designed to prevent or minimize potential program-related accidents. While the risk of injury or death is highest in such outdoor recreation pursuits as sky-diving, mountain climbing, scuba diving, hang-gliding or skiing, or in active team sports such as football, ice hockey, or basketball, the reality is that a wide range of program elements involve safety hazard. Arts and crafts that make use of chemicals, cutting tools, or power tools also have a high hazard factor. Sledding, in-line skating, and skateboarding frequently result in accidents.

Leisure-service agencies may minimize the threat of accidents in several ways: (1) by ensuring that all facilities and equipment are as safe and well maintained as possible; (2) by establishing strict rules and procedures governing participant behavior and the supervisory responsibilities of leaders; and (3) by initiating a total risk-management plan that includes systematic assessment of all accidents and injuries and their causes, safety education of all participants and staff members, and a set of detailed procedures to be followed in the case of accidents, in terms of first aid or lifesaving methods, notification of parents and guardians, requesting emergency assistance, or filling out accident reports.

Playground Safety

This area represents the chief concern of public recreation and park officials who seek assistance from the National Recreation and Park Association. As a result, the National Playground Safety Institute and the U.S. Consumer Product Safety Commission have published extensive guidelines and standards that include playground inspection and audit forms, staff training outlines, and recommended procedures for preventing injuries. One major concern has to do with playground equipment, in terms of its design, selection, and maintenance. Ken Kutska writes:

> Seventy percent of all playground injuries are caused by falls. Replace hard surfacing with appropriate impact-attenuation surfacing.
>
> Cover over, pad, or remove exposed concrete footings. Fix, dispose of or remove broken equipment.
>
> Remove broken glass and other debris from the playground area.
>
> Replace worn swing chains and connectors.
>
> Remove equipment not recommended for public playgrounds according to the new CPSC [Consumer Product Safety Commission] Guidelines, such as heavy flying animal swings, multiple occupancy swings . . . rope swings, swinging exercise rings, and trapeze bars.
>
> Remove equipment that is known to have caused a reported injury because of poor maintenance, lack of repairs, or poor design that is not in compliance with the CPSC guidelines or ASTM [American Society for Testing and Materials] standards.[7]

Beyond such recommendations, recreation leaders are urged to be proactive in their efforts to prevent accidents, by improving maintenance and inspection procedures, training staff members, carrying out appropriate documentation, and similar practices. Departments also should develop and enforce other safety rules governing playground activities, such as:

1. No bicycling, skateboarding, or roller-skating, except in areas specifically designed for these purposes.

2. Requiring appropriate safety equipment, such as batting helmets, for specific activities.

3. Separating activity areas with a potential for causing injuries, such as baseball fields, from other activity areas, such as outdoor picnic areas, play equipment for young children, or shuffleboard courts for elderly residents.

4. Strict rules governing all active games and sports, the use of possibly dangerous equipment or materials in arts and crafts, or other activities with the potential for injury.

Another area of concern that requires playground staff training and explicit guidelines is weather-related problems, such as risks stemming from lightning, heat exhaustion, and similar causes.

Water Safety

More deaths are attributable to drowning than to any other single cause, in outdoor recreation programs. Deaths may be linked to swimming, boating, scuba diving, waterskiing, and a number of other leisure pursuits and settings. Water safety therefore represents a major concern for recreation, park, and leisure-service program managers who operate swimming pools, beaches, or other types of aquatic facilities or programs.

Natural swimming locations like ponds, lakes, or oceanfront beaches represent a special problem because of the extensive areas to be covered, the water opacity and uneven depths involved, and surf and undertow dangers, particularly on ocean beach swimming areas.

Pool Safety.   To maintain swimming-pool safety, all recreation, park, and leisure-service agencies have clear responsibilities for:

1. Employing only qualified and certified life-saving or water-safety personnel, and assuring that they have appropriate orientations or pre-service training sessions.

2. Defining a strict set of rules, both for participants in the pool (related to diving, horseplay, staying within designated areas of the pool, or adhering to a buddy system) and for lifeguards on duty.

3. Other safety procedures, such as keeping needed rescue equipment on hand; maintaining proper chemical balance in the pool water; posting on towers and the perimeter of the pool the exact schedules of lifeguards, and enforcing those schedules; keeping dressing rooms, lockers, and all other pool areas clean, free of debris or broken glass; and maintaining fences and, if necessary, night-time patrols to prevent intruders or surreptitious swimmers.

In some cases, pool-management procedures may be extremely complex. For example, some large recreation and park departments have established water-play parks with wave pools that impose additional safety hazards. To illustrate, the Oakland County, Michigan, Parks and Recreation Commission operates an extensive water-play park with a wave pool and water slides, with several different depth areas and degrees of water turbulence. The park's operational manual for pool personnel contains a detailed diagram of the pool facility designating these areas, accompanied by rules governing the behavior of swimmers in each location, entry into roped- or chained-off areas, and precise lifesaving procedures, particularly in the wave-impact areas of the pool.

Other Accident-Risk Areas

Increasingly, both state governments and private-industry associations are instituting regulations to promote participant safety in such areas as bicycle riding and skateboarding; scuba diving and boating, including the use of jet skis; and varied forms of outdoor adventure recreation activities, such as mountain climbing. In some cases, agencies requiring that participants undergo mandatory education programs and gain certification, or that they wear designated safety equipment or take part in high-risk activities only in approved areas.

Managing Special Events

Finally, many recreation and park departments have been forced to consider the safety risks associated with their sponsorship of major forms of entertainment events, such as rock concerts, where crowd control and the risk of antisocial, violent behavior, or illegal drug use have represented a continuing problem.

When special events are on a large scale, attracting hundreds or thousands of spectators or participants, they may require complex logistical arrangements and preparation over a period of time. For example, the Department of Recreation and Parks of Nassau County, New York, issues the following guidelines to groups planning events in parks:

1. All plans for special events must be screened by the Assistant to the Superintendent for Program Development, to be cleared by the Park Director.
2. Each step of the program must be carefully planned, using a map of the individual park that shows all program aspects, such as access, parking, seating areas, program locations, etc.
3. In planning program activities, consider age, gender, and probable number of participants, the leadership and supplies needed, the goals of the program, possible hazards, and cost factors.
4. Develop options in case of adverse weather conditions, such as moving location to indoor facility, cancellation or postponement to "rain date."

5. Use all appropriate means to inform public of event, and make advance arrangements for photo coverage, preparation of signs and posters, and directional signs within the park.
6. Plan for needed crowd control, with stanchions, ropes and other control barriers as needed, along with police coverage for traffic entrance and exiting.
7. Make sure you have adequate first aid and emergency coverage, and portable toilets as needed, if department building with toilet facilities is not accessible or sufficient.
8. Determine whether pre-registration is necessary and plan accordingly. If there is to be registration at the event, or ticket sales, make necessary arrangements for tables and personnel.
9. Make maximum use of volunteers to cover or assist in varied program functions, with careful briefing or orientation, and ongoing supervision by regular staff members.
10. Make a full report on the special event, using department forms, and submit to the Special Events Director through the Office of the Park Director for review, filing and use for future planning.

Effective Supervisory Practices

In terms of successful program operations, the supervisor is responsible for making sure that all program plans are carried out in accordance with agency guidelines, that all leaders—whether paid or volunteer—are carrying out their tasks properly, and for dealing with problems or changing needs in a creative and responsive way.

In the past, supervision was viewed in a relatively authoritarian way, with little opportunity for leaders to have meaningful input into program planning or decisions. Today, there is much greater emphasis on a participative, humanistic approach to staff relationships. Instead of being viewed as a punitive figure, the supervisor is regarded essentially as a coach and a counselor, with the primary concern of motivating leaders to do their best work. The supervisor must also play a key role in dealing with problem situations that may occur during the course of program operations.

Problem Solving and Crisis Management

Obviously, the goal in conducting successful program operations is to have all activities and events carried on in a smooth, untroubled way, with a high level of patron participation and satisfaction, maximum financial return from fee-generating program elements, and full accomplishment of agency goals.

The reality, of course, is that few human enterprises are invariably successful. Instead, numerous problems may occur during the course of any recreation, park, and leisure-service program. These may involve leaders performing inconsistently, personality conflicts among participants, accidents and injuries, poor or declining attendance, breakdowns in facilities or support services, and varied other difficulties.

Some problems may be handled routinely, based on an agency's procedural guidelines, with the leader or supervisor making a simple decision or ruling. Others may require a fuller process of negotiation or administrative consultation, a staff reassignment, or other solution. Still other, more deep-seated problems may have their roots in the agency's structure, or in other neighborhood or community social conditions.

Common Examples of Problem Situations

Within leisure-service agencies themselves, programs may be affected by such problems as work overloads, administrative red tape, lack of adequate staff or maintenance support, conflicting goals or priorities, or other difficulties stemming from poor communication or interpersonal friction among staff members.

In general, such problems are at two levels:

1. Fairly routine kinds of difficulties that may be resolved by application of agency policies governing the situation, or by staff members' actions that mediate a situation and are generally acceptable to all parties involved; and

2. More serious problems, in terms of the issues involved, the deep-rootedness or longevity of the difficulty, its impact on the overall program, or the unwillingness of the people involved to accept agency leaders' decisions or actions.

Among program participants, conflicts may be caused by different leisure-related values and interests. For example, in wilderness recreation, there may be serious conflicts between recreationists who prefer active, noisy forms of travel such as snowmobiling or power-boating, and others who are environmentally minded and prefer cross-country skiing or canoeing.

Particularly in urban settings, there may be problems that stem from gender-related or race-related factors. In one large city, there have been numerous examples of male teenagers intimidating and sexually harassing girls in city pools, to the point that agency supervisors considered the possible need to segregate swimming by gender.[8] In another large city, there were race-related problems stemming from the rejection of a new white playground leader by primarily African American neighborhood youth, and there was a concerted attempt to prevent private, nonprofit rowing clubs from holding major regattas using public facilities, because their membership had few minority-group rowers.[9]

Problem-Solving Approaches

In the first type of situation, quick and automatic application of appropriate procedures is likely to be successful. In the more serious problem situations, it may be necessary to go through a process of investigation, analysis, discussion, and finally action. Elsewhere, the author has identified the sequence of steps that are commonly taken in dealing with such problems:

1. Recognize the problem, including not only its symptoms but also its apparent causes. This may involve varied types of difficulties such as: (1) problems of staff functioning or interpersonal relationships; (2) problems of interdepartmental or interagency relationships; (3) problems of community relationships; (4) problems between staff members and participants; or (5) problems of inadequate finances or other difficulties in the agency's environment.

2. Assign responsibility for solving the problem. This may be the task of a single program leader or supervisor or may be assigned to a small group or "task force" of staff members, depending on its severity and the resources required. At the same time, the desired objectives of the problem solution should be defined.

3. Investigate the problem and gather all relevant data. This may involve the examination of records, direct observation of a program or facility, interviews with concerned parties, or even formal hearings or other investigative sessions.

4. Identify alternative solutions. Here, several different strategies for solving the problem may be identified and balanced with each other both in their probable degree of success and in the difficulty that might be experienced in implementing them.

5. The solution that appears most logical and most likely to be successful, as well as the most feasible in administration, should be selected and put into action. When this is done, it is usually wise to inform all parties of the decision that has been reached or ideally to have this occur as part of the shared problem-solving effort.

6. When the problem-solving solution has been implemented, it must be carefully monitored and its success evaluated. If it is *not* working, or if new difficulties appear, reviewing the strategy that has been chosen and trying a new solution may be necessary.[10]

Race, Disability, and Gender Issues

In some cases, individual problems may be recognized as part of a broader complex of social, environmental, economic, or other concerns, and must be approached within the larger context. There is growing awareness that recreation, park, and leisure-service agencies have an important role to play in race relations and multicultural programming. For example, in Dallas, Texas, it was found that issues of racial and cultural sensitivity were affecting the operation of the city's Park and Recreation Department in numerous ways. Staff members had to face such questions as these:

> *Is an independent contractor at a public tennis facility treating African American and Hispanic patrons with the same respect as white patrons? Should a statue of*

a Confederate hero be removed from a Dallas park for the sake of patriotism and because it is an insult to liberal citizens [or racial minorities]?[11]

In an effort to get at the roots of this continuing problem, the Dallas Park and Recreation Department Board established a Minority Affairs Committee with substantial representation from both African American and Latino populations. The functions of this committee included examining and debating all issues related to interracial and intercultural programming, and making recommendations to the full board, in such areas as programming, fees and budget policies, special events, and overall policy development.

In many cases, program-related problems may have serious legal implications. Often this is the case with respect to issues of gender- or disability-linked discrimination. James Kozlowski, for example, cites numerous examples of lawsuits based on such claims. In one such case, Little League Baseball, Inc., was sued by a Little League coach who was confined to a wheelchair due to a spinal cord injury, and who was barred from serving as an on-field base coach by the organization's national policy—in violation, he claimed, of the civil rights protection provided by the Americans with Disabilities Act.[12]

In a gender-related case, a sixteen-year-old student who was the first female high school football player in Carroll County, Maryland, was injured in her team's first practice scrimmage, and then sued the county school board for the coaches' negligence in failing to inform her adequately of the physical dangers inherent in such contact sports as football.[13] In these and numerous other cases, it is necessary to obtain sound legal counsel in establishing agency policies—or, following that, when crisis situations or lawsuits occur.

When recreation and park agencies experience problems that are part of broader community conditions—such as those related to juvenile delinquency, gang activity, drug abuse, or adolescent sexual activity—they should attempt to deal with them both within their own programs and as part of community-wide efforts. In many cases, public and voluntary recreation organizations may be able to play a leading role in calling community attention to problems, and in developing interdisciplinary approaches to solving them.

Emphasis on Total Quality Programming

Summing up, the successful operation of program activities involves both the efficient, enthusiastic, and responsive leadership of all program elements and services, and the ability to respond to difficulties that may occur in a timely and responsible way.

These guidelines for the successful operation of leisure-service programs underline the recognition that recreation itself involves far more than the provision of light, enjoyable activities that are essentially an amenity or a disposable frill for participants. Instead, the guidelines make it clear that recreation and other leisure-related activities and services have the potential to meet important individual and community needs, and that activities must be organized and administered so as to do this effectively and imaginatively, as a vital part of neighborhood and community life.

At the same time, it must be emphasized that leisure-service agencies must also be able to promote their programs to community residents or organization members *as* recreation, providing exciting, rewarding, and pleasurable experiences that meet personal needs for sociability, self-expression, and other play motivations.

Finally, program operators must bear in mind the fundamental precepts of the marketing orientation in terms of accurately identifying the needs and wishes of participants, treating them efficiently and with courtesy, and making the satisfied "customer" a key priority in ongoing operations. To this end, many public recreation and park departments, and other types of leisure-service agencies, have evolved marketing and service-delivery policies aimed at achieving maximum patron satisfaction.

Total Quality Programming

Christopher and Susan Edginton describe the concept of "total quality programming," which demands a commitment to quality from top management through every level of recreation, park, and leisure-service staff members. It focuses on achieving the highest possible level of quality and value, through innovative, customer-sensitive practices that rely on the use of benchmarks, statistical analyses, and continuous measurement of achievement in reaching standards of performance.

The Edgintons identify a number of key elements of total quality programming. They include the following:

Innovation—programs that are constantly evolving to meet customers' needs and improve the quality and value of services.

Future orientation that addresses not only quality issues of today, but that focuses on future needs, trends and strategies.

Continuous improvement, that seeks to do things right the first time, but that then constantly looks for new ways to do things better and with greater cost efficiency.

Staff development, with constant, ongoing upgrading of leisure-service programmers' knowledge and skills.

Attention to detail that emphasizes the little things that distinguish higher-quality programs from mediocre ones.

Use of performance measures of elements such as customer numbers, customer survey results, program costs, behavioral outcomes, with action follow-up based on findings.

Elimination of mistakes and *"negativeness,"* with emphasis on error-free operations, and stress on being energetic, enthusiastic and zestful.

Assuming personal responsibility for quality, making use of teams or "quality circles," to improve joint planning, cooperation and supportive staff involvement.[14]

Ronald McCarville provides a number of useful guidelines for achieving the critical goal of client or participant satisfaction, emphasizing the expectations that program participants have, through which they evaluate agency performance. He writes:

Brochures, program entrances, and telephone contacts, often the first contacts between the agency and client, are examples of key encounter points. First impressions that set the stage for subsequent interactions with staff may deter-

mine how an entire agency is perceived by a client. Programmers must identify these encounter points and ensure that the experience is positive for their clients.[15]

On the other hand, client irritation may be caused by having to wait a long time for service, failure to receive promised services, experiencing poor staff performance or unsatisfactory service quality, poorly maintained facilities, or restrictions stemming from agency policy.

"Customer-Driven" Emphasis

A vivid illustration of an agency-wide effort to develop the highest possible levels of program quality and value, and customer satisfaction, may be found in the Sunnyvale, California, Department of Leisure Services. Examples of its emphasis on being a "customer-driven" organization fall under the following headings:

1. *Organizational culture*—making use of a market-pricing philosophy; satisfaction guarantees for patrons; organizational restructuring designed to bring managers closer to customers; and educating staff members that change is the "new norm," and that change means success.

2. *Innovative business practices,* including use of agency "enterprise fund;" "bottom-line" budget management; phone-in registration and reservations; use of credit cards; discounting for special purposes, "prime-time" and "non-prime-time" rates; and multi-tiered program offerings with value added at different levels of participation.

3. *Staff development,* with market-impact teams; focus on "little wins and improvement"; Disney training for selected staff members; appointment of training teams; training "swaps" with other organizations; and internal recognition from peers.

4. *Maximizing facilities* and *services,* with upgraded audiovisual equipment; in-house graphic artists and desktop publishing methods; renamed meeting rooms and quality renovations; cultural diversity approaches; lengthened outdoor season; party-planner services offered to public; corporate outreach for business meetings and seminars; and restructured youth services program.[16]

Underlying all these innovative strategies is the emphasis on "listening" to customers through surveys, focus groups, and exit interviews; and the emphasis on market feasibility surveys, and on constant measurement of the Sunnyvale program's success in meeting its established goals and objectives. While other organizations may differ in their specific priorities and methods, clearly the "total quality" and "customer satisfaction" approaches that have just been described represent the wave of the present and the future for leisure-service agencies of every type.

Summary

Effective preliminary planning should have laid a solid foundation for the actual implementation of recreation, park, and leisure-service programs. This chapter describes several key stages of program operations, beginning with publicity and registration procedures, and ending with problem-solving methods and an emphasis on total program quality that achieves a high level of patron and community satisfaction.

Throughout, several ways are shown to approach each operational task. Within each approach, however, staff commitment to approved agency policies and procedures, systematic risk management, and consistent, sensitive responsiveness to the needs and interests of program participants, are essential.

Even in the best of circumstances, conflicts and crises may occur. The chapter suggests appropriate problem-solving approaches at different levels of difficulty. Race, gender, and disability factors are cited as focal points of such problems. Interpersonal difficulties among staff members or participants, as well as other problems linked to social or economic conditions, or to the behavior of participants, may also be sources of difficulties. As leisure-service professionals confront and succeed in overcoming such problems, they realize an essential goal of the benefits-driven programming approach.

Student Projects or Assignments

1. Assume that you are going to conduct a new program venture, such as a sports tournament for disabled participants, a community art or folk festival, or a volunteer park cleanup project. Outline a publicity campaign and prepare a news release to promote the event.

2. Continuing with the first task, or selecting a new program activity such as a weekend camping trip to an environmental center, or a company-sponsored fitness fair, outline the various tasks to be carried on in sponsoring the fair. Prepare a set of guidelines for the major steps after publicity, such as registration, presenting program activities, assuring crowd and safety control, overseeing transportation, setting up booths, or other tasks.

By forming a steering committee, with one person assigned to manage each of these functions, develop an overall event plan.

3. Individual class members may interview staff members of a leisure-service agency to gather case studies of typical problems or crisis situations faced in program operations. Alternatively, class members may develop accounts of crisis situations they have faced or observed in recreation settings. After presenting these in detail to the class, the class may form small groups for buzz sessions to develop solutions or strategies to solve each problem. These may be shared with and discussed by the entire class.

References

1. Richard L. Fuller, "Fifteen Years on the Edge," *Parks and Recreation,* Nov. 1993, pp. 34–35.

2. Michael Corwin, "Sharks in the Parks," *Parks and Recreation,* Jan. 1994, pp. 62–65.

3. David M. Dale, "Mainstreaming Fitness at Ashland Oil, Inc.," *Employee Services Management,* Aug. 1995, pp. 27, 30.

4. Alan Bright, "Information Campaigns That Enlighten and Influence the Public," *Parks and Recreation,* Aug. 1994, p. 49

5. Edward H. Szillat, "Wanted: Superhuman Worker to Manage Membership and Access," *Parks and Recreation,* June 1994, p. 50.

6. *Operations Manual* (Williamsport, PA: Little League Baseball, 1994), p. 19.

7. Ken Kutska, "Public Playground Safety: Paradigm or Paradox," *Parks and Recreation,* Apr. 1994, p. 48.

8. Douglas Martin, "After Sexual Attacks, Segregation of Pools Is Weighed," *New York Times,* July 7, 1994, p. B–1.

9. Amy Rosenberg, "The Dad Vail Manages to Right Itself," *Philadelphia Inquirer,* Apr. 22, 1994, p. B–1.

10. See Richard G. Kraus and Joseph E. Curtis, *Creative Management in Recreation, Parks and Leisure Services* (St. Louis: Times Mirror/Mosby, 1990), p. 189.

11. Tracy H. New, "Group Addresses Issues Affecting Dallas Minorities," *Parks and Recreation,* Mar. 1993, pp. 8, 10.

12. James C. Kozlowski, "Banning Wheelchair from Sidelines Violates ADA," *Parks and Recreation,* June 1994, pp. 18–22.

13. James C. Kozlowski, "First Female in Football Program Claims Negligent Failure to Warn of Risks," *Parks and Recreation,* Dec. 1994, pp. 20–23.

14. Christopher R. Edginton and Susan R. Edginton, "Total Quality Program Planning," *Journal of Physical Education, Recreation and Dance,* Oct. 1993, pp. 40–42.

15. Ronald E. McCarville, "Keys to Quality Leisure Programming," *Journal of Physical Education, Recreation and Dance,* Oct. 1993, p. 36.

16. "Organizational Culture: A Customer-Driven Organization," Presentation by Carl Clark, at National Recreation and Park Congress, San Jose, CA, Oct. 1993.

Chapter 11

Program Evaluation Methods and Management Information Systems

Facility attendance is up, it appears that the place is busier than ever and no one has come to complain to you about anything. You must be doing a great job, right? Maybe. Then again, you may be losing business even though it looks like things are booming. How can you tell if you are meeting your users' needs? How can you keep ahead of your competition? Are you providing the quality services that you think you are providing?[1]

Usually defined as a systematic process of judging the quality or effectiveness of agencies or programs, evaluation traditionally has been considered to be a key element in recreation, park, and leisure-service programming.

Evaluation may focus on an agency's success in achieving its stated goals and objectives, as a key element in the benefits-driven approach. It may also measure its quality with the use of professionally accepted performance standards and criteria. This chapter describes both quantitative and qualitative research methods used in program evaluation, and gives examples of evaluation in different types of agencies.

The topics presented in this chapter relate to the following undergraduate curriculum objectives established by the NRPA/AALR Council on Accreditation:

Knowledge of the purpose, basic procedures, and interpretation, and application of research and evaluation methodology related to leisure services. (8.24)

Understanding of principles and procedures for evaluation of leisure programs and services. (8.26)

Understanding of and ability to apply techniques of program evaluation and policy analysis which measure service effectiveness and the extent to which programmatic and organizational goals and objectives have been achieved. (9A.05)

Understanding of the nature and implications of professional standards of practice and external accreditation standards relative to therapeutic recreation service. (9D.05)

Meaning and Purpose of Program Evaluation

Evaluation in recreation, park, and leisure-service agencies is often described as the process of measuring the extent to which program goals and objectives have been successfully achieved.

In a broader sense, evaluation may be used to judge the quality of programs and agencies as a whole, making use of standards formulated by professional societies or by authoritative practitioners and educators in the field. Evaluation also may be used to examine specific components of recreation, park, and leisure-service agencies, such as personnel, facilities, or management practices.

Each of these purposes of evaluation is discussed in this chapter. It should be emphasized that evaluation, in order to be credible, should be carried out in systematic, objective ways, using techniques drawn from research methodology, such as the use of valid, reliable instruments, representative sampling of subjects or program elements, objective recording, and systematic analysis of data.

When it meets such requirements, evaluation may play a key role in the development of management policies and strategies, as well as in ongoing and future program planning. It also may contribute to another important need of the recreation, park, and leisure-service profession: the development of a body of knowledge about the proven benefits and outcomes of organized recreation programs.

Evaluation of Program Effectiveness

There are several ways in which the effectiveness of recreation programs may be meaningfully evaluated. These include the following:

1. Measuring the program's success in achieving its goals and objectives, chiefly in terms of participant outcomes.

2. Surveying and analyzing the views and satisfaction levels of program participants.

3. Measuring the program's success in meeting administrative goals with respect to attendance, fiscal viability, or other criteria.

Success in Meeting Participant-Centered Goals and Objectives

This approach tends to be the most valid and easily applied measure of program effectiveness, provided that program goals and objectives have been clearly stated at the outset, and that they were keyed to specific measurable outcomes, such as changes to be achieved in participant skills mastery, social behavior, values or self-concepts, or other desired benefits.

As Chapter 5 shows, program objectives frequently involve the teaching of skills, with clearly defined performance measures. In many recreation programs, for example, swimming represents a popular instructional activity, with specific skills that are to be learned in sequence. Daily or weekly records may be kept of the success of class members, as shown in Figure 11-1, thus providing a sound basis for measuring the program's success at its conclusion.

In a second example of the use of skill objectives and performance measures in swimming, the Center for Human Development in Plymouth, Michigan, outlines a sequential series of twenty-one swimming skills in working with developmentally disabled children and youth. Several of the simpler skills are shown in Figure 11-2 as illustrations of the overall sequence.

Performance measures of this type may be used to assess program effectiveness in terms of the progress of individual participants, or in terms of the degree to which the overall group or class of participants has mastered the targeted skills.

Evaluation may also be used to measure other aspects of participant change, in terms of behavioral objectives, improved social involvement, or strengthened self-concept. Chapter 5 provides illustrations of such program objectives in treatment protocols or other client-centered plans in therapeutic recreation settings.

In some cases, program participants may be asked to record their own perceptions of the extent to which personal goals have been achieved. For example, Figure 11-3 shows a section of a survey conducted by the Department of Parks and Community Services in Fort Worth, Texas, in cooperation with the Department of Recreation, Park and Tourism Sciences at Texas A & M University. The survey queries youth who have taken part in the Fort Worth Youth Sports Soccer Program about areas of personal change with respect to knowledge, abilities, understanding, or personal values.

Instructor: _____   Day: _____   Time: _____

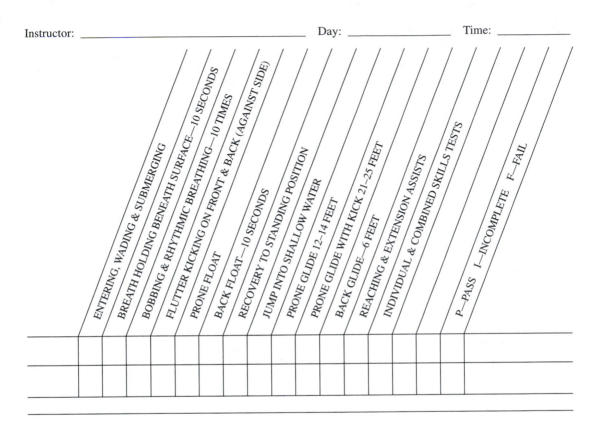

Figure 11-1. Record of individual skills performance—"Pollywog" Class, Santa Monica, California, Recreation and Park Department.

Swimming Pool Skills	Objective	Acceptable Performance
1. Locate the steps into pool	Orientation and pool safety	To locate and use steps properly when instructed to do so
2. How to enter pool from steps	Pool safety	Enter, walk forward using handrail
3. Walk in waist-deep water assisted	Confidence and adjustment to deeper water	Walk in waist-deep water 20 feet with assistance of instructor
4. Walk in waist-deep water unassisted	Confidence and adjustment so deeper water	Walk in waist-deep water 20 feet without assistance
5. Bob in water assisted	Confidence, breathing and coordination	In waist-deep water, feet on bottom, stand and squat four times in succession, breathing inwhile standing, breathing out with face in water

Figure 11-2. Measurement of swimming progress—Plymouth, Michigan, Center for Human Development.

This part of the survey asks you questions about the Fort Worth Youth Sports Soccer Program in which you recently participated. For each of the statements below, circle the response that best describes how much you increased your knowledge, abilities, understanding, etc., due to your participation in the soccer program.

As a result of participating in the Fort Worth Youth Sports Soccer Program, I increased:	Increased A Lot	Increased Some	Increased A Little	No Impact
my ability to talk with other children . . .	A Lot	Some	A Little	None
my athletic ability	A Lot	Some	A Little	None
my knowledge of safe places to play	A Lot	Some	A Little	None
my ability to get along with other family members	A Lot	Some	A Little	None
my respect for coaches and referees	A Lot	Some	A Little	None
my understanding of the importance of teamwork	A Lot	Some	A Little	None
my interest in other recreation activities .	A Lot	Some	A Little	None
my number of friends	A Lot	Some	A Little	None
my ability to control anger	A Lot	Some	A Little	None
my desire to keep playing sports	A Lot	Some	A Little	None
my ability to be creative	A Lot	Some	A Little	None
my knowledge about other community activities	A Lot	Some	A Little	None
my ability to be a good sport	A Lot	Some	A Little	None
my understanding of the importance of doing one's best	A Lot	Some	A Little	None
my ability to play with other children . . .	A Lot	Some	A Little	None
my ability to express ideas more clearly .	A Lot	Some	A Little	None
my respect for the rules	A Lot	Some	A Little	None
my understanding of the importance of staying out of trouble	A Lot	Some	A Little	None
my understanding of the importance of physical fitness	A Lot	Some	A Little	None
my ability to play sports	A Lot	Some	A Little	None

Figure 11-3.   Section of self-reporting form, used in evaluation of Fort Worth Youth Sports Soccer Program.

Measurement of Participant Satisfaction

A second common approach to evaluating program effectiveness consists of having participants fill out an evaluation form at the conclusion of a trip, class, tournament, or similar recreation event. Typically, respondents reply to a series of questions about the activity, using a numbered scale of quality or satisfaction for each item. For example, Figure 11-4 shows how a suburban YMCA has its members evaluate the agency's facilities and services on a four-point scale.

Using an evaluation instrument that focuses on the judgments of four classes of program participants, the U.S. Navy's Morale, Welfare and Recreation program employs a Likert questionnaire approach, which measures respondents' agreement or disagreement with a number of statements about recreation facilities, staff members, and operations (see Figure 11-5).

---

1. What membership type are you?

   Check one   **Check one**

   _____ Full Facility   _____ Fitness Center   _____ Youth _____ Couple

   _____ Swim   _____ Basic   _____ Adult _____ Family

2. Rate the facilities used by you and/or your family over the past year.

   1-Excellent   2-Good   3-Fair   4-Poor

   Circle one   **Circle one**

Pool	1	2	3	4	Nursery School Building	1	2	3	4
Fitness Center	1	2	3	4	Preschool Center	1	2	3	4
Steam/Sauna	1	2	3	4	Annex Building	1	2	3	4
Gymnasium	1	2	3	4	Parking	1	2	3	4
Locker Rooms	1	2	3	4	Whirlpool	1	2	3	4

3. Please check the approximate number of time you utilize YMCA facilities per week:

   _____ **less than one** _____ **one** _____ **two** _____ **three** _____ **four or more**

4. How did you hear about the YMCA?

   _____ **Newspaper** _____ **Brochure** _____ **Word of Mouth/Friend** _____ **Other**

5. Please rate our services.   *1-Excellent   2-Good   3-Fair   4-Poor*

   Circle one   **Circle one**

Registration process	1	2	3	4	Maintenance of equipment	1	2	3	4
Staff and instructors	1	2	3	4	Communication with members	1	2	3	4
Building cleanliness	1	2	3	4	Facility hours	1	2	3	4
Maintenance of building	1	2	3	4	Scope and variety of programs	1	2	3	4
Babysitting service	1	2	3	4					

6. Other comments and/or suggestions _____

Figure 11-4.   Ambler, Pennsylvania, YMCA membership survey form.

Activity: _____ **Date:** _____

Gender: ☐ Male ☐ Female **Status:** ☐ Active Duty ☐ Spouse ☐ Retired ☐ Civilian

Please rate the extent to which you feel the program in which you are now participating has the features described by each of the following statements. Circle your responses.

Item	Not Applicable	Strongly Disagree	Disagree	Neither Disagree or Agree	Agree	Strongly Agree
1. The facility is up-to-date and well equipped.	0	1	2	3	4	5
2. The activity/event/service starts on time.	0	1	2	3	4	5
3. The staff is willing to go an extra step.	0	1	2	3	4	5
4. The hours of operation are convenient.	0	1	2	3	4	5
5. The staff is trustworthy.	0	1	2	3	4	5
6. The staff has enthusiasm.	0	1	2	3	4	5
7. The staff gives individual attention to you.	0	1	2	3	4	5
8. The staff responds to requests quickly.	0	1	2	3	4	5
9. Information provided is accurate.	0	1	2	3	4	5
10. The facility is attractive.	0	1	2	3	4	5

Note: The overall survey form contains 25 items. All of them are positively stated. In such evaluation forms, it may be desirable to include a number of negative items as well, to obtain a fuller, more accurate response.

Figure 11-5. Service quality in U.S. Navy MWR programs.

Most evaluation instruments of this type use closed-end questions; participants simply check a box or indicate a numbered rating, in response to each item. However, some evaluation surveys also use open-end questions, which permit respondents to give a broader range of detailed reactions.

Evaluation in the Research Literature

When success in meeting program goals is recorded as a routine part of daily program operations, evaluation is normally the responsibility of staff members who conduct specific activities, or of their supervisors. However, if the evaluation is part of a purposeful research effort intended to determine the efficacy of a particular treatment service, it must meet a set of scientific research criteria:

1. The evaluation procedure should be based on a formal, written plan, which outlines its purposes, the steps of the study, and the instrument or other methods to be used;

2. The program treatment, or intervention, should be precisely defined and uniformly applied;

3. There should be careful controls over the program, to exclude other factors that might influence participants or cause behavioral change;

4. Where possible, measurement procedures that have been shown to be valid and reliable should be used, and should be applied by outside evaluators or observers, rather than by program leaders themselves; and

5. In most cases, quantitative information that can statistically analyzed should be used to identify significant evaluation findings.[2]

Numerous examples of evaluation research efforts to determine the effects of specific recreation programs or strategies are found in the literature. For example, Mactavish and Searle measured the effects of a physical activity program on selected groups of older men and women, and found that participation resulted in improved levels of perceived leisure competence and self-esteem.[3] Numerous other evaluation studies have documented the positive outcomes of therapeutic camping or Outward Bound-type programs on adolescents who are disturbed or delinquent.[4]

Formal evaluation of this type has also been done in outdoor recreation and park settings. For example, Vander Stoep and Gramann tested the effectiveness of verbal appeals and incentives in reducing vandalism and other destructive behavior among youthful visitors in a national military park in Tennessee.[5]

Numerous other studies examining levels of participant satisfaction with recreation and park programs and facilities have been published in recent years. Some of these measure both the importance of different program or facility factors, and the degree to which they are satisfactorily provided. Examples include the following:

Vaske, Donnelly, and Williamson summarize the findings of report cards distributed each year to thousands of visitors to over thirty New Hampshire state park units, including historic sites, day-use areas, campgrounds, and beaches.[6] Respondents were asked to rate the area they visited on a five-point scale, in terms of eleven variables, such as helpfulness of staff, cleanliness of restrooms, safety and security, ease of access, hours of operation, and overall satisfaction.

Hollenhorst, Olson, and Fortney describe the use of importance-performance (I-P) analysis in evaluating park cabins operated by the West Virginia state park system.[7] Using a mailed questionnaire survey addressed to past cabin users, they determined which aspects of park cabin usage were more important (including such elements as cleanliness, reservation system, seclusion, scenic views, and access to park recreational features), and how well they were being provided.

Success in Meeting Administrative Goals

Another approach to measuring the effectiveness of recreation, park, and leisure-service agencies involves determining whether they have successfully achieved administrative goals and objectives.

As Chapter 5 indicates, these should include specific performance measures, which can be monitored during and at the conclusion of program units or seasons. Figure 11-6

Key Objectives

1. Provide social and recreational activities to 5.5% of Kansas Citizens 65 years of age or over.
2. Plan and coordinate monthly meetings for the various Golden Age clubs.
3. Conduct special citywide events for older adults.
4. Arrange and conduct a travel program for Golden Agers.
5. Provide weekly instruction, competition, physical recreation and social activities for 200 disabled children and adults.

Performance Measures

1. Percent of target population of elderly being served	5.5%
2. Number of Golden Age clubs	13
Number of monthly meetings	32
Average attendance per meeting	69
3. Number of special events	13
Average attendance per special event	902
4. Number of trips for seniors	59
5. Weekly participation by persons with disabilities	132
Number of special events for persons with disabilities	1
Average attendance per event	125

Figure 11-6. Project objectives and performance measures in Kansas City Senior Center and Disabled Participants Program.

illustrates a number of objectives and the performance measures attached to them, in Kansas City, Missouri.

In some cases, evaluation may focus on a specific aspect of agency management, as shown in Figure 11-7, which shows how quantitative performance measures may be established to improve the program registration process for classes and workshops in Sunnyvale, California.

Measurement of Program Quality

A second important thrust in the evaluation of leisure-service programs consists of efforts to measure the overall quality of recreation and park organizations and their operations. The most widely used approach to this task involves the use of professionally developed standards and guidelines.

Essentially, standards represent approved guidelines or descriptions of recommended practices, which have been formulated by authorities in the field or developed by professional organizations to provide tools to be used in accreditation or certification processes. Standards usually are considered to be statements of minimal levels of quality or performance, rather than optimal or best levels.

	1993/94 Planned	1993/94 Actual
Performance Indicators:		
1. Number of Customers registering for class/workshop programs completing and returning surveys rating customer service (timeliness of response, knowledge, etc.) as meeting or exceeding their expectations, and percentage to returned surveys.	51 85%	_____ _____
2. Number of user concerns which were resolved to satisfaction of concerned party, and percentage to concerns returned.	5 55%	_____ _____
3. Number of Mail-in program registrations process before first day of Walk-in registration, and percentage to Mail-in registrations received.	13,800 100%	_____ _____
4. Number of program registrations taken by mail or phone, to increase 5% each year to maximum of 85%, and percentage to total registrations.	16,100 70%	_____ _____
5. Number of Customer refunds processed within one week of Customer request or class cancellation and percentage to total refunds.	1,710 95%	_____ _____

Figure 11-7.   Performance measures for registration upgrading: Sunnyvale, California.

NRPA Standards

In the mid-1990s, a national committee on accreditation formed by the American Academy for Park and Recreation Administration and the National Recreation and Park Association developed evaluation guidelines and a self-assessment manual, based on 152 standards in 10 categories. Under the heading of *Program and Services Management,* this new manual presented thirteen standards to be used in evaluating public recreation and park programs, as shown in Figure 11-8.

The overall self-assessment manual can be used in two ways: (1) as a key element in the agency accreditation procedure developed by the National Committee on Accreditation; or (2) simply to assist local recreation and park departments in evaluating their own performance with the purpose of self-assessment and self-improvement.

Other specialized leisure-service fields have also developed standards to be used in evaluating program services.

National Youth Sports Camp Standards

For example, the National Youth Sports Camp, a program funded by the United States Congress and administered by the National Collegiate Athletic Association, sponsors

6.1   Program/Services Determinants
       The program and services provided shall be based on:
       conceptual foundations of play, recreation, and leisure that enhance positive leisure
           lifestyles
       constituent needs
       community opportunities
       agency philosophy and goals
       experiences desirable for clientele

6.1.1 Participant Involvement in Planning
       Development of program should involve the participants.

6.2   Nature of Services
       Services shall be delivered in a variety of ways, such as:
       structured programs, outreach, user services, rentals

6.2.1 General Supervision
       The program should provide for recreation opportunities under general supervision

6.2.2 Structured Leadership Programs
       The program should provide recreation opportunities under direct face-to-face leadership,
           including skills instruction

6.2.3 Facilitator
       Services should be provided to individuals and small groups . . . to stimulate and assist
           them to become independent of the supervision and control of the recreation agency

6.2.3 Services for a Fee
       Services should be offered for a fee to augment basic recreational opportunities

6.3   Objectives
       There shall be specific objectives established for each program element and service

6.4   Outreach
       The programs and services shall be available to all cultures and populations resident of and
           visitors to the community

6.5   Scope of Program Opportunities
       The agency's programs shall provide opportunities in all program fields for various levels
           of proficiency, ages, and gender, in accordance with the agency's statement of mission

6.6   Selection of Program Content
       The selection of program content, specific activities, and opportunities shall be based on an
           understanding of individual differences and the culture of the community

6.7   Types of Participation
       The program shall provide structurally for a wide range of types of participation

6.8   Education for Leisure
       There should be a plan of education for leisure.

Figure 11-8.   AAPRA/NRPA Self-Assessment Manual (Section on Program Evaluation).

Note: Each of these standards is followed in the Manual by a Commentary that explains it in detail and gives examples of its application. This is followed by a statement titled *Suggested Evidence of Compliance,* which suggests ways in which the agency that is being evaluated can document its compliance with the standard.

numerous summer day camp programs for disadvantaged children in inner-city neighbor-hoods. Each such camp is evaluated annually by a visiting team that employs a manual with 106 standards that cover such areas as these: institution, participants, activities, enrichment program, and project schedule.

For example, seven specific items are listed under the heading of "Institution" including "Cooperation afforded by several departments in the University or College," "Lockers used daily by each participant," and "NYSP shirts provided to all participants." In scoring the evaluation, a maximum number of 180 points may be gained by programs that satisfy all 106 standards. Depending on its total score, an institution may be approved fully for funding in the following year, approved conditionally (based on improving in certain areas), or disapproved.

Standards in Therapeutic Recreation Service

The field of therapeutic recreation service has also been active in developing standards that are useful in evaluating the programs designed to serve special populations in clinical treatment settings. As early as 1980, the National Therapeutic Recreation Society developed a statement of approved standards of practice for such programs. One section of it, on documentation, illustrates the emphasis on measuring patient progress and determining the outcomes of professionally directed programs (see Figure 11-9).

Standard IV-Documentation

Standard: Therapeutic recreation personnel record specific information on assigned clients for the client/participant's record on a regular basis, in accordance with the policies and procedures accordance with the policies and procedures of the agency.

Criteria

A. The individualized therapeutic recreation treatment/program plan is recorded in the client/participant's record. It should include:
  1. The referral document or reason for
  2. Assessment data.
  3. Identification of client's problem and needs.
  4. Treatment objectives.
  5. Methods and plans for implementation of the therapeutic recreation program.
  6. Methods and plans for evaluation of the objectives.
B. Progress of the individual and his/her reactions to the therapeutic recreation program are systematically recorded in the client/participant's record and reported to all

appropriate parties (e.g., Interdisciplinary team, parents, etc.)
  1. Subjective Interpretation of client progress is supported with concise behavioral observations.
  2. An assessment of the client's current level of leisure function.
  3. Recommendations for post-discharge transition planning.
  4. Information regarding appropriate community recreation resources and referrral information as indicated.
C. Client records are reviewed regularly by therapeutic recreation staff in accordance with standards of regulatory agencies and documentation of such

Figure 11-9.   Therapeutic recreation: example of standards of practice.

Today, there is an overriding tendency in the therapeutic recreation field to apply systematic self-evaluation measures—even when accreditation is not a primary concern. Jeff Witman reflects this thrust in a suggested checklist that therapeutic recreators may use in examining their own practices with respect to the documentation of outcomes (see Figure 11-10).

Armed Forces Management Guidelines

Another example of the use of standards and guidelines to direct and evaluate agency practices is found in military recreation management manuals. To illustrate, the Navy MWR

Our therapeutic recreation department (check all which apply):

☐ Establishes measurable goals and objectives for clients and for programs based upon assessed needs

☐ Can demonstrate the relevance of our services to our agency's mission and goals

☐ Regularly receives feedback (e.g., processing at the end of groups/programs, exit interviews) from clients.

☐ Has an active role in our agency's Quality Improvement activities.

☐ Conducts effectiveness studies of various program offerings.

☐ Is able to cite specific benefits of, as well as contraindications for participation in various program offerings specific to clients' problems/diagnoses.

☐ Is included in agency efforts (e.g., surveys, interviews) at determining client satisfaction with services received.

☐ Conducts inservice, orientation and other programs for those in our agency beyond our own department which detail our program activities and outcomes.

☐ Is sharing through publications and/or presentations with the community and with professionals from other agencies regarding program activities and outcomes.

☐ Is conversant with what other programs and projects (e.g., the Temple University efficacy project) have done in the outcomes area.

Key: 8–10 checks—keep up the good work. Be a resource for others and a catalyst for collective/collaborative actions:

4–7 checks—you're doing some good things. Consider how you can generate more resources to expand your efforsts:

0–3 checks—time to get moving. The client you are better able to service (and perhaps the job you save) may be your own!

Figure 11-10.   Outcomes: a self-assessment tool for therapeutic recreation departments.[8]

program publishes management "tool kits" that prescribe detailed controls over financial practices in various revenue-gathering activities. One manual of operations presents detailed questionnaires governing such elements as the use of cash funds and receipts, amusement machines, and other practices involving procurement and receiving, accounts payable, and cash disbursements (see Figure 11-11).

Name of Fund: _____   **Review Date:** _____

Activity: _____

Program/Function: _____

Questions	Answer			
	Yes	No	N/A	Remarks
Bingo				
1. Is the playing of bingo limited to authorized patrons and their bona fide guests?				
2. Are employees, fund managers, and direct line supervisors of the activity sponsoring bingo and their immediate family members prohibited from playing bingo or accepting prizes?				
3. Are reusable bingo cards validated with a mark or date stamp at the time of sale?				
4. Are all throwaway bingo cards prenumbered, and issued and sold in numerical order?				
5. Are bingo receipts controlled through the use of a cash register and/or prenumbered coupons or tickets?				
6. Do Bingo Special Events Reports contain the: a. Name of the winner?				
b. Rank of the winner (if applicable)?				
c. Social security number of the winner?				
d. Organization of the winner?				
e. Telephone number of the winner?				
f. Signature of the winner?				
g. Name of the sponsor when the winner is a guest?				
7. Are cash prizes within authorized limits paid from an imprest fund or by a properly authorized check?				

Figure 11-11. Navy internal control questionnaire: bingo operations.

Leadership evaluation

In addition to determining whether agency practices conform to established guidelines or standards such as those that have been illustrated, many leisure-service organizations conduct regular assessments of their staff members' on-the-job performance.

In the past, it was customary to rate leaders based on a set of desired traits, such as initiative, responsibility, human relations skills, or other job-related capabilities. Recently, more comprehensive approaches to leadership evaluation have assessed individuals' effectiveness on the job, in light of their assigned functions, agency priorities, and program strategies. As an example of the current use of evaluation in program management, the Recreation and Park Department of Edmonton, Alberta, has developed a three-part form that identifies the primary functions of managerial employees; rates them on knowledge, personal qualities, on-the-job performance, and strengths and weaknesses; and outlines a plan for professional development.

The Edmonton approach illustrates a key principle of all forms of evaluation—that evaluation is not intended solely to document outcomes, or to provide a score or performance rating. Instead, it should consistently be used to improve practices and upgrade the quality of programs and services. When used to assess leadership performance, it may also reveal factors about the agency's practices with respect to orientation and in-service training, assignment practices, and supervisory relationships that need to be reviewed and improved. Figure 11-12 shows a section of the rating form used in this system.

In some cases, recreation staff members may be asked to suggest several challenging objectives that they would like to accomplish during the next rating period, including both regularly assigned job responsibilities and new projects or program initiatives. In such cases, estimated dates of project completion and detailed measures of successful performance should be included.

Facilities Evaluation

A final element that should be regularly evaluated, one that is closely linked to successful program operations, consists of areas and facilities used by the agency. This process may involve a systematic assessment of the adequacy of facilities based on established space-and-facility standards. For example, traditional classification systems have included such recommendations as the following for sports areas:

> *Ice hockey requires an area of 22,000 square feet, including support areas; one such indoor rink should be provided for each 100,000 in population, and may be expected to serve people within a ½ to 1 hour of travel time.*
>
> *Tennis requires an area of 7,200 square feet for a singles court; one court should be provided for each 2,000 in population, and should serve people with a service radius of ¼ to ½ mile.[9]*

While such guidelines may not be applied as absolute standards, recognizing the wide variations among communities, they provide a useful basis for examining the degree to

The supervisor conducting the evaluation is required to indicate his/her plans for having the employee improve in areas of weakness revealed in the assessment of job performance, using the form below.

Priority	Subject	Type of plan(s)	Tentative timetable	
			Begin: mo.-year	End: mo.-year
1				
2				
3				

Subject

1—Managerial techniques

2—Supervisory techniques

4—Personal facts or habits

5—Communication skills

6—Technical knowledge or subject matter (specify type)

7—Other (specify)

Type of plan

1—Directed self-development (reading, self study, etc.)

2—In formal training—(ed. dept. courses)

3—Outside educational programs (seminars, courses)

4—Counseling, coaching

5—On-the-job training

6—No plan at present

Figure 11-12. Section of Edmonton employee development plan.

which recreation and park agencies are providing needed physical facilities for sports and other program activities.

Other evaluative tools may include guidelines or schedules for the efficient operation and maintenance of facilities. This kind of evaluation often makes use of written plans that outline all tasks and responsibilities in simple terms, including: the acceptable level of condition or repair for all areas, facilities, and equipment; methods and schedules of performance at different times of the year; and personnel assignments and descriptions of equipment and time needed to carry out maintenance functions.

An example of facilities evaluation may be found in the operating manual of Little League Baseball. Because of the shortage of ball fields in many communities, a growing number of leagues have installed artificial lighting to permit extended hours of play, rather than construct new fields. To guard against mishaps that might occur because of faulty lighting systems, the operating manual defines a set of required minimum standards and optional-but-desirable features that govern the installation of metal halide lamps, the placement and height of poles, electrical wiring systems, environmental impact on adjacent residential neighborhoods, and similar elements. The Little League Manual includes provision for regular testing of poles and base-plates, lamps, cables and conduits, and grounding connections.

Accessibility as a Concern

A related factor that is closely linked to program planning is the accessibility of recreation areas and facilities for individuals with disabilities. As this text has shown, meeting the needs of physically or mentally challenged people has become a major priority for leisure-service agencies, based both on a morally imposed responsibility to serve them, and on the legal imperatives stemming from the Americans with Disabilities Act and other legislation or court decisions.

For example, the National Institute on Disability and Rehabilitation Research has provided information, materials, and technical assistance to varied types of organizations to ensure access for people with disabilities. At the simplest level, ensuring access may involve the elimination of physical barriers to participation by individuals in wheelchairs or with limited mobility, and the provision of doorways, entrances, restrooms, ramps, elevators with slow closing speeds, drinking fountains, telephones, and other equipment that is accessible.

At a more complex level, providing for accessibility may include the construction of special facilities such as parks and playgrounds for individuals with visual disabilities or other impairments, including nature trails with guide ropes and Braille markers or taped interpretive messages.

A number of states have developed architectural guidelines for barrier-free environments, and on the national level the Architectural and Transportation Barriers Compliance Board is charged with ensuring that facilities designed, constructed, or altered with federal funds provide access to disabled people.

Evaluation's Contribution to Management Information Systems

This chapter has described a number of the most widely used approaches to recreation-program evaluation. Traditionally, evaluation was considered to be a *summative* procedure—that is, it was carried out at the end of a program to assess its effectiveness and to make recommendations for future action. Today, much evaluation is conducted within a *formative* model. This means that it is done while a program is being carried on, with immediate feedback that is used to modify activities, services, and leadership methods.

Within both models, evaluation contributes significantly to the recreation agency's management information system. This system consists of a total body of comprehensive, accessible, and relevant data drawn from continuous monitoring and reporting of program operations. It should include data on enrollments and registration, staff performance, program costs and revenues, facilities usage, accidents and injuries, and a host of other operational functions.

Such pieces of information provide more than just facts and figures. They assist in problem solving and decision making, and in evolving management strategies to overcome barriers to programming success. Such functions have become increasingly sophisticated in recent years with the development of computerized data-processing hardware and software that record, store, and analyze an immense range of program-related information.

Use of Computerized Data-Processing

As in business, health care, education, and other major social systems, in recreation, parks, and leisure services computers contribute immeasurably to a variety of management functions.

For example, in terms of financial management, computer software has been designed to assist with general ledger and financial reporting, budget worksheets, payroll and personnel record-keeping, accounts payable, cost accounting, cash receipts, purchasing procedures, and tracking of budget balances and expenditures through the year.

With respect to program operations, computers are widely used to facilitate, process, and record memberships, registrations, and reservations, class or course enrollments, sports league scheduling, participant usage rates, staff and facility scheduling, accidents or safety statistics, and other specialized functions.

In the important management area of budget controls, computers offer major assistance to recreation and park managers. For example, Bitner and Bitner describe the accounting process:

> *Each month as purchase orders are issued, vouchers are entered and paid and payroll is calculated and paid, the transactions automatically post to the general ledger. The accounting of software automatically keeps track of the budget vs. the actual expenditures, including encumbrances and variances from the budget. You can get a printout at any time during the accounting period.*[10]

Obviously, computers do not provide a magical solution to all agency operations. Often, staff members with limited background in their use are resistant to learning needed skills, and the management of a computer system—including the purchase of appropriate equipment and software—too often is marked by poor decisions or negative events such as system breakdowns and program failures.[11] However, with growing availability of computer training workshops, like the highly successful annual Computer Use Institute cosponsored by the National Recreation and Park Association Resource Development Division and the Oglebay, West Virginia, Department of Continuing Education, such problems are steadily becoming less serious.

Qualitative Evaluation Methods

Certainly, from the perspective of program monitoring and evaluation needs, automatic data-processing capabilities are essential in terms of maintaining an ongoing management-information base. At the same time, it should be stressed that not all useful information is the kind of quantitative data that can best be processed through computer analysis and record-keeping.

Over the past two decades, there has been growing interest in the use of investigative methods that are qualitative (sometimes called naturalistic), in both evaluation and formal research studies.

Qualitative research involves the kind of data-gathering and analysis that does not rely on rigidly structured research designs and instruments, experimental and control groups, numerical findings, and statistical analysis. Instead, it tends to be more flexible and intuitive, involving study designs that examine human relationships and interactions, and probing more deeply into subjective and emotional factors that are often intertwined with leisure motivations and outcomes.

Christine Howe suggests that when recreation, park, and leisure-service programs are evaluated, two essential aspects are critical: *efficiency* and *effectiveness*. When efficiency is the primary concern, she writes, quantitative data having to do with such elements as pricing or participation rates are obviously important. However, when effectiveness is the key issue—meaning whether a program is enjoyable, meaningful, and satisfying for participants—Howe suggests that qualitative or naturalistic methods of inquiry lend an important dimension. She writes:

Qualitative methods to collect and analyze open-ended, written, spoken, or observed information can be used (e.g., What does participating in the low-impact aerobics program mean to you? Why did you discontinue attending the stamp-collecting club?). . . . In naturalistic evaluation, the information gleaned from participants through observing their behavior over time, in-depth interviewing, or examining items they have created (drawings, stories, etc.) is key to evaluating the program. The judgment criteria or evaluation questions concentrate on participants' enjoyment, meaning, and satisfaction.[12]

Seen in this light, qualitative methods of evaluation seek to go beyond the facts gathered through quantitative methods, to uncover the meaning behind them. Interviewing, participant observation, content analysis, and other forms of in-depth inquiry make it possible to understand the real impact of leisure-service programs.

Evaluation as Source of Outcomes Documentation

Qualitative evaluation can be particularly useful in terms of the ability of the recreation, park, and leisure-service field to document its positive contribution to community life—a key element of the benefits-driven approach to programming.

While it would be ideal to be able to prove recreational social value in statistical terms—such as a quantitative reduction in juvenile delinquency, births to single teenagers, or heart attacks or other illnesses—it is often difficult to do so in terms that would be acceptable to social scientists, through traditional quantitative research methods. In many cases, it is impossible to maintain the kinds of experimental and control groups in real-life situations that formal, positivistic research requires to confirm cause-and-effect relationships.

At the same time, the kinds of real-life experiences that provide the basis for human interest stories in newspapers and television accounts, or the actual encounters that millions of North Americans have with the positive outcomes of varied forms of recreation, offer another kind of impressive documentation of the value of quality recreation. Whether in sports, creative arts, outdoor recreation and travel, social activities, or other forms of leisure involvement, there is little doubt that recreation is capable of satisfying important human needs in both personal and societal terms.

Evaluation that gathers this kind of vivid evidence may be used by recreation programmers in their public-relations efforts. An example of such publicity is found in newspaper articles featuring the innovative "Code Blue" operation, a late-night youth and young-adult program sponsored by the Fort Worth, Texas, Park and Recreation Department, in cooperation with police and other agencies (see Figure 11-13).

Qualitative evaluation methods may be used to provide anecdotal, narrative, and other descriptive kinds of evidence to enrich journalistic reports of recreation program outcomes. They may also be used in agency reports that summarize program operations and accomplishments for public consumption.

Example of Annual Report: Westchester County, New York

As a single example, the annual report in a recent year of the Department of Parks, Recreation and Conservation of Westchester County, New York, provided a detailed report of the agency's administrative management and budgetary operation, as shown in Figure 11-14.

In addition to these events and campaigns, the county's annual report featured details of an extensive learn-to-swim program, and numerous other activities and events serving youth, senior citizens, physically challenged or emotionally disturbed persons, and those with developmental disabilities.

TUESDAY, JULY 21, 1992   FORT WORTH STAR-TELEGRAM   PAGE 13

Playing it safe
Night program offers youths fun, advice

BY MATT WOJICK
Special to the Star-Telegram

FORT WORTH — It's just before midnight on Saturday, and most of the homes and businesses along Sycamore Street lie dark and quiet.

But at the Sycamore Recreation Center, a bright yellow glow spills through the windows reflecting the activity buzzing inside.

A basketball tournament is under way, and the bleachers at courtside are filled with adults, teen-agers and younger kids who have just watched the Dream Team beat the Hattie Street Posse in a heated contest.

At such a late hour, when most people in this east Fort Worth neighborhood have called it a night, two more teams quickly weave their way through the crowd and onto the court to begin warming up for the next game. A game that won't end until after 2 a.m.

The nocturnal activity is part of Code: Blue, a series of programs funded by the city and aimed at stopping the spread of youth gangs
(More on PROGRAM on Page 18)

Fort Worth Star-Telegram / REX CURRY
Kenneth Wilkes listens to a lecture about AIDS

Figure 11-13.   Example of Fort Worth Code Blue newspaper coverage.

Where PRC'S Money Comes From

Golf Courses 18% $3,710,800.00 *

Parks/Parkways 10% $2,080,600.00 *

Park Pass 1% $375,000.00 *

State Aid 2% $445,500.00

County Taxes 27% $5,578,242.00

Playland 36% $7,376,930.00*

County Center 6% $1,100,000.00 *
Recreation 0% $55,000.00 **

* Revenues generated from departmental operations
** Less than 1%

How PRC'S Money is Spent

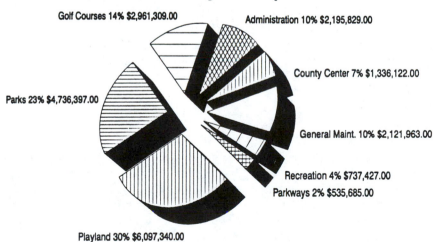

Golf Courses 14% $2,961,309.00

Administration 10% $2,195,829.00

County Center 7% $1,336,122.00

Parks 23% $4,736,397.00

General Maint. 10% $2,121,963.00

Recreation 4% $737,427.00
Parkways 2% $535,685.00

Playland 30% $6,097,340.00

Figure 11-14.   Budget analysis in annual report, Westchester County Department of Parks, Recreation and Conservation (1992).

Beyond this statistical financial breakdown, however, the Westchester County report also stressed in detail the accomplishments of its recreation program, including such elements as these:

Over 250,000 attended more than 87 major programs that stressed healthy, substance-free, and environmentally-aware lifestyles.

One example was "Celebrate a Drug-Free Life," an event designed to provide support and guidance for substance-free lifestyles, cosponsored by the county and several public and private agencies. Similarly, a "Just Say No Pool Party" was a major county-sponsored alcohol-free social event, as was a huge alcohol-free

New Year's Eve Party at the Westchester County Center, with over 1,500 people attending.

"Celebrate the Earth Day," cosponsored by various businesses, public, and private conservation agencies, also drew thousands of participants for a combined Earth Day and Arbor Day celebration at the official opening of a new arboretum.

Personal health and fitness issues were the focus of the Great Westchester Walk-In, with over three thousand people attending, in conjunction with the Department's publishing a "Guide to Walking in Westchester" and sponsoring numerous walking clinics.[14]

The Westchester County report shows clearly how contemporary recreation, park, and leisure-service agencies are increasingly providing a broader range of services, many of them clearly linked to a benefits-driven approach aimed at meeting significant community needs in such areas as substance abuse, environmental concerns, health and fitness, and the needs of people with disabilities. In a broad sense, they show how recreation has become a major player within the fields of personal and public health, and that it can work effectively with huge segments of the population attracted to its positive goals.

Both quantitative and qualitative evaluation of leisure-service agencies and programs can thus produce convincing evidence that documents the value of organized recreation and park activities and that contributes meaningfully to their improvement. Seen in this light, evaluation represents a vital aspect of the recreation programming process and deserves full administrative support and staff commitment.

Summary

Systematic evaluation measures the effectiveness and quality of recreation, park, and leisure-service programs. This chapter describes several different approaches to evaluation, including: (1) analysis of program success in achieving stated goals and objectives; (2) measurement of agency quality, defined by professionally approved standards of performance; and (3) use of surveys or other methods of judging participants' satisfaction with program-based experiences.

When evaluation seeks to measure program outcomes as part of formal reports or within a research context, it must adhere to approved scientific standards of investigation, including the use of valid and reliable instruments, sound sampling procedures, and objective observers. In addition to measuring program effectiveness and quality, evaluation may also focus on agency policies and procedures, staff performance, facility maintenance, and similar elements.

Most evaluation is regarded as quantitative, making use of factual data that can be statistically analyzed. However, qualitative evaluation that relies on more subjective, anecdotal, or observational kinds of data, can also yield information that gives depth of understanding of an agency's performance. Both quantitative and qualitative approaches can be used to contribute to an agency's management information system, and to improve program planning and recreation service delivery. Finally, both approaches are useful in familiarizing the public with the important benefits of recreation, park, and leisure-service programs.

Discussion Questions and Class Assignments

1. What are the key purposes of evaluation in recreation, park, and leisure-service programming? Identify and describe three chief methods used in this process (e.g., standards approach). What are the strengths and weaknesses of each approach, in your judgment?

2. Formulate an evaluation instrument to rate participant satisfaction in a single recreation activity, such as a class, workshop, festival, or tournament. Indicate the major areas of information to be covered, as well as sample open- or closed-end questions within each area. Finally, indicate how you would apply the instrument, and how you would tally and interpret its findings.

3. Formulate an evaluation instrument making use of standards and criteria, for measuring the quality of a program, such as a Boys and Girls Club, a hospital therapeutic recreation program, a church-sponsored family camping program, or a college intramural sports and outdoor recreation program. What sources would you use to validate your standards?

4. This chapter points out that both quantitative and qualitative forms of investigation may be used in leisure-service evaluation. What are the differences between these two methods, and what kinds of information would they be expected to yield? In particular, what are the strengths and weaknesses of qualitative evaluation?

References

1. Bruce I. Lazarus and Jane Kaufman Broida, "How Are We Doing?" *Parks and Recreation,* Sept. 1992, p. 80.

2. For a fuller discussion of research-based evaluation methods, see: Richard Kraus and Lawrence Allen, *Research and Evaluation in Recreation, Park and Leisure Studies* (Scottsdale, AZ: Gorsuch Scarisbrick, Inc., 1997).

3. Jennifer B. MacTavish and Mark S. Searle, "Older Individuals with Mental Retardation and the Effect of a Physical Activity Intervention on Selected Social Psychological Variables," *Therapeutic Recreation Journal,* 1st Q. 1992, pp. 338–347.

4. Harve E. Rawson and David McIntosh, "The Effects of Therapeutic Camping on the Self-Esteem of Children with Severe Behavior Problems," *Therapeutic Recreation Journal,* 4th Q. 1991, pp. 41–49.

5. Gail A. Vander Stoep and James H. Gramann, "The Effect of Verbal Appeals and Incentives on Depreciative Behavior Among Youthful Park Visitors," *Journal of Leisure Research,* 2nd Q. 1987, pp. 69–83.

6. Jerry Vaske, Maureen Donnelly and Bradford Williamson, "Monitoring for Quality Control in State Park Management," *Journal of Park and Recreation Administration,* Vol. 9, No. 2, 1991, pp. 59–71.

7. Steve Hollenhorst, David Olson and Ronald Fortney, "Use of Importance-Performance Analysis to

Evaluate State Park Cabins: The Case of the West Virginia State Park System," *Journal of Park and Recreation Administration,* Vol. 10, No. 1, 1992, pp. 1–11.

8. Jeff Witman, "Demonstrating Treatment Outcomes in Therapeutic Recreation," *Parks and Recreation,* Apr. 1994, p. 87.

9. For a fuller listing of facility standards, see R.D. Buechner, Ed., *National Park, Recreation and Open Space Standards* (Washington, DC: National Recreation and Park Association, 1969).

10. Dick Bitner and Mary V. Bitner, "Automating Park and Recreation Operations," *Parks and Recreation,* June 1991, pp. 41–42.

11. Steven L. Sims, "The Drawbacks of Computerization: Half-Truths and Horror Stories," *Parks and Recreation,* June 1991, pp. 48–52.

12. Christine Z. Howe, "The Evaluation of Leisure Programs: Applying Quantitative Methods," *Journal of Physical Education, Recreation and Dance,"* Oct. 1993, p. 43.

13. Matt Wojick, "Playing It Safe: Night Program Offers Youth Fun, Advice," *Fort Worth Star-Telegram,* July 21, 1992, p. 19.

14. *Annual Report,* Westchester County, N.Y. Dept. of Parks, Recreation and Conservation, 1992, p. 19.

Photo Credits

(t) = top; (c) = center; (b) = bottom; (l) = left; (r) = right

page 8: (all) Westchester County, New York, Department of Parks, Recreation and Conservation.

page 25: (all) Phoenix, Arizona, Parks, Recreation and Library Department; (c) Courtesy Bob Rink.

page 27: (tl, tr, and bl) Vero Beach, Florida, Center for the Arts; (br) Montgomery County, Maryland, Department of Recreation, courtesy Geri Olson.

page 46: (t) James Brennan, Outdoor Recreation Intern at Ft. Wainwright, Alaska, courtesy Bob McKeta, U.S. Army Community Recreation Public Relations; (cr) Patti Kim, Army Recreation Intern at Camp Zama, Japan, courtesy Bob McKeta, U.S. Army Community Recreation Public Relations; (cl and b) Boys and Girls Clubs of America, National Office.

page 54: (tl) Kamloops, British Columbia, Canada, Parks and Recreation Services; (tr) Northeast Passage, University of New Hampshire, Department of Recreation Management and Policy, courtesy Janet Sable; (b) National Foundation of Wheelchair Tennis, courtesy Wendy Parks.

page 58: (tl) Conoco Co., Houston, Texas; (c) Parsons Corporation, Pasadena, California; (b) CoreStates Financial Corporation, Philadelphia, Pennsylvania.

page 69: (all) Kamloops, British Columbia, Canada, Parks and Recreation Services.

page 130: (t) Little League Baseball, Public Relations Department; (c) Westchester County, New York, Department of Parks, Recreation and Conservation; (bl) National Association of Police Athletic Leagues, Inc.; (br) Washington State University Public Relations.

page 133: (tl) National Outdoor Leadership School; (tr) U.S. SPACE CAMP photo, courtesy Edd Davis; (cl) Silver Springs, Florida; (b) Sugarbush Resort, Warren, Vermont

Index